THE GLORY AND SHAME OF ENGLAND

The Development of Industrial Society Series

C. Edwards Lester

THE GLORY AND SHAME OF ENGLAND

Volume 1

IRISH UNIVERSITY PRESS
Shannon   Ireland

First edition New York 1841

Second edition New York 1866

This I U P reprint is a photolithographic facsimile of
the second edition and is unabridged, retaining the
original printer's imprint.

© *1971 Irish University Press Shannon Ireland*

All forms of micropublishing
© *Irish University Microforms Shannon Ireland*

ISBN 0 7165 1789 2 Two volumes
ISBN 0 7165 1790 6 Volume 1
ISBN 0 7165 1791 4 Volume 2

T M MacGlinchey Publisher

Irish University Press Shannon Ireland

PRINTED IN THE REPUBLIC OF IRELAND BY
ROBERT HOGG PRINTER TO IRISH UNIVERSITY PRESS

The Development of Industrial Society Series

This series comprises reprints of contemporary documents and commentaries on the social, political and economic upheavals in nineteenth-century England.

England, as the first industrial nation, was also the first country to experience the tremendous social and cultural impact consequent on the alienation of people in industrialized countries from their rural ancestry. The Industrial Revolution which had begun to intensify in the mid-eighteenth century, spread swiftly from England to Europe and America. Its effects have been far-reaching: the growth of cities with their urgent social and physical problems; greater social mobility; mass education; increasingly complex administration requirements in both local and central government; the growth of democracy and the development of new theories in economics; agricultural reform and the transformation of a way of life.

While it would be pretentious to claim for a series such as this an in-depth coverage of all these aspects of the new society, the works selected range in content from *The Hungry Forties* (1904), a collection of letters by ordinary working people describing their living conditions and the effects of mechanization on their day-to-day lives, to such analytical studies as Leone Levi's *History of British Commerce* (1880) and *Wages and Earnings of the Working Classes* (1885); M. T. Sadler's *The Law of Population* (1830); John Wade's radical documentation of government corruption, *The Extraordinary Black Book* (1831); C. Edward Lester's trenchant social investigation, *The Glory and Shame of England* (1866); and many other influential books and pamphlets.

The editor's intention has been to make available important contemporary accounts, studies and records, written or compiled by men and women of integrity and scholarship whose reactions to the growth of a new kind of society are valid touchstones for today's reader. Each title (and the particular edition used) has been chosen on a twofold basis (1) its intrinsic worth as a record or commentary, and (2) its contribution to the development of an industrial society. It is hoped that this collection will help to increase our understanding of a people and an epoch.

The Editor
Irish University Press

THE

GLORY AND SHAME

OF

ENGLAND.

BY

C. EDWARDS LESTER.

VOLUME I.

NEW YORK:

BARTRAM & LESTER, PUBLISHERS,

118 BROADWAY,

1866.

NEW YORK:
E. O. JENKINS, PRINTER AND STEREOTYPER,
20 NORTH WILLIAM ST.

CONTENTS.

Volume One.

Volume Two.

THIS WORK IS DEDICATED,

𝔚𝔦𝔱𝔥 𝔕𝔢𝔰𝔭𝔢𝔠𝔱 𝔞𝔫𝔡 𝔄𝔣𝔣𝔢𝔠𝔱𝔦𝔬𝔫,

TO

HONORABLE WILLIAM E. DODGE,

BY HIS FRIEND AND FELLOW CITIZEN,

THE AUTHOR.

NEW YORK, *June 1st,* 1866.

BOOK I.

INTRODUCTION.

INTRODUCTION.

I.

THE true object of an Introduction should be to give the reader a correct idea of the book. I will try to do this by hinting the subjects I treat of, and what I meant in writing this work.

With the restoration of peace at home, we have time to look abroad; and while no good citizen desires a conflict with England, there is a universal and settled determination to call her to an account, sooner or later, for the enormous wrongs and depredations she has allowed her subjects to perpetrate upon our Commerce, our Peace, our Union and Prosperity. She was unfriendly to us in our weakness—she can hardly ask us to be friendly to her in our strength.

I intended not only to display the power, resources and grandeur of the British empire, with whatever constitutes its title to enduring glory, but to lift the veil from her crimes, in oppressing the masses of her own people at home; her cruelties to Ireland, and her helpless hundred and fifty millions in Asia; the corruptions of her "Established Church," as a State Religion; and, in a word, the atrocities of her Oligarchical System, which dresses one man in gold and sends him to the House of Lords, and another in rags and sends him to the Workhouse; a system which has only one scope in Foreign Policy, viz. : to oppress and rob nations, to sweep all commerce but her own from the sea, and above all, to break up the Great Republic of the United States.

Since my first work under the same title appeared, many years ago, I have made repeated visits to England, and spent seven years on the continent, chiefly in the Public Service. I have rewritten and greatly enlarged the original work, bringing it down to 1866—thoroughly exposing the conduct of England towards this country during the period of our great trouble, and showing just how she stands to-day before the gaze of the world.

I do not expect much good-will from the British Government, or most of the British aristocracy, for writing this book. I am working for the emancipation of whole nations, and the elevation of all men. England has always been working for the overthrow of rival nationalities, and the political subjection of men. England fights for the few—I for the many. She for Aristocracy—I for Democracy. She for the present—I for the future. No wonder we should not agree any too well. In justice to myself, however, it should be always held in mind, that, in speaking of England, I mean the Government and the ruling classes of the British empire—not the British people, for whom I entertain all the sympathies which spring unbidden from the common fountains of kindred, language, laws and religion.

II.

I BY no means wish to inflame a feeling of animosity between my own countrymen and Englishmen. This is the last thing I would attempt, unless provoked to it by acts of wrong which could not be atoned for except by justifiable retaliation. But there has been solid ground for American complaint against the English Government at many periods of our history—especially since our home troubles began. The barometer of British feeling towards us, during our Rebellion, was graduated exactly to the wavering fortunes of our armies in the field. When victory was on our side, the Government and the press of England were partially with us. When the armed insurgents had the best of it, England and most Englishmen were against us.

It would be wasting time and type to show that England has never treated us with much respect or complacency, except where it was for her immediate interest to do so. She shifts her policy towards all strong nations to suit the hour—towards weak ones, to suit her convenience.

Now, this may do very well in the *short run*, but will it do in the *long run?* Individuals are short-lived—they can easily forget; *but nations are long-lived, and have a plenty of time to remember.* The embers of a bitter war may seem to have smouldered into ashes; but a coming breeze may blow those ashes into thin air, and set the world on fire.

Yes, causes of complaint against Great Britain do exist—provocations have been given; and they are of too serious a nature to be overlooked, or treated with levity. A contest between the British Monarch and the American Republic has begun, and it is too late to arrest it by any policy on our part, which any American statesman or party would dare to propose. How serious this contest may grow, will depend on England alone. The solution of this problem is no longer in our hands. She alone can quiet the disturbed elements—she alone can avert the gathering storm.

These questions must be discussed; the day of mealy-mouthing diplomacy is over; the ground of our complaints must be carefully explored; the causes and nature of British provocations must be clearly stated; the issue cannot be much longer postponed—we must get ready to meet it.

It would seem that the politicians who manage the British empire have a chronic complaint, from which few of them ever recover, of dealing with us as "old-fashioned colonies;" as, in some sort, dependencies still of the English crown! They seem to look on us as a kind of *tributary*—not exactly as an independent nation—but somehow or other, an *attaché de l'empire.* The Revolution of 1776 ought to have blotted this idea out; but it did not. The war of 1812 should have ended it. But this same idea exists to-day ; and Englishmen of state must get rid of the foolish fancy before they can deal with us successfully. They must put themselves *omnis in hoc* with our political system.* They are *monarchical ;* we are *democratic.* We do not bandy words about *forms* of government ; we want *substance*—the real substance of liberty. Englishmen will choose their own forms ; they have chosen them ; and under these forms they manage to get a plenty of liberty for the privileged classes, while God, and a few good people, take as much care of the poor as they can. What we want, and claim to have in America, is a *magna charta* for the whole people, which means—First : Suffrage for all duly qualified classes of the people and none others ; Second : The vote by ballot, which is the chief guaranty of independent suffrage ; Third : A just distribution of paternal estates among all legitimate children, which annihilates the hereditary rights of primogeniture, and thereby lays the axe at the root of this Upas tree of family aristocracy ; Fourth : Universal religious (not toleration) *protection*, thus dissolving the harlot embrace of Church and State, and ending the foul system of a state religion ; and last of all, the education of *all the people as a public duty—as a cardinal maxim of State*. When the first civil structures were reared by the infant American Colonies, they put this great thing in : " Our children's education must be provided for, and zealously looked after, as one of the first

---

* I am fully aware this is no easy work for an English statesman. It is only now and then that it has been achieved. Burke, Fox and a few others understood us during our revolutionary struggle. At a later period such men as Canning and Huskisson did. But in our immediate times, the number of public men and journals in Great Britain that have displayed any adequate comprehension of our political and social system could be counted on the ten fingers. Even so illuminated and liberal a thinker as Macaulay was a dupe to the same English delusion; for English the delusion is. Neither De Tocqueville nor any other great continental writer on the American system, fell into such a delusion. Even Macaulay said that our territory was too vast to be held together by the feeble hands of a Democratic Government, and that our Union would fall asunder by the weight of its component parts.

duties of a God-fearing commonwealth ; for ignorant children will make bad citizens." Milton, Blackstone, Burke and Brougham never had anything to say against this. This mode of ruling nations England has yet to learn ; she will yet pay dearly for not having learned it before.

III.

I DO not forget here, nor elsewhere, the great and welcome fact, that we have friends in England : friends of our Government and its perpetuity ; friends of its cardinal Democratic principle of the equal political rights of all men ; friends of the Republic which has emerged from the waves of a dreadful civil deluge, stronger than ever ; and which is now ready on all proper occasions to vindicate throughout the world, if need be, the right of men to govern themselves. It is all bootless now to make out a case against the British Government. Our case is made out. England herself has made it out. Events have helped her. It is now summed up. She must be friendly to us, or she will be sorry for it. This is no threat—for threats are mean things at best ; not fit for men nor nations. But England must be ready to answer the People of the United States these questions : Why did you take the first chance you had to turn the cold shoulder on us ? Why did you not do it in the day of our strength, when we were a united nation ; when we were too formidable for your assaults ? Why secretly build, and then clandestinely despatch your pirate steamers to sink our honest merchantmen on all seas, from the Equator to the Poles ?

THE BLOW LEVELED AGAINST AMERICAN COMMERCE by British cruisers, was far more complete than it could have been had war actually existed between England and the United States. Then, all seas would have swarmed with our privateers, and it would have been the same straightforward game the two nations played in their contest of 1812. In making up, therefore, any sort of an estimate of the commercial losses this Country suffered through the course England thought proper to take in the very beginning of the Rebellion, we have scarcely reached the threshold by simply counting the two hundred and seventy-five peaceful merchantmen sunk or bonded by British cruisers. This covered only so many tons of shipping—and perhaps twelve or fifteen million dollars of value in ships and goods. It was an item too inconsiderable to demand much attention, compared with the stupendous loss of the carrying trade with foreign nations, then in our hands. We glance at the commercial condition in 1860, when, although the clouds were lowering over the political horizon, commerce had not yet shortened its sails, nor altered its courses.

The following figures are from the Treasury Reports, which show our commerce and navigation with all countries for the financial year, ending June 30, 1860 : Domestic produce, exported, $373,189,274. Foreign, exported, $26,933,022. Total exports, $400,122,296. Total imports, $362,166,254. Total exchanges, $762,288,550. *Entered, American tonnage*, 5,921, 285. *Cleared, do.* 6,165,924. *Foreign tonnage entered*, 2,353, 911. *Cleared*, 2,624,005. *Our exports had risen in eight years, one hundred and seventy millions;* a commercial growth unparalleled in the history of any nation.

The figures for the next five years will be given in the body of the work, with much valuable information derived from the Records of the New York Chamber of Commerce. To show the vigilance with which that important Institution guards the commercial interests of this country, and the feelings with which its members contemplated the whirlwind which swept our commerce from the sea, I have only to cite below a few passages from the proceedings of the Chamber, January 2, 1863.*

---

* "*Whereas*, It is alleged that the Alabama is continually supplied from Great Britain with coal and ammunition, by means of which she is enabled to continue her piratical course against American commerce, the consequence being to raise the premium of insurances on American vessels and their cargoes, and to depress the rate of freights in American ships, and to transfer our carrying trade to vessels of other nations, this Chamber is led to the following conclusions :

Could we not have our share of blue water ?   Could not our
Republic live, and your oligarchy too, at the same time?
Must you humiliate us in order to save your own pride ?

England has yet to learn the great lesson *that Democracy is
hereafter to be the law of the human race.*   Monarchy and despot-

" *First.* That through the active instrumentality of the subjects of Great
Britain, the so-called Confederate States are furnished with ships, men, arms and
ammunition with which to war on the commerce of the United States.

" *Second.* That without such foreign aid the States in revolt against the government of the United States would be powerless to effect any injury to American commerce on the high seas.

" *Third.* That this war on American commerce, carried on by ships built and
manned in Great Britain, if not rebuked by the British press generally, is not
discouraged by the public sentiment of a once friendly nation, claiming to be
guided by high and honorable principles, and is not effectually and thoroughly
arrested by the strong will and stronger arm of the British government.

" *Fourth.* That as a result of the foregoing facts and conclusions, the merchants of the United States are subjected, in a certain degree, to the evils which
would attend a state of war with Great Britain, and are compelled to witness the
carrying trade of their country transferred from their own vessels to British
bottoms, under all the sanctions and advantages of peace and neutrality to the
latter, while the source of this great peril, threatening to drive American commerce from the ocean, is of British origin ; now, therefore."

In the autumn previous (Oct. 22, 1862,) the Chamber had used the following
language in another memorial to the President of the United States :

" Now it cannot be said that the government of England, and the merchants of
England, indeed, every body in England, are ignorant of this, or of the further
fact, that vessels are to follow the " Alabama " and other privateers intended to
operate against our commerce on the seas, when they leave the shores of England, with cargoes of arms, guns, and munitions of war, and crews made up of
British subjects, all which are to be transferred to these piratical vessels for the
purpose of destroying American ships and American commerce.

" Therefore, we say that this Chamber ought publicly to express the opinion
it set forth seven years ago, when the situation of the two countries was revers-
ed, when England was at war, and we were at peace. The sentiments we then
expressed, when vindicating our character and our honor against unfounded
aspersion, we may well, and should emphatically express as our sentiments to-
day, and hold them out for the consideration of the people of England, with
whom it has ever been our desire to live on terms of friendly intercourse. It
will be for them to consider what impression it will make on the American mind
that British built ships, manned by British seamen, are sent out to burn and destroy our ships pursuing their legitimate courses upon the ocean, and to commit

ism may live for a while *in form;—in spirit* they are dead. They can, hope for no resurrection. The world is not wide enough any longer for monarchy, hierarchy, superstition, or oppression, of the bodies, souls, or spirits of men. The emancipation of men everywhere from the thraldom of man, is the enchanting watch-word of the last, and better half of the Nineteenth Century. The world has heard the shout of Freedom, and is straining on its fetters. It is saying to its oppressors : " The cup of bitterness you have so long pressed to our lips, we will drain no more forever."

IV.

ENGLISH critics and statesmen must not grow restive or angry at us because we turn the tables, and speak with some freedom about them, and their social and political system. Again and again we say, we do not care for your form of government, nor do we claim that Republican forms are necessary to the existence or perpetuity of liberty. You call your form a *monarchy*, by which you mean an *aristocracy*, as strong and impregnable as you could make it. You care not much more for your Queen than we do, and many of you not half as much. But you use her as a foil, a pretext, a sham, behind which you hide your unearned, often unjustly gotten, but always conveniently inherited wealth and titles. *You are the monarchy—* not the royal family. *You* rule—not the Queen. You feast —the masses starve. I know that the word American Democ-

---

their crews to chains. And because the law of nations, more careful it seems of personal interests than the interests of humanity, has so shut these pirates out from the ports of every civilized country, that they cannot take in their prizes for condemnation in the rightful way of law, they must, therefore, condemn them by fire on the seas.

" Sir, as a great commercial people, holding and anxious to hold friendly relations with the government and people of Great Britain, we have a moral right to present these views to the government at Washington, and to ask the Secretary of State for the United States, through our diplomatic agents abroad, to lay these resolutions before the government and people of Europe."

racy grates harshly on English ears, but that alters not the case. There is no throne, nor mitre, nor class that can withstand the tide of the age.

And tell us!—should not the time come, sooner or later, when the many may have justice? When hunger among the neglected millions may drown the noise of pomp and splendor, and hush its revelry in a festival for the wronged, the outraged and the forgotten classes?

You know little of the sufferings that surround your own palaces. Through those noiselessly swinging doors the plaints of sorrow never pass. But those hearts that beat outside may be as warm as yours, and perhaps as divine music may be heard in heaven when those heart-strings are touched by angel fingers. Your own *Dickens*, whose suffering heroines you have read of, has taught you these lessons of sympathy long ago. If not, no word from this side of the Atlantic could reach your hearts.

But although I am writing with few of the restraints of arrangement which writers commonly impose upon their pens, I am admonished that I am encroaching unnecessarily upon ground which I have gone over more thoroughly in the body of the work. Therefore, at the risk of the imputation of egotism, I come to a brief account of the circumstances which led me to choose England as the theme of my first book.

v.

THE friends of an author are entertained by incidents which illustrate his personal history, or the history of his writings. The public care little about either, till the fame of the writer has become the property of the world. It will therefore be understood, that the plain account I give in these introductory pages of the history of this work, is intended chiefly for those who on both sides of the Atlantic, have, during long years, sent or given me friendly greetings.

My health had given way, and my physicians told me that nothing could save my life but a voyage to sea, and in May,

1840, I sailed for England, uncertain whether the voyage would cure or kill me. I had to leave my wife and child behind me, and I need not say, it was a painful separation : and yet there was the relief of excitement about it—the inspiration of hope. Such a dash could not but change the current of my fortunes, for it seemed to me my last chance to live had come, and if there were a chance I should seize it,—if it were an *ignis fatuus* which lured me on, we would both disappear together.

There are periods when even Nature herself relies on extraordinary remedies, and Providence resorts to them so often in guiding our destinies, that uncommon exposures and bold designs often turn out to be the only means of success, or even of safety.

All that books and teachers could do for a boy of my age had thus far been done. I had no idea of becoming an author, or trying to do anything to arrest the attention of mankind. To be well again I did not hope, but to die I could not think of.

What men call fortune, I was born with. It had melted away. I did not dream of recovering it again, and as for fame, it had nothing to do with my thoughts. I know, in recollecting that period, that I only hoped I might return and live a few quiet years, pursuing my studies unmolested by poverty, garnering up my treasures in the bosom of my family, with a home which I knew would be a happy one, so long as beings who loved each other so well, were not separated by death. I remember very distinctly that, while I was looking back to catch the last sight of my cottage door on the morning I started for Europe, I felt, with more intensity than I had ever before felt a sentiment in my life, a desire to live to come back. It seemed to me that I could not, must not, die so young, so happy.

VI.

A STORM swept our vessel to England in fifteen days. As I look back on it, that voyage is almost a blank. It would have been quite such but for my sufferings. I remember little but the terrible monotony of creaking rigging, hoarse orders, deck tramping and the angry surgings of the ocean. After making half the passage, the storm suddenly left us rocking among the waves. We now prepared ourselves for a long, tedious calm. Towards sunset the next day we saw a column of smoke rising up into the clear heavens on the western horizon, and we knew the "Great Western" was behind it. In a few hours she came up, and went sweeping by majestically over the now calm sea, leaving our sails to flap away interminable days without moving twenty miles in twenty-four hours.

So we all thought then, and wished we were on board the steamer. A consciousness of the power of the steam engine on the ocean, I then felt for the first time. All the fleets of England, without steam, never could have impressed me as did that solitary steamer. But while we were lamenting our fate, and the sailors were beginning to get sulky, and the old captain was pacing the deck impatiently, whistling for a wind, far away to the north-west a cloud came rising which made the sea black as it came. First it struck the main-top-gallant-sails, and slowly we began to move once more through the waters. The ship soon lifted and shook herself and began to leap through the sea. The breeze freshened ; we flew through the ocean. The next day a gale brought us where we saw the "Great Western" pitching and floundering heavily among the waves, while we were rushing by her shortly afterwards before the storm. We passed the steamer and saw no more of her, but we took with us her news to England, and stood on that island three hours before her passengers.

VII.

IT was a warm summer day when the glorious Welsh mountains rose up out of the ocean. The glass brought the farm houses, the quiet flocks, the green fields, close up to the eye. I cannot describe the feeling with which I gazed for the first time on that ancient land which had been the home of my fathers. I seemed to be returning to the graves of my ances-

tors, who had been long dead, and a new feeling came over me
that I myself had been almost as long a wanderer. A great
many associations which no one but an American whose ancestors came from England can ever feel, crowded on my mind,
and the history of the Anglo-Saxon-Normans, their struggles
and triumphs, came fresh to my memory. I began to find even
before I landed what was only confirmed by experience, that I
should enjoy England as she had been, more than England as
she is. Up to the time of the embarkation of our fathers, England was their country, and our history was the history of
Britain. The great writers of England, till the period of the
Commonwealth, wrought and thought for my fathers as much
as for the fathers of any living Englishman; and I have as many
associations to bind me to them and their times, as though I
had been born on that island.

VIII.

AROUND English history there is a charm which can be
found in no other. The recent and the remote—the plain
and the obscure—novelty springing up by the gray remains of
antiquity—all the elements of the touching, and the beautiful,
the gloomy, and the grand, mingle in the chronicles of our
fatherland.

With us at home all is familiar and modern.* It is true we

---

* In illustration of this, I cite a few passages from the pen of Goldwin Smith,
the noblest Englishman who has trod our soil during the present century.—(*Atlantic Monthly*, December, 1864.)

"But you have a real and glorious history, if you will not reject it—monuments genuine and majestic, if you will acknowledge them as your own. Yours
are the palaces of the Plantagenets—the cathedrals which enshrined our old
religion—the illustrious hall in which the long line of our great judges reared,
by their decisions, the fabric of our law—the gray colleges in which our intellect
and science found their earliest home—the graves where our heroes and sages
and poets sleep. . . . . . You are heirs to all the wealth of the Old World, and
must owe gratitude for a part of your heritage to Germany, France and Spain,
as well as to England. Still, it is from England that you are sprung; from her

read with pride and ambition of our fathers' struggles, when the story leads us through the toils of the Revolution back to the gloom of the green old forests and the bleak desolation of Plymouth landing : but there the story ceases in America, and we must cross the water for an account of our antecedent national existence. We then have an interest, and can betimes forget America as it slumbered on unwaked by the sea-gun of Columbus, while we retrace the story of our ancestors through preceding generations, to the time when the Roman conqueror first planted the eagle of Italy on the rocks of Britain, and returned to tell of a stormy island in the ocean, and of the rugged barbarians who dwelt in its glens and hunted on its cliffs.

you brought the power of self-government which was the talisman of colonization and the pledge of your empire here. She it was, that, having advanced by centuries of effort to the front of the Old World, became worthy to give birth to the New. From England you are sprung; and it is because you are Englishmen that English freedom, not French or Spanish despotism, is the law of this continent. From England you are sprung; and if the choice were given you among all the nations of the world, which would you rather choose for a mother?

"England bore you, and bore you not without a mother's pangs. For the real hour of your birth was the English Revolution of the Seventeenth Century, at once the saddest and the noblest period of English history—the noblest, whether we look to the greatness of the principles at stake, or to the grandeur of the actors who fill the scene. . . . . . But before 1783 you had founded, under the name of an English Colony, a community emancipated from feudalism; you had abolished here and doomed to general abolition hereditary aristocracy, and that which is the essential basis of hereditary aristocracy, primogeniture in the inheritance of land. . . . . . You had created the system of common schools, in which the sovereignty of the people has its only safe foundation. You had proclaimed, after some misgivings and backslidings, the doctrine of liberty of conscience, and released the Church from her long bondage to the State. All this you had achieved while you still were, and gloried in being, a colony of England. . . . . .

"In England the Revolution of the Seventeenth Century failed. It failed, at least, as an attempt to establish social equality and liberty of conscience. The feudal past, with a feudal Europe to support it, sat too heavy on us to be cast off. By a convulsive effort we broke loose, for a moment, from the hereditary aristocracy and the hierarchy. For a moment we placed a popular chief in power, though Cromwell was obliged by circumstances, as well as impelled by his own ambition, to make himself a king. But when Cromwell died before his hour, all was over for many a day with the party of religious freedom and of the

It is natural and proper that an American should read with stirring interest of the defeats, the struggles, the triumphs of Englishmen in those rude times, and think with the indignation of a free man and the love of a brother, on the sufferings of his kinsmen who dwell there now. The starving peasant and the pale operative are the sons of those who not long ago dwelt with our own fathers on the banks of the Tweed, the Thames and the Severn ; and why should we not feel for them as for brothers ?

Nurtured too in a Republic which had not only proved great in times which had tried the stability of older states, it seemed to me natural that I should carry with me into any land,

people. The nation had gone a little way out of the feudal and hierarchical Egypt; but the horrors of the unknown Wilderness, and the memory of the flesh-pots, overpowered the hope of the Promised Land ; and the people returned to the rule of Pharaoh and his priests amidst the bonfires of the Restoration. . . . . . English society had made a supreme effort to escape from feudalism and the hierarchy into social justice and religious freedom, and that effort had failed.

" Failed in England, but succeeded here. The yoke which in the mother-country we had not strength to throw off, in the colony we escaped ; and here, beyond the reach of the Restoration, Milton's vision proved true, and a free community was founded, though in a humble and unsuspected form, which depended on the life of no single chief, and lived on when Cromwell died. Milton, when the night of the Restoration closed on the brief and stormy day of his party, bated no jot of hope. He was strong in that strength of conviction which assures spirits like his of the future, however dark the present may appear. But, could he have beheld it, the morning, moving westward in the track of the Puritan emigrants, had passed from his hemisphere only to shine again in this with no fitful ray, but with a steady brightness which will one day reillumine the feudal darkness of the Old World.

" The Revolution failed in England. Yet in England the party of Cromwell and Milton still lives. It still lives : and in this great crisis of your fortunes, its heart turns to you. On your success ours depends. Now, as in the seventeenth century, the thread of our fate is twined with the thread of yours. An English Liberal comes here, not only to watch the unfolding of your destiny, but to read his own. . . . . .

" It is of want of sympathy, not of want of interest, that you have to complain. And the sympathy which has been withheld is not that of the whole nation, but that of certain classes, chiefly of the class against whose political

and through any clime, not only the principles in which I
had been educated, but the pride of country, which will forever
in the breasts of all true Americans, remain inseparable from
their nature. Penetrated with the deepest belief, not only of
the capacity of intelligent men (none others) for self-government, but that Republican institutions are the mightiest of all
agencies to develope whatever is great in human nature, I
thought the feeling might perhaps be stronger in me than
among the men I was about to look on, and talk with.

It has always been a common, and rather an odious slur in
England upon our countrymen who go abroad, that they carry
their Republicanism with them. Although this is often meant

interest you are fighting, and to whom your victory brings eventual defeat.
The real origin of your nation is the key to the present relation between you
and the different parties in England. This is the old battle waged again on
a new field. We will not talk too much of Puritans and Cavaliers. The soldiers
of the Union are not Puritans, neither are the planters Cavaliers. But the
present civil war is a vast episode in the same irrepressible conflict between
Aristocracy and Democracy; and the heirs of the Cavalier in England sympathize with your enemies, the heirs of the Puritan with you.

"The feeling of our aristocracy, as of all aristocracies, is against you. . . . . .
Therefore, as a class, the English nobility cannot desire the success of your
Republic. Some of the order there are who have hearts above their coronets,
as there are some kings who have hearts above their crowns, and who in this
great crisis of humanity forget that they are noblemen, and remember that they
are men. But the order, as a whole, has been against you, and has swayed in
the same direction all who were closely connected with it or dependent on it.
It could not fail to be against you, if it was for itself. . . . . .

"The clergy of the State Church, like the aristocracy, have probably been as
a body against you in this struggle. In their case too, not hatred of America,
but the love of their own institution, is the cause. If you are a standing menace
to aristocracies, you are equally a standing menace to State Churches. A State
Church rests upon the assumption that religion would fall, if it were not supported by the State. . . . . . The Englishmen of this day will not prevent those
who come after them from being proud of England's grandest achievement, the
sum of all her noblest victories—the foundation of this the great Commonwealth
of the New World. And you will not prevent the hearts of your children's
children from turning to the birth-place of their nation, the land of their history
and of their early greatness, the land which holds the august monuments of your
ancient race, the works of your illustrious fathers, and their graves."

as a sarcasm, I have always taken it as a compliment; for in all nations respect has been felt for those men who have not forgotten the land of their birth, when they lost sight of their habitations. But if this feeling were a crime, Englishmen should never impute it to us; for in what part of the world has an Englishman ever been found who had not carried with him a good many testimonials that John Bull was his father! This *hauteur* that Englishmen never can get rid of, and perhaps never should, sometimes makes them very disagreeable; but it is part and parcel of that national sentiment which, however disagreeable it may make some Englishmen, makes England very great.

These were the feelings with which I landed on the shores of England, went through her islands, and looked on society and government. The standard by which I judged government and the organization of society, was that which all men of sense will say is founded in justice. My premises were facts which I saw and learned for myself. My logic was that of the Declaration of Independence and my own heart, between which there was no collision. My conclusions were honestly drawn, and without pausing to think of the consequences, I published them to the world.

IX.

I HAVE never entered the lists with critics or enemies to defend my book on England. Attacks without number were made on it (and in this country on its writer) on both sides of the Atlantic, but I never had a disposition to reply, and if I had felt like it I never should have found the time. My faith in authorship and fame is summed up in a word; if a book has not enough truth and vitality in itself to live, all the bolstering in the world will do no good. Who knows but the Spartans were right after all, in putting their sickly children out of the way. It seldom pays to raise them, especially literary bantlings. Time, the great regulator, will do justice at last to every volume, and every man. It is a good maxim, that if you cannot put fire into your book, put your book into the fire. Whatever is necessary or useful to the progress of mankind, mankind will take care of. I am willing and glad to be tried in whatever I have written, or done, or may write, or do, hereafter, by that impartial tribunal. For I do not yet know of an instance, in which any contribution made in a proper spirit to the good of mankind has ever been allowed to die. As the stream of time moves on, it can and will bear on its bosom every thing that is buoyant enough to sustain itself. All else must sink, and ought to. Neither the partialities nor the prejudices of contemporaries can alter the decisions of the future. The judgments of men cannot be swayed for any great length of time by the petty strifes of contending rivals, or parties of the brief hour of struggle.

One of my most candid critics said, I could not have become qualified to write about England when I had passed hardly a year there. This struck me as a new sort of objection to urge against the correctness of a man's vision, because he spent so short a time in looking at the objects he described. There are men who might gaze, like Newton's dog, for years on Newton's stars without making much progress in the science of astronomy. Another of my English reviewers remarked, in speaking of these same critics, that " it would be more just to inquire whether what the writer saw and said was really so." I account for the fact that I did say some things about England that other visitors had not remarked, by giving an idea of the manner in which I economized my time. A residence of many years in Europe since that period, has only illustrated an observation I made when I first went abroad, that most travelers, especially Americans, are equally prodigal of their time and their money. I remember that when I reached England I was impressed with the feeling of how much my time would be worth there, if it were well spent. I have always found in my travels and sojournings, that a few hours, or even a few minutes, well spent at the right time, would

multiply forever my resources of happiness. I felt this when
I looked for the first time on the frowning rock of Gibraltar ;
the sun-clad mountains of Grenada ; the tideless bosom of the
Mediterranean ; the mosaic shores of Italy ; the dome of St.
Peter's ; the frost-work of the Duomo of Milan ; so felt I when
first standing on the fields of Montenotte and of Marengo.

X.

I WAS very young when I went to England. The first man
I ever saw in my life who was famishing with hunger, I saw
in London. The first female I ever looked on in the streets,
whose raiment could not cover her form, was in London. The
first structure raised by the hand of man that overwhelmed me,
was Westminster Abbey. The first prison that made me shud-
der as I gazed on it, was Newgate. The first throne I ever
saw was the throne of the then youthful and still beloved Victoria. These things struck me deeply ; I felt deeply ; I saw
clearly. I described with earnestness and honesty what I saw
—from the palace, with all its splendors, to the underground
homes of the heathen in the collieries—from the dizziest heights
to the lowest depths, I scoured through England for myself. I
saw with my own eyes. I turned England inside out and up-
side down straight before the eyes of Englishmen themselves ;
and, forsooth, because I showed them what they never had seen
before, and told them what they did not know, they said it was
all made up. Well it was made up—of facts. My statements
have stood the test of twenty-four years, and all my pictures
of the vice, the degradation, the sufferings, the sottishness, the
heathenism of the masses of the British people, have been out-
done since, by Reports made to the British Parliament on the
horrors of the Collieries, the barbarities practiced in the Work-
houses, the worse than slave toil of the Factories, the plethora
of the Prelacy, the spiritual as well as the physical poverty of
their flocks, the ignorance of the great herd of England's home
subjects, and, in a single word, the· accursed system of govern-

ment and society which is made for the express purpose of dressing one Englishman in gold and sending him to the House of Lords, and another Englishman in rags and sending him to the workhouse.

In some departments, my teachers then and my defenders since, have been the first men of Great Britain. Brougham, in his better days, before he began to drivel ; Carlyle, in his better days, before he began to scold and drivel ; Cobden, then glowing in, and since passed from the furnace, one of the greatest and most admired of the men of our times ; Bright, the great Quaker man of State ; Mill, the public economist of the world ; Goldwin Smith, of Oxford ; Daniel O'Connell, the Irish liberator ; Dickens, who had partly before, and who has entirely since, torn off the garb of hypocrisy under which the British aristocracy had enwrapped itself in the dreadful work of embruting and enslaving the largest portion of the people ; Thackeray, who shows the honeycomb system of villainy, fraud, dissipation and rottenness on which the aristocratic structure of England stands : so, if my work was the work of a boy, I am not utterly ashamed to own it as a man ; for unworthy as it may have been of the favor it received, it was written in an honest and truthful spirit, and for the good of mankind.

XI.

I HAVE given pretty liberal space to the course of the Government and the press of England towards us during our civil war.

England is responsible for the losses occasioned by the "Alabama," *First*, not because of the violation of any act of Parliament which could neither increase nor diminish her responsibilities, but because upon the principles of international law, which she has no right to modify by any statute, she neglected, after due notice from our Government, to arrest the departure of the "Alabama."

Second. Because her own revenue officers at Liverpool were fully apprised of the intended departure of the "Alabama," and knowingly assisted in her leaving port as a Confederate cruiser.

Third. Because after England, by the order of arrest, had acknowledged that the departure of the "Alabama" for such a purpose was contrary to law, neglected to send British cruisers to seize her.

Fourth. Because she sent no notice to any of her colonial ports to seize the "Alabama."

Fifth. Because the "Alabama" was received into British colonial ports after her departure, in violation of law, and instead of being seized by the Colonial authorities, she received the hospitalities of a national vessel.*

* As these proof sheets are leaving my hands, the first Annual Message of President Johnson is received. His language on this subject is clear and unequivocal:—" Our domestic contest, now happily ended, has left some traces in our relations with one at least of the great maritime powers. The formal accordance of belligerent rights to the insurgent States was unprecedented, and has not been justified by the issue. But in the systems of neutrality pursued by the powers which made that concession there was a marked difference. The materials of war for the insurgent States were furnished, in a great measure, from the workshops of Great Britain, and British ships, manned by British subjects, and prepared for receiving British armaments, sailed from the ports of Great Britain to make war on American commerce, under the shelter of a commission from the insurgent States. These ships, having once escaped from British ports, ever afterwards entered them in every part of the world, to refit, and so to renew their depredations. The consequences of this conduct were most disastrous to the States then in rebellion, increasing their desolation and misery, by the prolongation of our civil contest. It had, moreover, the effect, to a great extent, to drive the American flag from the sea, and to transfer much of our shipping and our commerce to the very Power whose subjects had created the necessity for such a change. These events took place before I was called to the administration of the Government. The sincere desire for peace by which I am animated, led me to approve the proposal, already made, to submit the questions which had thus arisen between the countries to arbitration. These questions are of such moment that they must have commanded the attention of the Great Powers, and are so interwoven with the peace and interests of every one of them as to have insured an impartial decision. I regret to inform you that Great Britain declined the arbitrament, but, on the other hand, invited us to the formation of a joint commission to settle mutual claims between the two

This expresses the convictions and the feelings of the American people, and further than this I have no desire to go.

XII.

I HAVE spoken of the policy of Palmerston and Napoleon concerning this country, for they had to be considered together. That policy was early matured, and it was afterwards clearly developed. It has ceased to be even a matter of curiosity to get at the secret history of the conferences and intrigues of these subtle statesmen at the commencement, and during the continuance, of the rebellion. Events have withdrawn the veil from the innermost penetralia of every cabinet in Europe, as far as we are concerned. The first object of Napoleon was to imperialize the governments of all the Latin nations in the Western hemisphere. His plan embraced the overthrow of the Mexican Republic, and placing an emperor on the throne—the annexation of the Central American States—the intervention of Spain for the subversion of all the Republics of South America, and the establishment of a vast empire,

---

countries, from which those for the depredations before mentioned should be excluded. The proposition, in that very unsatisfactory form, has been declined.

"The United States did not present the subject as an impeachment of the good faith of a power which was professing the most friendly dispositions, but as involving questions of public law, of which the settlement is essential to the peace of nations; and, though pecuniary reparation to their injured citizens would have followed incidentally on a decision against Great Britain, such compensation was not their primary object. They had a higher motive, and it was in the interests of peace and justice to establish important principles of international law. The correspondence will be placed before you.

"The ground on which the British Minister rests his justification is, substantially, that the municipal law of a nation, and the domestic interpretations of that law, are the measure of its duty as a neutral; and I feel bound to declare my opinion, before you and before the world, that that justification cannot be sustained before the tribunal of nations. At the same time I do not advise to any present attempt at redress by acts of legislation. For the future, friendship between the two countries must rest on the basis of mutual justice."

which would blot out every republic in the New World except our own, (which was to be broken up,) and thus make Imperialism the Law of Government for the entire Latin race of the West.

Under treaties with England and Spain, Louis Napoleon went to Mexico with the most solemn pledges not to interfere with her government, but to unite with Spain and England in demanding security for certain English, French and Spanish claims from the Mexican Republic.

When, in violation of that treaty, he announced his determination to overthrow the Republic of Mexico, the troops of Spain and England at once withdrew from the conflict, and returned home.

When the French troops were being more than decimated by yellow fever at Vera Cruz, Louis Napoleon was permitted to remove them to a high and healthy position on the way to Mexico, and thus saved his army from destruction, with a most solemn pledge, that if such a movement were permitted by Mexico, he would take no advantage of this position to assail that government. This engagement he most certainly violated, by moving from this interior position so evidently secured to overthrow that republic.

The movement was exclusively in hostility to the United States, to the republican system of the world, and to make monarchy or imperialism universal. It was not a mere movement against Mexico, for in his published letter on that subject, when he thought our rebellion would succeed, he announced his purpose to be to establish the equilibrium of the Latin race on this continent. By the Latin race he meant the whole American continent, from Texas and California to Cape Horn : in other words, he *desired to monarchize or imperialize that whole region*. In the meantime he was under secret confidential arrangements with the so-called Confederate government for moral aid and support. Whilst we were engaged in civil war, he made three desperate efforts to render the rebellion successful, by three separate attempts to induce the British govern-

ment to unite with him in recognizing the independence of the
South. Two of these efforts were diplomatic: the third was by
two of his emissaries—Roebuck and Lindsay, in the House of
Commons of the British Parliament. By recognition, had he
succeeded, he meant, of course, war by England and France
against the United States in favor of the Southern rebellion.
He meant war by this recognition, because by acknowledging
the South as an independent nation, France and England would,
of course, have made commercial treaties with the South as an
independent power, embracing reciprocal free trade, and dis-
criminations against the United States, necessarily leading to
the breach of the blockade, and to war. His object was, having
monarchized Mexico and Central and South America, and
established a slave-holding oligarchy in the South, to split the
North into separate States, leading first to anarchy, and then to
a military despotism. He was defeated in this project by the
unanimous refusal of the British Cabinet to unite with him in
recognizing the independence of the South. His hostility continued until he received the intelligence of the reëlection of
Mr. Lincoln, in November, 1864. In the event of McClellan's
election, he had prepared, as a *coup d'état,* acknowledging the
independence of the South, and appealing to all European
powers to unite with him, upon the ground that the American
people, by endorsing the Chicago platform upon that election,
had declared that the war to suppress the rebellion *was a failure,*
and therefore, by the principles of international law, acknowledged by Europe and America, it was the right and duty of all
neutral powers to acknowledge the admitted fact of the independence of the South. The reëstablishment of our Union necessarily involves the defeat of his Mexican scheme, and his whole
imperial and monarchical policy. If we do not drive him out
of Mexico, he will soon have to leave it himself, because
he can never be tolerated by the Mexican people. It will
be a continued struggle against the French usurpation. No
revenue can be collected by the satellites of Napoleon in
Mexico, and France will not submit to the further and useless

waste of her blood and treasure in a contest so wicked and fruitless.*

On this ground the whole nation will stand.

XIII

ENGLAND was inspired by far different motives. Her sole object was to appease her lust for gain ; and this she could do, only by maintaining her commercial supremacy throughout the world. In adhering to this cardinal tradition of her empire, she had kept the temple of Janus open for hundreds of

---

* The President has, in few words, disposed of the whole question of the Monroe Doctrine:—" From the moment of the establishment of our free Constitution, the civilized world has been convulsed by revolutions in the interest of democracy, or of monarchy ; but through all those revolutions the United States have wisely and firmly refused to become propagandists of republicanism. It is the only government suited to our condition ; but we have never sought to impose it on others ; and we have consistently followed the advice of Washington, to recommend it only by the careful preservation and prudent use of the blessing. During all the intervening period, the policy of European powers and of the United States has, on the whole, been harmonious. Twice, indeed, rumors of the invasion of some parts of America, in the interest of monarchy, have prevailed ; twice my predecessors have had occasion to announce the views of this nation in respect to such interference. On both occasions the remonstrance of the United States was respected, from a deep conviction, on the part of European governments, that the system of non-interference and mutual abstinence from propagandism was the true rule for the two hemispheres. Since those times, we have advanced in wealth and power ; but we retain the same purpose to leave the nations of Europe to choose their own dynasties, and form their own systems of government. This consistent moderation may justly demand a corresponding moderation. We should regard it as a great calamity to ourselves, to the cause of good government, and to the peace of the world, should any European power challenge the American people, as it were, to the defence of republicanism against foreign interference. We cannot foresee, and are unwilling to consider, what opportunities might present themselves, what combinations might offer to protect ourselves against designs inimical to our form of government. The United States desire to act in the future as they have ever acted heretofore ; they never will be driven from that course but by the aggression of European powers ; and we rely on the wisdom and justice of those powers to respect the system of non-interference which has so long been sanctioned by time, and which, by its good results, has approved itself to both continents."

years. It was a ceaseless battle of English aggression all round the world. She was in open encroachment, or remorseless hostilities in some part of the world, steadily through successive centuries. Her mighty armaments never sailed from that miniature island without laying tribute upon the helpless nations. This is the history of her hundred colonies. Commerce then being her life, and the amount of her profits dependent upon the monopoly of the seas, she had successively broken the commercial power of every rival—the Dutch, the Danes, the Spaniards, the Portuguese and the French, till she found in the United States the most formidable contestant she had ever encountered.

It was plain enough to everbody that England's sceptre was trembling in her grasp. Something thorough must be done. In her dilemma, fortune seemed to come to her aid. The earthquake burst under the Great Republic, shaking its foundations, and opening gaping seams in the superstructure.

XIV.

IRELAND—It is a sad word ; the saddest of all the names, and all the nations. No people have been immolated as heartlessly, nor so long. This book is too narrow for the recital of her wrongs, or to hold even the catalogue of her sufferings. Indeed, they are nowhere portrayed with half adequate intensity, except in those mournful ballads which have descended for centuries from maternal and maiden lips, as they melted into the star-lit air. They are the richest volume in the Green Island's library—her unwritten literature. Why did not Moore do for his nation what Scott did for his. We had almost said that the "Scottish Ballads" and "Border Minstrelsy" would outlive "Waverley" and "Ivanhoe."

But brief as must be the space we can give to Ireland, it would be filled with a more touching story than could be told of any other people, if the writing were worthy of the subject or the poor words of the writer could do any justice to his heart.

The plain truth plainly stated, is that England never had a shadow of right to put her foot on the soil of Ireland ; to touch it one moment.   To England, Ireland is indebted only for invasion, robbery, murder and centuries of insolent oppression. Ages of insult and wrong, have not, and cannot sanctify her bloody title to that dewy land.   Ireland is now preparing for one more struggle for freedom.   When the hour of her emancipation may come, the God of freedom alone can tell.   But that it will come, and may sooner, perhaps, than British statesmen suppose, no thinking man can doubt.

The Independence of Nations is the Common Law of the world.   Nations have as much right to be free as men.   Why *thraldom?* Who wants it? Who shall be the serf? Shall it be the Polander, or the Hungarian? The Italian or the Greek? Least of all, shall it be the generous Irishman, whose first impulse is to strike for freedom and the right?   The crimes of England towards Ireland, as in all cases of oppression, will yet be avenged—not in blood, we trust—for there is a nobler vengeance than that.   The pen outlives the sword.   Truth will outlive oppression—the pencil and the chisel survive the injustice of thrones.   With these instruments of justice—these messengers and servants of the Eternal, the oppressed and trampled nationalities of the present hour will yet inscribe upon the falling palaces of their tyrants, what Ireland can now say to England—you *may* die—we *shall* live.   Your oppression has driven half our nation to the New World.   The rest will follow if you do not grant our independence.   *Your* Ireland may be depopulated ; *our* Ireland is in America to-day.

It should be plain enough to the obtusest reader of history, that this is the Period which will be hereafter known as the Age of free Nations and free Men.   Nearly a century ago, England had to let the Thirteen Colonies have their nationality. Next Spain had to concede the independence of all her colonies in North and South America.   Then the Turk took his polluting hand from the bosom of Greece.   Again the hour of Italy's redemption came.   Now the future of other nations is pressing its images of freedom into the lenses of history. Russia, at one blow, strikes the chains from twenty million serfs ; America from four million slaves ; the spoilers of Poland must strike off her fetters ; Austria must take down her hated standard from the towers of Venice, and England must give back to the Emerald Isle her ancient liberty.

The nation which has done wrong, but will do so no more ; which will swing her ship of state gracefully into the irresistible stream that, in its swelling, is to bear its precious freight to a calm and secure harbor, will hear the shouts of gratitude pealing from myriads of peoples. But those nations that try to stem this torrent, will be swept away. The shores of Time's great river are strewn with the wrecks of fallen empires. God—who always tells the truth—says, in pleading for the freedom of man everywhere from the thraldom of tyrants : " The nation that will not serve me shall perish."

The great crime of England lies in sustaining a system which oppresses, starves, and brutalizes the masses of her subjects. These fruits are legitimate, in Ireland.

XV.

PRIVATE benevolence, and alms-giving, cannot make up for *this system of wrong which England inflicts on her people.*

No men, no women, no community on the earth will so willingly put kerchief to the eye, or quicker thrust hand into the pocket, to relieve an individual case of helplessness. But the sympathy of individuals, only helps individuals. This help is all noble and generous ; but good as the motive may be, it has been proved ten thousand times that private efforts to do good in England, are blotted out by public determination to do wrong. No Atlas of the earth has yet appeared who could bear all our burdens, except our Divine Master.

The Government of England makes poor men poorer, and rich men richer. The fault is not in the noble men and women

of England, for God knows they do well. But what is their
drop in the bucket ? It is only to help keep the kettle full,
while the holes in the bottom are left. Philanthropy pours
into the cask ; Aristocracy keeps the spigot open.

It is *the system* of Government which makes things get so
much out of joint—which makes everything go so badly. Who
could grow vergaloo pears from such thistles ?

What I complain of in English statesmanship is this— *Why
cannot England take care of all her people ?* If she cannot,
it would seem to be only fair, at least, to let them take care of
themselves. But I complain of the English system because it
does sacrifice most of her subjects to pamper the rest. If I
am disputed in this statement, her own writers and public men
will come to my rescue.

So far back as the elder Greeks, I may go for my justification in saying, that *any Government which takes liberty out
of the hands of the people, must see that the people do not
starve.*

Twenty-three hundred years have rung out their requiems
over the age of Pericles and his scholars, philosophers, sages,
poets, and comprehending men ; but modern governments have
yet to show why the helpless masses must still be crushed into
the mire.

That *mire* means ignorance, because it cannot become intelligence ; it means helplessness, because it *is* ignorance ; it
means hopelessness, because it sees no light in despair.

XVI.

LET England explain to her own people, if she can, why a
system of Government should be obstinately adhered to,
which can, has and will, as long as it lasts, foredoom one class
to opulence and idleness, and another, and infinitely the larger
class, to hopeless poverty and exhausting toil.

The worst attribute in African slavery has been this—forcing men to work hard to keep them from starving ! This is all

England has done for hundreds of years. She has millions of her own home people who know no more about Jesus Christ than about Mahomet, or Confucius. I have proved this, and (if it be possible) things still worse.

I therefore say that no population can be found on the earth, who live so near Christianity, that know so little of it; that see so much luxury, and have so few of the necessaries of life; that dwell in such filthy holes and dens; that bask in so little of the sunlight of Heaven.

Who made this system? Who keeps it up? What good is there in the Established Church and its Thirty-nine Articles, when you come to the question of bread and butter? What creed will stand between the stomach of a hungry man and a new or oldfangled creed about the Trinity, or the Unity? Christ came to see and help the poor, the forsaken, the despairing. The Established Church came to tax them, and enrich a prelacy.

It is too late in the day to set up screens between the masses and the few; between Democracy and mankind. The man of Nazareth tore those screens away long ago—and His work once done, lasts. Christ had to die but once; He had to proclaim the Redemption of mankind but once, and it was done forever. Governments must comply with this philosophy or be overthrown.

Either the present British system of society must go down or it must be changed. It cannot last as it is. The men who do the work must be paid—their children must be educated—or a wild mob of wronged men will call somebody to a serious account. Let England take her choice now while she can.

XVII.

I DO not know, in my whole life, when I have suffered so much by looking on human misery, brought about by a system of government which grows out of society and makes society, acting and reacting, as during my first visit to England

—confirmed, deepened more indelibly by subsequent visits. I had read and heard somewhat of the poor of the British Islands. The essays of Elia, Dickens' Nicholas Nickleby and Oliver Twist, and some other works telling much about this state of things, I had regarded more as the limnings of romancing pencils, than sober every-day truths. But none of these gave me any adequate idea of the enormity and extent of the sufferings of the trampled herd of British people. England is a country of almost incomprehensible extremes. She is every thing that is glorious, and everything that is shameful. She has in government, what some of the old masters were so fond of showing in their *chiaro oscuro* pictures. Overgrown power is balanced in her cartoons by despairing helplessness. One portion of society dies slowly by surfeit—another rapidly by famine. One section of the Established Church gropes back through formulas to scholasticism and the creed of Hildebrand, without his heroism or evangelical devotion to the Founder of the Christian faith ; while the other throws off its plethoric humors in the fox chase, and sanctified indulgences. The science of the universities had degenerated into learned ignorance till such men as Brougham, Arnold, Macaulay, Bulwer and their great *confreres* touched them with the wand of genius, and brought them somewhat nearer to, but a still dim comprehension of, the objects of Letters, Learning and Science. The other extreme left the lower classes in sottishness incomprehensible.

The condition of the helpless classes of England, Thomas Carlyle considered to be a subject worthy of the serious attention of statesmanship. Every thinking, reading man knows something of Carlyle's pamphlet : " The Condition of England Question." It is safe to say that a majority of the men of Great Britain know not how to gain enough by their honest labor to secure themselves and their families from want. This is a pretty important item in the estimates which England is making for herself in the future. Into these limits are crowded all the elements of England's " yet to be." The sulphur, the saltpetre and charcoal are there, and the strong arm of power cannot forever keep them asunder. The trouble will come when they begin to mingle. The middle classes are safe, because they are right. They are free from those wretched and dangerous elements which have, in all nations that have passed away, laid the mains which by the explosion overthrew governments and society.

XVIII.

BUT the great work of regeneration is slowly going on in England, and she may thank her fortune that her Constitution is unwritten. She makes her Constitution as she goes along. It began with the Magna Charta, and it has been like many of her old structures, growing part by part, and all the time making in the concrete a pretty complete whole ; so that without any further form than concurrent votes of both houses of Parliament, and decisions in courts of final appeal, she is saved from those necessities that have sometimes pressed on *us*, to go through the forms of constitutional amendments, to which we are so rigidly held by the conditions of our own Federal Constitution. In this respect, England appears more Democratic than we. She has, indeed, a refined and eliminated element of Republicanism which sometimes shows itself. When all England is roused, and the angry cry for bread comes howling up to the British Parliament from the starved millions, if some relief is not given or promised, a single vote of lack of confidence in the ministry brings a change and saves a revolution ; while under our boasted Democratic liberty, if we happen to put into power, as we have two or three times, a bad or incompetent man, and with him a bad and incompetent set of counsellors, we must either rely upon the omnipotent power and beneficent mercy of Almighty God to remove the President and his creatures of mischief to better or worse worlds, or grin and bear it till the four constitutional years of humiliation and disgrace are passed, and we can once more go on our way.

This elasticity of the British Constitution, and this inherent love of justice and of liberty, and this sacred regard which British monarchs and British nobles must pay to the rights of the people, when the people demand them, is a great lack in our American system of government; so that the American who goes bragging around the world about the intrinsic superiority of our administration of government over that of all others, is the fair object of ridicule. I love justice, and above all I love it as towards foreign men, and foreign governments. The recent events that have occurred in the United States, may well humble us, and put an end to all this balderdash about the essential superiority of Republican over monarchical forms. What I have complained of most, and shall complain of still, is, that England in the comprehension of her statesmen has not yet found herself generous, or just, enough to concede a better system of social life, and remuneration for labor that would lift her valleys up, without tumbling her mountains down.

XIX.

YES, the great work of regeneration is going on in England. Her statesmen know enough to yield to the pressure which would force a reform, rather than defy it and provoke a Revolution. This was proved when the great Reform Bill was passed, and the rotten borough system partially abolished. It was made true again, when O'Connell, outside of Parliament, carried the Catholic Emancipation Bill through over the heads of the House of Lords. This was true when the Corn Laws were finally abolished. This was true when the Irish Encumbered Estates Bill became a law. This was true when, in name at least, property in human flesh and soul was abolished throughout the empire. This was true when a larger liberty of voting was granted. Again, when some concession was made, small as it was, from the Government to take a portion of some of the fruits of heavy taxation, to devote to the education of a few of the people. It will be true hereafter, when any well-prepared

English boy can enter an English university—when the sacred right of the ballot shall be conceded :—above all, when such a union of Church and State as the union which now compels the believer in one religion which he loves, to support another which he abhors, shall be abolished.

The legislators of England have generally had among them brave, bold and humane advocates of the rights of the people. And looking back over the last two or three decades, I cherish with glowing earnestness the hope which has dawned through many clouds of distrust and despondency, that a complete regeneration of the condition of the British people will be achieved, without much of the violence and blood of Revolution.

The beneficent changes which have occurred, have not been ushered in by tempests. They have been wrought out silently and effectually, as far as they have gone. The surface has remained the same, while the center has changed. England may be no nearer a Republic now, than she was a century ago, not half so near as in the time of Cromwell. But she is nearer liberty. The spirit of Reform has entered British legislation, and it will do its perfect work ; for what Anglo-Saxon-Norman men undertake, they are sure in the long run to perform. Conservatism itself has achieved reforms against which the Whigs fought twenty years ago. England is nearer free-trade with all the world, than either of the great parties of this Republic have ever been willing to come. Her great statesmen have at last made the discovery, which the political writers of Italy made more than two hundred years ago, that civilization, and the true policy of every nation require that all obstacles which the barbarism of former ages had raised to the free and unobstructed intercourse of mankind should be leveled. And in the abolition of her navigation laws, she has shown a more liberal policy towards foreign nations, than we have ever offered in any period of our history.

XX.

I HAVE said that I never desired to make out a case against
Great Britain as towards the United States, since she has
made it out herself.   Efforts enough were put forth by good
citizens in the United States, and good subjects in Great Britain,
during a long course of years, to heal the wounds that had been
made between the two nations, from the Stamp Act to the sailing of the pirate "Alabama."   But the most peacefully disposed
men on both sides have lost their courage, because they have
lost confidence in their ability to work, through peaceful means,
the accomplishment of results which seem now to defy even destiny itself.   It is more true with nations than with individuals,
that ages are sometimes crowded into hours—that the flash of
a sabre may do, in a second, what a whole generation has grown
tired in waiting for—that exhausted patience among men and
governments may assume the prerogatives of the Almighty,
and make the bolt and the flash come together.   Beware, however, where the bolt may strike.

This is all true in our own history of later days.   The enemies of our own household undertook the overthrow of our
Union, and to wind up our history as a first-class power.   England has given them all the encouragement, aid and comfort
which she dared to give.   The course she has taken now looks
strange enough, and in after times neither she nor her historians
can explain her conduct to themselves.   Men forget, on both
sides of the Atlantic, that England will live in America when
she shall have died at home.

XXI.

ENGLAND owes much of her progress to the spirit of
liberty caught, at first, from her own wild hills ; a spirit
which was kept alive and invigorated by the fierce struggles
through which she had to pass.   More favorable circumstances
than those in her history could not have combined for the

formation of a free, brave and generous people. In the freedom of her political institutions, she was for ages in advance of the rest of the world ; for the democratic principle had crept into her Constitution, long before mankind had elsewhere begun to question the *divine right of kings*. Many a time were English tyrants made to bow before the indignant Briton. Thus was the pride of the Norman princes humbled, when upon King John the assembled barons imposed the Magna Charta. Thus, too, did the nation avenge the insolence and tyranny of the Tudors, on their weakened and helpless successors, when a haughty line of monarchs went down in misfortune and blood, and the sceptre was grasped by the great Cromwell.

XXII.

MUCH has been said against Cromwell ; but none deny that it was under his splendid administration English liberty assumed its broadest character. Scenes of riot and anarchy existed, it is true ; but they were accompanied with blessings, for the absence of which nothing could atone. They waked in the bosom of the people those fires of liberty which have been the hope of England to this hour ; fires, too, from which our own altars were kindled. For it was during that great struggle, with the sound of contention still in their ears, and the shout of liberty, mingled with prayers to God, still on their lips, that the Puritans bore away with them all England had ever known of political or religious freedom. England was unconscious at the time, that the greatest of her offspring were taking with them the fruits of that Revolution to a forest home, where they would rear an empire that could not be conquered.

History tells us, that after a great effort the human mind settles into repose, and rests satisfied with past achievements. After the restoration of Charles II., who never should have been permitted to wear a crown, the flames of liberty seemed to go out, and the reign of tyranny again commenced. From that time, the mass of the people have sunk down in uncomplaining silence: "Now and then, indeed, they have bustled about and shook their chains," but to little purpose.

XXIII.

THE nation has increased in power, wealth, arts and learning; but the progress has been confined to the higher orders. The mass have been below the current of advancement—busy in toiling for bread. What has England's prosperity been to the poor? Machinery has only lessened the value of their honest labor; commerce only increased the luxuries of the rich; books, though abundant as the productions of the earth, have done nothing for the toil-worn craftsman, whom drudgery has left no time to read. The world has moved on, but brought to him none of the blessings civilization should profusely scatter in her progress; and while every other land is filled with the elegant productions of English art, the poor enjoy none of the abundance they so liberally dispense. Commerce, which in our times seems to unite with Christianity in achieving the world's redemption, is to him a bitter curse.

Is this the nation once the freest on earth? It is now more polished, opulent, and splendid than ever; but it has also within its bounds, deeper suffering and more crying wrong than it ever had in the days of its ancient obscurity; and this suffering and wrong seem the more intense and unnatural, in contrast with the spirit of the age.

XXIV.

BUT there is a point where degradation passès the bounds of endurance; and England's people, who have so long bowed down in silent sorrow to the cruel arm of tyranny, are starting from their dream-like stupor. The sun of liberty, now advancing high in the heavens, begins to throw some glancing beams through the gratings of their prison; they are looking anxiously abroad to find the occasion of their miseries; and wo to those from whom they conceive their miseries to flow. They drop the hammer upon the anvil; they pass from the clank of the factory, and ask for bread; it is not given: they *will* know why it is the English laborer must starve in a world of plenty. Once deeply stirred to a sense of injury and wrong, these men will not be silenced:

> " Not poppy, nor mandragora,
> Nor all the drowsy syrups of the world,
> Shall ever medicine them to silence."

English legislators begin to feel this; and ever and anon Committees are appointed, Reports made, so charged with human wo that they almost drive the reader's brain to madness; and bills are passed ostensibly for relief; but the evil is not reached: it is all shallow legislation.

Says Carlyle: " You abolish the symptom to no purpose, if the disease is left untouched. Boils on the surface are curable or incurable; small matter, while the virulent humor festers deep within, poisoning the sources of life; and certain enough to find for itself new boils and sore issues; ways of announcing that it continues there, that it would fain not continue there."

Thus England's wise men cheat themselves, and—the people *for a while*, by passing laws to quiet their discontent, grown fierce and mad. It is a silly expedient to play this game. " It is the resource of the ostrich, who, hard hunted, sticks his foolish head in the sand, and thinks his foolish unseeing body is unseen too."

XXV.

SOME men think England now more powerful than ever; but such persons forget *the wild boiling sea of smothered discontent, which is heaving under the throne and the aristocracy.*

It is as certain that the English Government will be overthrown, as that it is God's sublime purpose to emancipate a
long-fettered world, unless she shall cease her obstinate and
blind opposition to the progress of freedom, and grant the
people justice. No man who feels in his own soul the lofty
spirit of the age, and tracks the progress of the car of Liberty
as it rolls among the nations, can believe that England will be
able much longer to breast herself up against the advancement
of humanity : the majestic movements of God's Providence
can be clearly seen ; a train of causes are in operation too
mighty to be resisted by the crumbling thrones of despotism.
No ; England can do all mortal man can do ; she never vacil-
lates, is never faint-hearted : but she cannot successfully oppose
the spirit of the age. She has rife within herself the fiercest
elements of disorder, revolution, and decay. These are her
internal foes.

XXVI.

BUT, more than this, a deep-seated indignation against her
is manifesting itself throughout the world. Ambition
and injustice have made up the history of her diplomacy for
centuries past ; and her navy has been the grand executor of
her will. By it, she has acquired her foreign power ; and
through it, for nearly three centuries, she has possessed facilities for visiting every country to which wind and wave can
bear ; and these facilities have been most actively improved.
She has become familiar with every point of great commercial advantage, and appropriated to herself all the solitary
and unclaimed islands, and many of the claimed ones, she has
found straggling at a convenient distance from the mainland.
By discovery, conquest, and usurpation, she has reared an
empire upon which the sun never goes down ; and this she
has accomplished by being able to traverse the ocean without
fear or molestation.

Distance had hitherto formed a limit for conquest ; and
Alexander himself would have been a harmless assailant

against an island standing off a few leagues at sea. A few months have sufficed to transport her armies to the most distant countries; and that, too, frequently in an unexpected hour for her enemies. The naval supremacy of England once established, her political supremacy followed as a matter of course. By various devices she has extended her acquisitions alike in peace, and in war; and whatever she has acquired she has steadily retained. Thus, by discovery, silent assumption, or conquest, her claims have continued to grow; and when open plunder would not do, she has tried her hand at private filching. Accordingly, we see her asserting some new pretensions almost every day.

XXVII.

BUT her navy can no longer secure to Britain, the same supremacy as in former times. The rivalships of nations are not now, as once, of a warlike character—they are struggling for the mastery in commerce. The motive of national glory has in a measure given way to that of interest; and the acquisition of wealth is the principal advantage a nation now promises to itself in diplomacy. A great struggle has commenced in those arts which humanize mankind. This, it is true, is not yet the full result; it is only the tendency of affairs. Preparations for war are still made; national antipathies are still indulged; but these are hourly growing feebler and less rancorous. Such enterprises are looked upon with coldness and disapprobation; and the madness of plunging nations into war for trivial causes, is constantly becoming more and more palpable.

It is therefore to be hoped, that the extensive possessions of Britain will be made only the means of extending civilization, and enhancing her commercial importance; that they will no longer be turned into pretexts for quarrels and wars; that her grasping ambition will stop before she shall have kindled against her *universal* exasperation. The political equality of nations, was recognized long before the political equality of men ; and in attempting, therefore, to overshadow and trample upon the kingdoms around her, England is violating an older and longer established principle, than when she dresses one man in gold and sends him to the House of Lords, and another in rags and sends him to the workhouse. But this last practice may prove sufficiently dangerous, as the first may prove sufficiently fatal.

XXVIII.

ENGLAND is glorious by reason of her age, her ruins, her power ; her commerce, which has extended over the world ; her Christian missionaries, who are calling the pagans from their idols ; and her bards and orators, whose names stand bright on the records of mankind. But we cannot admire the spirit of that policy which, in giving the nation power and consideration abroad, leaves it weakened and wretched at home ; which, in providing the rest of the world with the elegancies and luxuries of civilized life, leaves the crowded masses of its own poor, in ignorance and starvation ; which, in its efforts to keep up the nation's outward pomp and display, takes no heed of its sickness and suffering within.

Let her remember that no sadder aspect in the decay of civic society can be presented, than when honest laborers, by millions, are perishing with want, while an aristocracy around them are rolling in voluptuousness ; that while the great middle class of her citizens are clamorous for their political rights, the lower classes at the same time are clamorous for bread ; that her provinces are held by a frail tenure ; that the branches of her power are already grown too large for the parent tree : that the heart of an empire may decay, while a distant dependency continues to flourish. Let her remember, too, that a Power greater than her own, has left no traces of its political existence in Italy ; and that the barbarian's steed long ago made his manger in the Golden House of Nero !

BOOK II.

———

THE POWER AND MAGNIFICENCE OF THE BRITISH EMPIRE.

POWER AND MAGNIFICENCE OF ENGLAND.

"That power whose flag is never furl'd—
Whose morning drum beats round the world."

"The future historian of a *decline* and *fall* hereafter, not less memorable than that of Rome, will probably commence his work with a corresponding account of the power and extent of the British Empire under William the Fourth and Queen Victoria. What Rome was in its influence over the destinies of mankind in the 1st Century, England is now in the 19th; while not merely in regard to rank in science and civilization, but also in the territorial extent of its possessions, on which the sun never sets, England occupies a prouder position than ancient Rome." *Westminster Review, Ap.* 1842.

THE POWER AND MAGNIFICENCE OF THE BRITISH EMPIRE.

I.

NINETEEN hundred years ago the Roman Standard first floated on the shores of Britain. Then a race of barbarians, clothed in the skins of wild beasts, roamed over the uncultivated island. The tread of the legions was then heard on the plains of Africa and Asia, and the name of Rome was written on the front of the world. Nearly two thousand years have rolled by, and Julius Cæsar and all the Cæsars, the Senate, the people, and the Empire of Rome have passed away like a dream. Her population now falls short of that of New York State,—while that Island of barbarians has emulated Rome in her conquests, and not only planted and unfurled her standard in the three quarters of the globe that owned the Roman sway, but laid her all-grasping hand on a new continent. Possessing the energy and valor of her Saxon and Norman ancestors, she has remained unconquered, unbroken, amid the changes that have ended the history of other nations. Like her own island that sits firm and tranquil in the ocean that rolls round it, she has stood amid the ages of man, and the overthrow of empires.

II.

A NATION thus steadily advancing over every obstacle that checks the progress or breaks the strength of other governments, making every world-tumult wheel in to swell its triumphal march, must possess not only great resources, but great skill to manage them. Looking out from her sea-home she has made her fleets and her arms her voice. Strength and energy of character, skill, daring, and an indomitable valor exerted through these engines of power, have raised her to her present proud elevation.

Her navy embraces *six hundred vessels.* Besides these she has fleets of steamships and packets so constructed as to be easily converted into war ships. In the short space of two months she could send 150 more steam frigates well equipped to sea, making in all 750 war vessels ; so that she could stretch a line of battle ships from Liverpool to New York, each separated only four miles from the other. Thirty millions of people in the three kingdoms sit down in the shadow of her throne. In the East, 150,000,000 more come under her sway, besides the vast number, civilized and uncivilized, that inhabit her provinces in every quarter of the globe.

III.

SALUTES in honor of the birth of the Prince of Wales were fired in America,—on the shores of Hudson's Bay, along the whole line of the Canadian Lakes, in New Brunswick, Nova Scotia, Newfoundland, in the Bermudas, at a hundred points in the West Indies, in the forests of Guinea, and in the distant Falkland Islands, near Cape Horn. In Europe—in the British Islands, from the Rock of Gibraltar, from the impregnable fortifications of Malta, and in the Ionian Islands. In Africa—on the Guinea coast, and St. Helena and Ascension from the Cape to the Orange River, and at the Mauritius. In Asia—from the fortress of Aden in Arabia, at Karrack, in the Persian Gulf, by the British arms of Affghanistan, along the Himalaya Mountains, the banks of the Indus and the Ganges, to the Southern point of India, in the Island of Ceylon, beyond the Ganges in Assam, at Prince of Wales' Island, and Singapore ; on the shores of China, at Hong Kong and Chusan, and in Australia, at the settlements formed on every side of the Australian continent and Islands, and in the Straits which separate these Islands of the New Zealanders. No Prince has ever been born in any other country, in ancient or modern times, whose birth was hailed with rejoicings at so many different and distant points in every quarter of the world.

After glancing over this catalogue of countries, we might well inquire, what spot is there where English cannon do not speak of English power? Along the St. Lawrence, Lakes Ontario, Erie and Michigan, one long booming shot rolls down over these free states, saying, "England is here." The wandering tribes of the western prairies and Guianian forests hear it and cower back to their fastnesses, for England is there. It sends terror through millions of hearts as it thunders from the harbors and fortresses of the East Indies. The vessels entering the Mediterranean turn an anxious eye to the rock of Gibraltar, as the smoke slowly curls up its sides ; and the report of a thousand cannon says in the most significant language, that England is there. To the reflecting man there is *meaning* in that shot which goes round the earth. England sends her messengers abroad to every nation, and the insignia of her power are scattered among all the tribes of the great family of man ; while she sits amid the sea, as if her power were the centre of tides, whose pulsations are felt on every shore, and up every continent-piercing river.

IV.

THERE is something in the name of England which awes mankind. The pressure of her hand is felt on every government, and her voice is heard at the council board of every nation. To one who looks only on the territory of England proper, the extent of her dominion seems incredible. That a small island should rule half continents, is indeed strange. No other nation since Rome, has so expanded herself, reached out such long arms, and with them grasped so much, and so strongly. How so small a body can extend and wield such immense limbs surprises those who calculate power from physical strength. It is the *moral* power of England that has carried her so high. Mind and skill multiply physical power a thousand-fold. It is as true of nations as of individuals. Every able-bodied man has two arms, and five fingers at their extremities; yet who estimates the power of the body so much as the power of the will that controls it? An ox can draw more than fifty men, it may be; but a single man can set in motion machinery which wields a power greater than that of the fabled Cyclops. China, with her vast territory and exhaustless population, can be brought to her knees by a few English ships and a few English cannon, guided and pointed by English *mind*. The few on one side, are governed by mind; the many on the other by ignorance. It is this which has enabled England so long to stand at the head of Europe, and send her mandates over the world. No throne since the world stood, has had such intellects gathered round it as the British throne. The clear heads that encircled it have ever been her firmest bulwarks. The intellect of Pitt, or Canning, can do for England in diplomacy, what Malta and Gibraltar cannot. English monarchs have in most instances been mere puppets—the wires that moved them were in the hands of such men. It was this moral power alone that made America her successful antagonist. Hitherto she had met physical force with moral power; but when she made her onset *here*, then "Greek met Greek." In the conflicts of ignorant nations, it is only a trial of muscles and bones, like the strifes of brutes; but in those of enlightened nations, it is the struggle of souls. England's *soul*, not her arms, has impressed itself on the world. It is the intelligence with which she speaks, that swells her voice so far, and makes it remembered so long. It is the intelligence that guides her fleets and armies, that renders them so formidable.

v.

BESIDES, there is a humanity about her when not crushed out by pride and love of power. The Commons of England have often shown a steadfast resistance to tyrants, that has blessed the cause of human freedom the world over. They have cut off one king's head, and can another's when necessary. The yeomanry of England were superior to those of any other nation in Europe. Bold, intelligent, and upright, they ought still to constitute no small share of her glory. Even amid the terrors and lawlessness of civil war, they acted with moderation and humanity. When king and commons, tyranny and aristocracy, were arrayed against each other, under the ascending star of Cromwell, civil law in England lost little of its sacredness. There is a love for the right and the true in the yeoman which equally resists lawlessness and oppression. There is also a religious feeling pervading this class, which, mingling with the rough elements of the old Norman and Saxon character, gives double power to them as a body. It is the intelligence and morality of these men, which *ought* to be the foundation of the English government, that will assert their power when revolutionary times come on again. There is no danger of the tyranny of British *kings* ever being reëstablished—all oppression now proceeds from the *aristocracy*—and the people are so fast advancing in a knowledge of human rights, and the consciousness of their power—which is always associated with intelligence—that the danger of the aristocracy is fast increasing.

VI.

IT will be unnecessary to say much of the manufactures of Britain. Most of my readers know that her machinery accomplishes more every year, than could be done by the entire population of the globe without it; the machinery of England does the work and puts forth the power, of a thousand million men, exceeding by one-half the entire number of men in the world. But I need not dwell on these facts, for they have been told a thousand times. England's commerce administers to the wants and the luxury of the world—finding its way to the farthest limits of the globe. Her merchants, like those of old Tyre and Alexandria, are clothed with scarlet, and dwell in palaces, while every nation, and every tribe of earth's great family, pour into her lap the gold, silver, precious stones and luxuries of every clime.

VII.

ENGLAND also stands unrivalled in the great men and the literature she has given to the world. From Alfred, who laid the foundation of British Glory, down through British history till now, she presents a galaxy of illustrious men, furnished in the annals of no ancient or modern empire. In her Milton she has more than a Homer; in her Bacon more than a Solon; and in her Shakspere, more than the earth has ever beheld in any other mortal mould. Her literature has done more for human freedom and civilization, than all the literature of other nations. Expansive in its nature, it has revealed the true sources of power, and taught men to know their strength. Bacon unbound the earth and set men acting intelligently, or rather marching forward, instead of marking time. Newton unbound the heavens, and bade them roll in harmony and beauty before the eye of intelligence. England has waked up the world. Not satisfied with knowing and improving the present, she has hastened the future. In her impetuous valor she has called on the tardy ages, as if in haste to meet their unknown events. But this she attempts no more. The future she invoked has come, and like Hamlet she starts at the spirit she has summoned forth. Having taught the people some knowledge—they are now sternly and intelligently demanding their rights; having taught the people strength—they are shaking the throne with its first experiment. Proud in her power, she has dared to do what no other nation has ever attempted—she has given her people the book of human rights, and yet told them not to ask for their own. She has told them they were free, and yet cheated them into the submission of serfs. In every other experiment she has been thus far successful—but here she has overrated her strength. If it could be done, England could do it. But it is attempting a contradiction, an impossibility ; and yet we can hardly see how she could escape the dilemma. Without being an enlightened nation, she could not have been great; and being an enlightened nation, she cannot exercise despotic power with safety. Yet starting on this broad basis, we cannot well see how she could have passed from it easily ; not that it would have been impossible had there been a will ; but taking into the account the prejudices of men, their love of power and wealth and pride, it is natural England should retain the form of government she adopted, even after its workings were seen to be evil. She could most easily have been a free and a great nation when in the transition state to which Cromwell brought her, had a second Cromwell been found to take the place of the first. Here Macaulay thinks England made her great mistake—" Either Charles the First never should have been brought to the block, or Charles the Second never should have been brought to the throne." Had the great Hampden lived, no man could say this consummation would not have been reached.

VIII.

TO do it now, would be to wipe out at one stroke the long line of Kings—bury the Peerage—rend Church and State from their harlot embrace—fling the reins of government to the people, and bid them guide their own destinies, and relieve their own wants. This, King, Peerage and Hierarchy will never willingly permit. To lay down their honors and ill-gotten wealth and, like the slaveholding aristocracy of the South, be reduced to the painful necessity of acquiring them by industry and merit, is a task they cannot perform. Honors they must have, and opulence too, though millions perish. Their rent-roll must be as great, though millions more fill the land with the cry for bread. To sustain the splendors of royalty, aristocracy, and hierarchy, there must be a perpetual drain of wealth from the people, to flow round the throne and privileged classes. This flow of wealth does not pass through the natural channels of trade. The people receive no equivalent for it. To go and take it from the poor man's pocket at the bayonet's point would be too bare-faced a robbery in the sight of the world. Hence inordinate taxation—tithes, church rates, excise and custom duties, etc., must be employed to legalize the robbery. The mass of the people behold this stream of gold incessantly flowing from them towards their idle and profligate oppressors, while there returns not even a scanty supply of bread. Such a sight naturally awakens the keenest inquiry, and as the injustice of it all forces itself upon them, the strongest, stormiest passions of the human soul are aroused.

IX.

THE English government is a *solid* one, but it must be infinitely more so to sustain itself amid such a wild waking up of men to their rights. There is a glory round her throne and her peerage, whose honors were laid in the days of Norman chivalry ; but it must be brighter than it has ever yet been, to dazzle the eyes of wronged and starving men, for the first time open to the true and only means of redress. The Church with its long train of mitred bishops, led on by Royalty itself, is an imposing spectacle, but it must invent some new majesty to awe a people that openly, boldly cry, " *Give us more bread and fewer priests !*" The throne of England towers as majestic as ever, but fearful shadows are flitting over it, the visages of famine-struck, hate-filled men. The chariot with its blazing coronet, and lazy lord within, rolls by as imposingly as ever ; but there is an ominous sound in the streets which the rumbling of its wheels cannot utterly drown ; it is the low, half-suppressed threat, YOUR TIME WILL COME ! Her cathedrals and bench of bishops retain their ancient splendor, but there are eyes looking on them with other purpose than to admire or revere.

To the careless observer, England is as powerful and magnificent as ever; all things yet remain as they were. But there is an under-working power which gathers strength from the very obstacles that bar its progress. The tremendous power exerted to restrain it from bursting forth, cannot make it cease working. Instead of expending its fires in eruptions, *it slowly eats away under ground*, hollowing out the whole mountain on which the Throne, the Aristocracy, and the Church rest. The greatest, keenest-sighted men of England know this, and they begin to study these new and alarming appearances, as philosophers study volcanoes—not to see what they shall do with the volcano, but what the volcano is going to do with them. And yet, after all, we think England could make as great an exertion (in certain directions) now as ever. In a crisis which should call forth all her resources, she would exhibit as much strength as she ever has done. A common danger would unite for a while all her jarring interests. No outward force, we imagine, can subdue her. Her provinces might be cut off in a general war, but her throne she would hold against the world. Her danger lies where the exertion of physical force would only increase it. Not abroad, but *at home*, are the elements of trouble. Not hostile armies, but her own subjects have become her greatest dread. She has reached that crisis from which most governments date their decline —*her foes have become they of her own household.*

In many respects she resembles the Roman Empire. Her own population bearing but a small proportion to the number of her subjects; like Rome her *external* growth has been more rapid than her *internal;* or rather, while she has been extending her dominion abroad, the elements of destruction have been gathering at home. Like Rome, too, her arms have become too long for her body. Even had not the Northern barbarians swarmed down on her, like giants drunk with wine, Rome would soon have reeled to her downfall. Nothing but a regeneration of the people could rescue her from the approaching ruin. But England is not threatened with *this* evil; her superstructure does not totter because it stands in the midst of an enslaved people, but because it is based on millions of agitated human hearts. It vibrates not so much because it has been wrong, as because the bowed necks on which it has so long rested, begin to erect themselves. England's greatness is in the past, not in the future. She looks *back* with pride, *forward* with shuddering.

X.

THIS truth was illustrated to me most forcibly as I passed from the crowded streets of London into the TOWER, that grand and gloomy treasure-house of England's Feudal and military glory. It was founded by William the Conqueror as a fortress, nearly eight centuries ago, and it speaks to us from the feudal age. As I entered its ponderous gates, crossed the ditch, and stood before the massive buildings, made gloomy by the terrible part they had played in the history of England, the past rose before me, haunted with majestic figures. For awhile the misery of England was forgotten—London was to me as though it were not—I stood in the shadow of past centuries.

I will not describe the Tower, but listen awhile to the language of this old home of the English monarchs. In one of the great chambers, the Horse Armory (the destruction of a large part of those valuable treasures of antiquity in this building by fire in 1841, was subsequent to the date of the visit here referred to,) were arranged, in regular and chronological order, twenty-two equestrian figures, many of them of the most celebrated kings of England, with their favorite lords ; all of them with their horses, in the armor of the ages in which they lived, surrounded by the insignia of their rank, and the trophies of their conquests.

In passing slowly by them, I met first, the figure of Edward, clad in the armor he wore 600 years ago, with hauberk and sleeves, and hood, and chausses of mail. Next came Henry VI. with his battle-axe, and knightly cap. Passing Edward IV. and Henry VII. I stood with a strange feeling, before Henry

VIII. in his gilt armor. As he scowled down on me in his
battle array, I wanted to whisper in his ear the names of his
murdered wives, and disinherited daughters. I imagined the
change that passed over that kingly face when he read the letter of the incomparable Anne Boleyn, written to him from this
very Tower, just before she was brought to the block. Though
his heart had become harder than the mail that covered it,
there were daggers in these dying words of a faithful wife that
found their way to its core :—" Let not your Grace imagine
that your poor wife will ever be brought to acknowledge a
fault, when not so much as a thought thereof ever preceded.
. . . Try me, good King, but let me have a lawfull tryall ;
and let not my sworn enemies sit as my accusers and judges ;
yea, let me receive an open tryall, for my truth shall fear no
open shames. . . . But if you have already determined of me,
and that not only my death, but an infamous slander must
bring you the enjoying of your desired happiness, then I desire
of God that he will pardon your great sin therein, and likewise
mine enemies, the instruments thereof, and that He will not
call you to a strict account for your unprincely and cruel usage
of me at His general Judgment Seat, where both you and me,
myself, must shortly appear, and in whose judgment I doubt
not, (whatsoever the world may think of me,) mine innocence
shall be openly recorded and sufficiently cleared, etc. From
my doleful prison in the Tower, this 6th of May. Your most
loyall and ever faithful wife, ANNE BOLEN." To that judgment he has gone.

As I looked on this long line of kings, sitting motionless on
their motionless steeds, the sinewy hand strained over the
battle-axe, the very swords they wielded centuries ago flashing
on my sight, and the very spurs on their heels that were once
driven into their war steeds as they thundered over the battle
plain, the plumes seemed to wave before my eyes, and the shout
of kings to roll through the arches. The hand grasping the
reins on the horses' necks seemed to be a *live* hand, and the
clash of the sword, and the shield, and the battle-axe, and the

mailed armor, rang in my ear. I looked again, and the dream was dispelled. Motionless as the walls around them, they sat, mere effigies of the past. Yet how significant! Each figure there was a history—and all monuments of England's glory as she was.

XI.

A T the further end of the adjoining room sat a solitary " Crusader on his barbed horse, said to be seven hundred years old." Stern, grim old figure! On the very trappings of thy steed, and on that thick plated mail, has flashed the sun of Palestine. Thou, perchance, didst stand with that gallant host led by the wondrous Hermit, on the last hill-top that overlooks Jerusalem ; and when the Holy City was lying like a beautiful vision below, glittering in the soft light of an Oriental sunset, that flooded Mount Moriah, Mount Zion, and Mount Olivet with its garden of suffering, and more than all, *Mount Calvary*, thy voice went up with the mighty murmur of the bannered host, *Jerusalem ! Jerusalem !* On that very helmet the scimetar broke ; and from that mailed breast the spear of the Infidel rebounded. Methinks I hear thy battle-shout, " *To the rescue !*" as thy gallant steed is borne into the thickest of the fight, where thy brave brethren are struggling for the Cross and the Sepulchre.

But Crusades and Crusaders are well-nigh forgotten. The dust of the desert has drifted for centuries over the bones of the chivalry of Europe. The Arab still spurs his steed through the forsaken streets of Jerusalem, and the Muezzim's voice sings over the Sepulchre of the Saviour.

I next passed into Queen Elizabeth's Armory, where rusty blades and enormous shields, picked from a hundred battle-fields, were gathered. The old glaive and bill, the boar-spear, halberds and pikes, the battle-axe, the mace and the cross-bow, with a thousand instruments of war and desolation, were piled around the room. Here also was the hideous apparatus of torture—the thumb-screw, the collar of torment, the bilboa—and there the beheading-axe, which severed the neck of the beautiful Anne Boleyn.

Omitting a thousand interesting objects, I at length entered the Small Arm Armory, a magnificent room, 345 feet in length —a wilderness of arms. Here were seen arms for over 100,000 men, all new flinted and ready for immediate use. In the Jewel Room are preserved the Crown Jewels, the Regalia, the Royal Communion Service, etc. The room is dark, and these superb jewels are seen by lamp light. It is a blaze of diamonds—the eye is dazzled with the glittering wealth scattered around. In other apartments I was everywhere met with emblems of England's power ; here she has clustered the crowns and jewels of whole races of kings.

XII.

WEARIED and overpowered with the feelings such objects awaken—borne over so many battle-fields, and startled at every step by some unexpected figure rising in my face from the past, scowled down on by kings from their war-steeds, with the battle-axes over my head—I was glad to escape into the pure air, and take one long look up into the far-spreading quiet sky.

From the Tower I ascended the Monument, which is near by, to look around on the *World of London*, heaving with its excited, busy millions, like a stirred ocean. I once more looked on the actual and the real. The rolling of ten thousand carriages, the sound of its mighty population going up in one ceaseless, confused roar to heaven, contrasted strangely with the silence and solitude of those fearful cells and chambers.

This, then, I exclaimed is England ! In a few moments I have passed from the feudal age with its gloom, to the turbulent scenes of action in our own times. England's Glory is in the *past*, her shame in the *present*, and her danger in the *future*. Proud of victories she has achieved, vain of splendor, she stands fairly represented in those trophies and jewels. And yet, who, of the thousand half-starved wretches that move in such masses below me, ever think of the Tower! The feudal age has gone by forever. That distant manufactory is greater than the Tower, for it is a *living thing.* That powerful steamship is an object of deeper interest than the relics of a thousand victories, *for it does something.* Men can no longer fall back on the past for support—they must move with the onward flow of the present—or be crushed by the trampling millions whom it were idle to dream of stopping, or staying. The aristocracy of England regard the Tower as they do the halls of their ancestors; they gaze on its treasures, and hug with greater tenacity the more it is assailed, the spirit of feudal times; they feel there is *something ominous to them* in the activity and restlessness of the present age.

XIII.

A S from this height I looked down on the miserable habitations of the poor, and cast my eye over distant Spitalfields, and thought of the 150,000 who knew not where they were to sleep that night—of the myriads crying for bread within sight of so much splendor—how that Tower sunk in my sight. It had but an hour ago stirred my heart like a trumpet-call; but now as I saw its white turrets against the sky, I loathed its grandeur. What were its emblems of greatness? Emblems of tyranny. The power that once wielded those instruments for self-aggrandizement, now use for the same purpose the sweat and toil of the poor. To gather these treasures, the blood of many thousands of England's subjects had been spilt. To sustain the pomp and royalty they minister to, tens of thousands now pine in ignorance and die of famine. Give me that Jewel-room to convert into *bread,* and I will send a shout of joy over the land that never before shook England. Give me the useless diamonds that glitter on from age to age by lamp-light in that dark and narrow cell, and before to-morrow night there shall go up more thanksgiving from London than ever before rose from its receptacles of woe. Convert these monuments of royal vanity into money, which shall clothe and feed the naked and the hungry, and in a day, they will purchase more happiness, than they will impart though they shine on for a thousand centuries. How strong must be the love of pomp, when it can overcome, not only sympathy for the suffering, but the fears and dangers of a mad and desperate population. Yes, I exclaimed, England's magnificence is based on suffering hearts, formerly purchased by *blood*, now by *tears*—formerly won in the hot fierce fight that filled hundreds of villages with mourning—now in the darker conflict of tyranny with liberty at home—of the few with the many—the rich with the poor, and which leaves the land filled with pallid poverty, wan famine, and scowling hate.

XIV.

WAR of some sort, England must wage to sustain her privileged classes—war with other nations, or war with her own subjects. *Spoils* she must win from somebody, or her oligarchy and hierarchy go to the ground. To support so large and unproductive a class, money must be obtained by unjust means. The spoils of war, or the spoils of home oppression, it matters not which, if they can but lay their hand upon them. Slothful and luxurious, they will not produce. Let another Tower be erected to trumpet forth England's magnificence, and all the trophies of it be gathered there. Let the relics be picked from every battle-field where the people's rights have fallen, and piled within. Place on his appropriate pedestal (a straw couch), that wan and haggard man who died for want of bread. Close by him, arrange the squalid family in the damp, foul cellar, famishing because an honest father can find no work. Arrange in imposing groups, the corpses of children that have perished in her manufactories. Bring in the men, women, and children, chained together naked in her coal mines. Let the rags and tatters be the Crown jewels, and take Pomp through the Museum, and bid her behold her appropriate trophies. Such a Tower would fill all London. Yet it would be more appropriate, more significant than the other—for England's present wealth and grandeur grow as really out of this suffering and destitution, as it formerly did out of her armies and navies ; or in other words, out of the sufferings and destitution of foreign foes. Idle and profligate pomp *must* live on open or secret spoils ; but spoils are not to be got without inflicting wrong and suffering *somewhere ;* and indeed a greater sacrifice of life is now demanded to sustain the feudal spirit and worthless magnificence of England, than when whole ranks were mowed down by the scythe of war.

But one who looks at England as she now is, must be struck with the moral change which is so rapidly working throughout her population. The reverence for symbols is fast passing away. The people no longer fight that a lazy lord may wear another star or ribbon. A feudal chieftain can no longer lead his vassals like sheep to the slaughter, to gratify his pride, or appease his revenge. Men begin to think for themselves : of every project of government, the subjects ask " Cui bono ?" Even they, thick-headed as their oppressors would fain have us believe them, are able to perceive some inconsistency in such piles of wealth being got without labor, while they who slave in sorrow, die without bread. Before that *cry for bread* titles and symbols disappear. Want sweeps distinctions to the grave. Famine is the greatest leveller on earth. Its hand will strike a lord as quick as a peasant. It will send its cry into the very heart of the palace, as soon as into the hovel. Men dare ask for bread *any where, of any man.* When men have abundance, they want glory ; when they lack bread, glory cannot satisfy them.

England seems now to stand as the representative head of the monarchies of Europe, and she is, as fast as she must, leading the van in the solemn conflict through which each is destined to pass—the conflict which is to decide whether governments shall be for the few, or the many, the rulers or the ruled. In that conflict, which no earthly power can long delay, thrones are to sink, the long line of kings disappear, and titles and estates vanish away.

XV.

IT brought a new joy over my heart when I saw the gray towers of Westminster Abbey rising above the stately elms of St. James's Park. The sight of the Abbey in the distance, with its deep-stained windows, its pointed turrets and pinnacles, and the thoughts they awaken, is worth a voyage to Europe. Sometimes the happiness of a life seems crowded into the short space of a few moments ; a sudden thrill of delight goes through the heart, which will not be forgotten in long years.

The legends tell that the Abbey was founded by Lucius, the first Christian King of Britain, as a burial-place for himself and his race. During the persecution of the Emperor Diocletian, it was converted into a temple to Apollo, and the heathen worship of Rome set up. But Sebert, king of the East Saxons, demolished it ; declaring, as he threw down its walls, that he would not leave one stone upon another of a temple where heathen gods had been worshipped ; and erected a church to the honor of God and St. Peter in its place. St. Augustine had baptized Sebert and his beautiful queen Ethelgoda, and consecrated Mellitus (a Roman abbot sent to Britain by Pope Gregory), Bishop of London. Sebert had freely expended his treasures upon the Abbey, and, for those times, raised a gorgeous structure.

The night preceding the day appointed for its consecration had thrown its shadows over the city, and its inhabitants were still in profound sleep, all save a fisherman, who was just preparing to cast his net into the Thames, which flows within a stone's-throw of the Abbey walls. As he was loosing his boat from the shore, some one called to him from the opposite side of the river to be ferried across. The fisherman afterwards remarked that there was something very peculiar in his voice, or he could not say that he should have left his net. But he obeyed the summons. He did not know who the stranger could be, but there was something celestial in his appearance ; and the light of his countenance cast a bright sheen upon the flowing water. When the boat touched the western bank, the stranger passed up to the Abbey, and the moment he reached it the doors opened of their own accord, and a bright light illumined every part of the building. A company of angels descended from heaven, and flocked around the portal. Music from seraphs' harps floated on the midnight air, with odors more delicious than ever perfumed the earth before. The honest fisherman gazed on the pageant with awe and admiration. Ever and anon, as some sweet strain broke forth from the church, and swelled up to heaven, it was answered by louder strains. The radiance became brighter, and the anthems so glorious that it seemed like the palace of an arch-angel welcoming the redeemed home to heaven ! As the daylight broke in the east the next morning, the lights faded, the music slowly died away, and the stranger who had crossed the river in the fisherman's boat, was seen ascending to heaven, with the angels at his side.

Strange reports of what he had seen, were circulated by the fisherman through London, and at the time appointed for the consecration, the white-robed Mellitus, with his ghostly brethren, led the expectant multitude to the church.

No sooner had the bishop thrown open the doors, than they saw enough to confirm the truth of everything the honest fisherman had said. Frankincense still lingered in the air ; twelve splendid tapers were still burning upon as many golden crosses before the altar ; the walls were anointed in twelve places with holy oil ; and the name of the Trinity in Hebrew was inscribed upon the pavement. " Can it be ?" " Yes," exclaimed the good bishop ; " Heaven has accepted the offering ; God has blessed us ; and St. Peter has been here with his attendant angels to consecrate our temple."

XVI.

TILL the time of Edward the Confessor, the first Abbey remained exposed to the sacrilegious fury of the times. At last it fell to decay, and that monarch rebuilt it upon a singular occasion. He had made a vow to the blessed Virgin during his exile, that if he should ever be restored to the kingdom of his forefathers, he would go on a pilgrimage to the tomb of St. Peter; and being once more firmly seated on his throne, he bethought himself of his vow, and prepared to set out on his pilgrimage. But his subjects gathered round his palace, and besought him not to leave them. They addressed a petition to his holiness the pope, who granted him a dispensation from his vow, on the condition that he should rebuild Westminster Abbey. The offer was joyfully accepted, and the monarch devoted a full tithe of all his possessions to the pious work. Shortly afterwards the Abbey rose from its ruins for the third time, and more beautiful than ever.

The king was buried in one of the chapels of the Abbey, and his shrine is still to be seen. In the revolutionary days of England, the shrine itself was plundered; but his body has been suffered to rest in peace there to this day. The Abbey is a vast repository of tombs, in which the progress of sculpture can be followed for nearly a thousand years. You can here see traces of the rude Saxon chisel in the early ages, when poetry, just struggling into existence, sought to perpetuate the deeds of the pious through enduring marble; and the Gothic architecture, in all its stages, from its first efforts, to the perfection of florid beauty in the times of Elizabeth. For several centuries none but kings, saints, and the founders of churches, were thought worthy to be interred in this house of God. Nobles and chieftains were content if they could but sleep beneath the *shadow* of this temple; while the common people did not expect anything better than an interment in unconsecrated ground. In course of time, the noble and learned had the privilege of burial in the Abbey gradually extended to them ; but it was considered a mark of the highest distinction to be permitted to rest in so holy a place.

XVII.

DURING the stormy days of Cromwell, few monuments were anywhere erected. It was an age of destruction, and the gray forms of oppression and power fell before the advance of the people. Instead of erecting new monuments, old tombs, where slept the illustrious dead, were defaced, and shrines were plundered of their ornaments and treasures. After the restoration of the Stuarts, (which was a darker day for the liberties of England than any she had seen under the great Cromwell) the triumph of wealth and dissoluteness began. The age of simplicity, of stern and bold primitive character, was past. The English people were yet too barbarous to enter fully into the wise policy of Cromwell : he achieved their liberty at a great price, but they were not yet prepared to receive and preserve it, or they never would have let Charles II. ascend the throne.

Wealth now became a passport to distinction during life, and the opulent, who had never rendered any service to humanity which would cause their names to be remembered, were determined that the marble at least, should perpetuate their fame. But it seems to be an unalterable law of Providence, that no man shall long be remembered with reverence, by a race whom he has not benefited ; and it is well that it is so. This world is not so sadly out of joint as to honor those men long, who have not rendered it some signal service.

At the period of which I speak, almost every church began to be lined with tablets, and crowded with monuments. You can hardly enter an old English church that does not abound in tombs and shrines. The Abbey walls were soon covered with tablets and inscriptions, and it became the first object in life, and the last hope in death, that the name should live in marble, after the body was turned to dust. We shall pass carelessly by the great mass of inscriptions; but there are names here we must read—names which will be known and honored when the walls of old Westminster shall have gone to decay; and I love to associate with them all the stories tradition has handed down from other times.

Who does not love to wander around the old structures of England, recall wild legends, and yield the heart up to the control and associations that are linked with the remembrances of childhood, and all that is entrancing in history.

XVIII.

I THINK the eye of any man, in whose veins the Anglo-Saxon blood flows, and who learned to speak the Anglo-Saxon tongue when he was a child, will, first of all, as he enters the "Poets' Corner," seek the monument of SHAKSPERE. And when he sees the tablet of the great Poet, and stands where he so often stood, he will feel that it is a crisis in his life. Said Pope, who was one of the committee to whom Britain gave the charge of erecting this monument, as he was asked to write an inscription, "No! I cannot write it. Let us have some of his own lines. No other man's genius is worthy to record his fame. Let us say nothing: we cannot praise Shakspere!" With great taste and judgment, they engraved upon an open scroll which forms a part of the tablet, these celebrated lines:

> " The cloud-capped towers, the gorgeous palaces,
> The solemn temples, the great globe itself,
> Yes, all which it inherits, shall dissolve,
> And, like the baseless fabric of a vision,
> Leave not a wreck behind."

What can a monument do for Shakspere! It seems strange, but it is nevertheless true, that the age which produces such a man, never knows fully what it has produced. His own generation cannot do him justice. While he is walking in flesh among his fellows, they little know of the sacredness of such a

gift from heaven. When after generations have read his words,
each leaving a tribute of more exalted admiration for his genius,
and entering with a warmer feeling into his spirit, tracing in
every book they write, and on every monument they raise to
his memory, one more tribute of devotion—then it is that the
world begins to know what kind of a being the great man was.
This reminds us of a custom among the simple but proud
American Indians : they come, one after another, on pilgrim-
ages from the Far West, whither our injustice has driven them,
each to cast a stone upon the spot where tradition says a great
Sachem of their tribe lies buried, and in time the monument
becomes a mountain.

Did Sir Thomas Lucy send Shakspere to the treadmill?
This Lucy's fame will be imperishable, from being associated
with that of the youthful deer-stealer of Stratford. How has
it been with great souls in all ages ? Dante was sent forth
from his country into banishment : his home, house and gardens sold by the Government. There is still to be seen in the
archives of Florence, a record which doomed Dante, whereso-
ever taken, to be burned alive !

Did not blind Homer beg his bread, and sing for a crust at
the gates of half a score of cities, which afterward fought for
the honor of having given him birth? No home for Homer, or
Dante in this world. But this is easy to be understood. They
were not fallen far enough from the empyrean of God's first
creation, to converse with the herd of mortals. They were too
great to be understood—made poor companions for the rest of
the world. Once Dante (so say Florentine books) spent an
evening in the brilliant halls of Della Scala, where buffoons
were playing their monkey tricks for the amusement of courtiers. Said the brainless Scala, addressing himself to Dante,
" How is it that these fools can do so much to amuse the court,
while you, a wise man, can do nothing of the sort? this is all
very strange." " No," said the indignant Dante, " it is not
strange, if you think of the old proverb, *Like to like*."

XIX.

IT is one of the mysterious but wise arrangements of heaven, that such great minds must battle, like the mountain oak, with storms ; naturalists tell us, that while the branches are striving against the winds, the roots are striking deeper into the earth.

The world is sure to do justice at last to every man. If the mass of mankind are forgotten, it is because they have no claim to be remembered ; and if the ambitious, the selfish, the cruel, are feared and courted by the men of their own times, posterity will reverse the decision.

It might not have been safe to have called Nero a bloody monster while he was emperor of Rome ; but it has been safe for 1700 years. Men spoke charily of the Virgin Queen while she wore the crown ; but since her death the world has not been afraid to say, that "she was a vain, selfish, jealous, proud tyrant." Nor does it follow that a man has forfeited all claim to our regard, because he has been gibbeted. How gloriously have the names of Sidney, Vane, Raleigh, Mary Stuart, and a thousand others, come forth from the eclipse which the dishonor of execution, for a long time, cast over their memories. "The walls of Elizabeth's sepulchre continually echo with sighs of sympathy heaved at the grave of her rival."

Shakspere was honored by his own age, but not as he has since been. It seems to be the opinion of mankind in this generation, that Shakspere was the greatest intellect that ever appeared in the world. There was one who knew the Bard of Avon well ; often heard him rehearse his own plays ; listened to his full musical laugh ; saw him buried in Stratford, and wept at his grave — "Rare Ben Jonson." *He knew what Shakspere was ;* appreciated his power ; revered his name ; and spoke of him as Johnson, Goethe, Carlyle, and others have since. Ben Jonson never wrote words for which his genius and his heart deserve more praise than the following :

"TO THE MEMORY OF MY BELOVED MR. WILLIAM SHAKSPERE AND WHAT
HE HATH LEFT US.

> " To draw no envy, Shakspere, on thy name,
> Am I thus ample to thy book and fame;
> While I confess thy writings to be such
> As neither man nor muse can praise too much.
>
> .   .   .   .
>
> Thou art a monument, without a tomb;
> And art alive still, while thy book doth live,
> And we have wits to read, and praise to give.
>
> .   .   .   .
>
> Triumph, my Britain; thou hast one to show,
> To whom all scenes of Europe homage owe;
> He was not of an age, but for all time.
>
> .   .   .   .
>
> Sweet Swan of Avon! what a sight it were
> To see thee in thy waters yet appear—
>
> .   .   .   .
>
> But stay! I see thee in the hemisphere
> Advanced, and made a constellation there:
> Shine forth, thou star of Poets."

It has been said that Jonson was envious of the fame of
Shakspere while living; but after death had thrown its sacredness over his memory, he wrote those touching lines, which he
could scarcely have written had he not loved the man. Ben
Jonson's mother married a bricklayer, who took Ben from
Westminster school to lay brick; and the story is told, that at
the building of Lincoln's Inn, he worked with his trowel in one
hand, and Horace in the other. The generous Sir Walter
Raleigh, thinking Ben would be of quite as much service to the
world in some other occupation, took him from his brick and
mortar, and sent him to the Continent with his son. Many
thanks to Sir Walter for that, as well as for other things.

XX.

AND there is the monument of the great Milton, who died poor, leaving three daughters unprovided for, to the charities of Englishmen, to whom he bequeathed a legacy worth more to them than all their foreign possessions. But rest thee peacefully, Milton! Thou art above the need of mortal pity now; for although the Paternoster publishers have grown rich from thy "Paradise Lost," they cannot rob thee of thy "Paradise Regained;" nor can they buy it of thee for £5, paid in three instalments.

Under Milton, is an elegant monument, lately erected to the memory of Gray, who has made every scholar weep as much for what he did not write, as over what he did. The Lyric Muse, in *alto-relievo*, is holding a medallion of the poet, and pointing to the bust of Milton, directly over it, with the inscription:

> "No more the Grecian Muse unrivall'd reigns,
>   To Britain let the nations homage pay;
> She felt a Homer's fire in Milton's strains,
>   A Pindar's rapture in the lyre of Gray."

Here is Dryden's plain, majestic monument. Sheffield showed much taste in the inscription: "J. Dryden, born 1632, died May 1, 1700. John Sheffield, duke of Buckingham, erected this monument, 1720." Nothing more was necessary. And here, too, are Cowley's monument and grave. The chaplet of laurel which begirds his urn, and the fire issuing from its mouth, are expressive emblems of the glory he has acquired by the spirit of his writings.

There sleeps Chaucer, the "Father of English poetry," who died 450 years ago. It was once a beautiful Gothic monument, but time has hardly spared the inscription. Near it is the tomb of Butler, the learned author of Hudibras, another of the great writers of England so neglected by his age that he often suffered severely from hunger. "The English are a wonderful people," says a certain English author. Yes, they are a *very* wonderful people.   They have erected palaces of gold for their oppressors, and left their illustrious authors to starve!   This is, indeed, wonderful!   John Barber, once Lord Mayor of London, a man distinguished for humanity, erected Butler's tombstone, "That he who was destitute of all things when alive, might not want a monument when dead."   Here we have the glory and the shame of England, side by side.

XXI.

BENEATH Butler's monument is the dust of Spenser.   The inscription is striking and appropriate.   "Here lies (expecting the second coming of our Saviour Christ Jesus) the body of Edmund Spenser, the Prince of Poets in his time, whose divine spirit needs no other witness than the works which he has left behind him.   He was born in London in 1553, and died in 1599."   Not far from Spenser is the grave of one of those choice spirits that from time to time come to us on earth, and over whose ashes the tears of all good men fall—Granville Sharp.   His record is in the hearts of all who love humanity.

In letting my eye wander back to Shakspere's tablet, I saw near it the monument of the author of the "Seasons," "James Thomson, Ætatis 48, obit. 27th August, 1748.   Tutored by thee, sweet poetry exalts her voice to ages, and informs the page with music, image, sentiment, and thought, never to die." The figure of Thomson leans its left arm upon a pedestal, holding a book in one hand, and a cap of Liberty in the other.

On John Gay's monument is an epitaph written by himself, which is no less shocking to good taste than to religion :

> "Life is a jest, and all things show it ;
> I thought so once, and now I know it."

John Gay was considered a sensible man ; but he has probably had occasion to change his opinion on this point.

There, are the ashes of one of those brilliant stars which **have** risen in Ireland, to shed honor upon the English name—Oliver Goldsmith ; and who does not love his name, Boswell notwithstanding ? Said that little, obsequious, but, after all, very useful slave of Johnson, one evening to Goldsmith, as he seemed to be attracting the attention of the company from the mighty lexicographer, " Oh, Goldy! you must not try to shine in the presence of Hercules." Goldsmith did shine, however, in the presence of Johnson, and every other man he met, when he condescended to.

XXII.

A LITTLE further on is a fine statue in relief, on a monument with a Latin inscription, calling upon the stranger, whoever he may be, to " Venerate the memory of Joseph Addison." Thou dost not need my praise, Addison ; but my heart responds to the call : I *do* venerate thee.

Near this is the last monument Roubiliac lived to finish : it is Handel's. The left arm of the statue is resting on a group of musical instruments, and the attitude is expressive of fixed attention to the melody of an angel, playing on a harp in the clouds above. Before him lies the celebrated " Messiah," opened at the sublime air, " I know that my Redeemer liveth ;" beneath only this inscription : " George Frederic Handel, Esq., born Feb. 23, 1684 ; died April 14, 1769."

I feel a great reverence for Isaac Barrow, who has a fine monument here : the last man we should expect Charles II. would have chosen for his chaplain. There is a curious story told of Barrow. When he was a boy, as has often been observed of others who afterward became illustrious, he used to indulge in fancies and day-dreams of young ambition. Isaac's parents felt no great admiration for such things ; and, besides, he would not work like his brothers ; and as his sire could perceive no value in a boy who would not work, the good man used to pray, that if it ever pleased the Lord to take away from him any one of his children, it might be Isaac! It is a good thing that even good men's prayers are not always answered.

"To the memory of David Garrick, who died in the year 1779, at the age of 63." When one is passing for the first time around the solemn walls of Westminster Abbey, it is difficult to feel much reverence for an actor, even though he were the greatest actor the world ever saw. Garrick was great and generous; but it is to be feared there was a part he never acted; a part, too, it were wise in every man to play, before the last fall of the curtain.

XXIII.

I COULD not but stop a few moments before the splendid monument of Major André. This monument is of statuary marble, and the figures were cut by Van Gelder. On a moulded, panelled base and plinth, stands a sarcophagus, on the panel of which is inscribed: "Sacred to the memory of Major André, who, raised by his merit, at an early period of life, to the rank of Adjutant-General of the British forces in America, and employed in an important but hazardous enterprise, fell a victim to his zeal for his king and country, the 2d October, 1780, aged. twenty-nine, universally beloved and esteemed by the army in which he served, and lamented even by his foes. His gracious sovereign, King George III., has caused this monument to be erected;" and on the plinth, "The remains of the said Major André were deposited, on the 28th November, 1821, in a grave near this monument."

The sarcophagus has projecting figures; one of them (with a flag of truce) presenting to Washington a letter André had addressed to his Excellency the night previous to his execution, and worded thus: "Sir, buoyed above the terror of death by the consciousness of a life devoted to honorable purposes, and stained with no action which can give me remorse, I trust that the request which I make to your Excellency at this serious period, and which is to soften my last moments, will not be rejected : sympathy towards a soldier will surely induce your Excellency and a military tribunal, to adapt the mode of my death to the feelings of a man of honor. Let me hope, sir, that if aught in my character impresses you with esteem towards me—if aught in my misfortunes marks me as the victim of policy, and not of resentment, I shall experience the operation of these feelings in your breast, by being informed that I am not to die on a gibbet. I have the honor to be, your Excellency, John André, Adjutant of British forces in America."

XXIV.

I HAVE some recollection, I think, that when I was a boy, I somewhere read a story like the following : After the retreat of General Washington from Long Island, by which it was left in possession of the British, that great commander applied to Colonel Knowlton to adopt some means of gaining information concerning the strength, situation and future movements of the enemy. The Colonel communicated his request to Captain Hale, one of the most brilliant and best educated young men in America, who had left the halls of Yale University to die, if necessary, for liberty. Young Hale immediately volunteered his services ; and, conquering his repugnance to assume a character foreign to his nature, in the hope of being useful to his country, passed in disguise to Long Island, and obtained all the requisite information. In attempting to return, however, he was apprehended and brought before Sir William Howe, who ordered him to be executed the next morning. This sentence (conformable, it is true, to the laws of war) was carried into effect in the most unfeeling and barbarous manner. He asked if he might see a friend (one he loved better than all things but liberty—one who had given him up to his country), and it was denied. He asked for a Bible ; it was refused ! He was soon to die ; and even his last request that a clergyman might be with him for a little time, was rejected with *noble* oaths, and *blasphemy and curses,*

(which we should not have mentioned but as furnishing a striking contrast to the conduct of Washington, who signed André's
death-warrant with tears, and, but for the advice of the court-
martial, would have granted his last petition) and, more cruel
than all this, Hale's letters written the night before his death,
to his betrothed, his mother, and other dear friends, and committed to his lordship for delivery after his execution, were broken open, read and burned,(*noble* conduct!) in order, as was said
by the provost-marshal, " that the rebels should not know that
they had a man in their army who could die with such firmness." I have also read that she who would have been his
bride, went with her father at night through the British lines,
and took his body from the gibbet, and carried it to their own
house! Spartan woman! my only regret is, that thy country
has not raised a monument to the memory of thyself and
lover.

XXV.

A LESSON of wisdom may be learned at every grave ; but
a voice comes forth from the graves of some men buried
here, which cannot but sink deep into the hearts of the living as
they stand over the dust of the sleepers.   The Earl of Chatham,
William Pitt, and his great rival Charles James Fox, Grattan,
Canning and Sheridan, all sleep close to each other ; their
strifes and heart-burnings, their lofty aspirings, their deep and
subtle intrigues, all sleeping with them.   In dying, these men
woke from the gorgeous dreams of life for the first time.
    The *elder* Pitt was the greater and better man. I always
admired the wisdom and the boldness of those prophetic words
of his to the English peers : "*To conquer America is an
impossibility.*"   He was familiar with the history of the
'injured colonies ; he knew that justice and heaven were on
their side when the struggle began ; and that love for homes
they had reclaimed from the wilderness ; love for liberty, their
wives and children, and for their posterity in all coming time,

would nerve the arm of Americans, as British gold never could the hired legions of England. One of the most preposterous notions which ever found its way into the human brain, was, that the descendants of the men who built their cabins on Plymouth Rock, could ever be conquered.

XXVI.

IT has always seemed to me that the embarkation of the Pilgrim Fathers must have been one of the finest spectacles ever presented. I have often thought, that when the Mayflower weighed her anchor, she must have seemed like a life-boat bearing away a few noble hearts from a sinking wreck—another ark freighted with men saved to people a New World. I once read a stirring anecdote of that Mayflower. It appears that one man, who had intended to sail in her, manifested some indecision when they were about to haul in the plank: "I don't know," he said, "as I had better go." "Well, then," exclaimed the brave commander, "jump ashore; if you want to go, you can go and have our fare; if not, you can stay. At any rate, we want no faint-hearted men among this crew." The man jumped ashore. The plank was the next instant hauled in, and in five minutes all her sails were set, and she was "leaving Old England's shores behind."

England has never been trod by a nobler company of men than the Pilgrim Fathers. They did not leave England because they were unwilling to struggle and die for their principles; but they saw the atmosphere of Europe was too cold and chilling for the growth of freedom, and they flung aside all but the hope that they might, in the fine language of Channing, "transplant the tree of liberty to a new and more congenial clime." There never had been a crisis in the world's history to call forth such men; they had never been needed before. *They* were true heroes—not in the common use of the term, for such heroes had driven them from their homes; but Christian, brave men, who could not be intimidated by the threat of tyranny, nor conquered by sword and cannon. They had no confidence in the weak panoply of the soldier, although they could fight when it became necessary. They afforded a strong proof of the truth of that wise saying of an old historian, " No man ever yet failed, who had faith in God and a determination to be free."

XXVII.

THE same despotism that oppressed the Puritans, urged their descendants into rebellion. There never was a greater outrage upon common sense, than the arrogant claim of England to tax the colonies with no representation in the legislature which governed them. The Americans rejected that claim with scorn, and the conflict began.

England could command the largest naval power on earth ; and what had America as an offset? Only a few rusty fire-locks laid by from the old French and Indian wars ; and, as old Stark said, a few kegs of powder, which " they were obliged to set fire to a week or ten days before they wanted to shoot." But then was raised the voice of Adams and Hancock, " To arms ; for our chains are forged, and their clanking may be heard on the plains of Concord, and Lexington and Bunker Hill!" What! subdue such men? England might as well have undertaken to chain the comets.

It makes one's blood thrill to think of the American Revolution. Rotteck says, that in the Declaration of Independence, " America planted herself between magnificence and ruin." It is a sublime idea. What a terrible thing it would have been even to England, if we had failed! Humanity would not have recovered from the disastrous blow in a hundred years. But to fail under such circumstances was impossible. The great Chatham foresaw all this ; and England, who never takes advice from her friends until it is too late—England, who commenced the war for the glory of her name and the wealth of her empire, might have saved herself millions of money,

and tens of thousands of lives, and the eternal disgrace of being expelled from the fairest portion of the habitable globe,
had she only listened to the voice of that tongue, turned to
dust in this grave.

XXVIII.

WE stopped a few moments before the superb monument of
Sir Isaac Newton. It is grand and expressive; worthy
of the illustrious man to whom it was erected. The inscription
is in Latin, short, but full of meaning. It concludes with this
beautiful sentiment: "Mortals have reason to exult in the existence of so noble an ornament to the human race."

After looking at the monuments of which I have spoken, I
directed my attention to the architecture of the Abbey. It is
an immense pile, built in the form of a cross, its length from
east to west being 416 feet, and its breadth about 200. The
two fine towers on the west end are 225 feet high. Around
the choir of the Abbey there is a succession of small chapels,
filled with curious antique monuments, and the effigies of royal
families lying in state.

We were led through every part of the Abbey by a pale old
verger, who had been so long cloistered within those sacred
walls, that he seemed to have lost all sympathy with the external world. His face was pale as marble; his step, as solemn
and still as you ever heard in the chamber of death; and his
voice seemed to come up as in hollow tones from the sepulchre:
a fitting representative of the spirit of the place.

We passed several hours among the chapels. The verger
seemed inclined to finish his explanations as soon as possible;
but we did not like the idea of being hurried through these im-
pressive chambers, and expressed a wish to remain a while:
this we were denied. But knowing that in such cases there is
one argument that never fails in England, I slipped a half crown
into the old fellow's hand, which settled the matter without
further words.

I will only speak of two of the chapels : St. Edward's and Henry the Seventh's. In the centre of the former stands the venerable shrine of St. Edward, which was once considered the glory of England. But the sepulchre was long ago broken open, and the ornaments stolen from his body. Edward was the last Saxon king of England. He died the year of the battle of Hastings (1066), and was canonized in 1269. Henry III. pledged the jewels belonging to the shrine of Edward to foreigners ; being compelled, as the record still preserved in the Tower states, to take this course "by heavy emergencies." No very creditable way for a *king* to raise money.

XXIX.

HERE Matilda, Queen of England, daughter of Malcolm, King of Scots, and wife of Henry I., is buried. It was her custom every day in Lent to walk from her palace to the Abbey barefoot, clothed in a garment of coarse hair, kissing the feet of the poorest people she met in her way, and dispensing charities. In this chapel, in a large plain coffin of gray marble, lies the body of the great Edward, called the English Justinian. He died in 1307. Four hundred and sixty-seven years after his burial, his tomb was opened by the Dean of Westminster. "The body was perfect, having on two robes, one of gold and silver tissue, and the other of crimson velvet ; a sceptre of gold in each hand, measuring near five feet ; a crown on his head, and many jewels quite bright : he measured six feet and two inches."

Here, too, Henry V., of Jack Falstaff memory, and victor of Agincourt, sleeps. In this chapel are also to be seen the two coronation chairs. The most ancient of these chairs was brought with the regalia from Scotland, by Edward I., in 1697 (after overcoming John Baliol), and offered at St. Edward's shrine. In this chair the monarchs of England are crowned, and to this place they come for their sepulchres.

Henry the Seventh's chapel is called " the wonder of the

world." It stands at the east end of the Abbey, and is so neatly joined to it that it seems to be part of the main edifice. It is adorned with sixteen Gothic towers, beautifully ornamented, and jutting from the building in different angles. It is built on the plan of a cathedral, with a nave and side-aisles. The entrance to this chapel is through curiously-wrought ponderous gates of brass. The lofty ceiling is worked into an astonishing variety of designs, and my surprise may be imagined when I was told that it was all wrought in solid stone. A celebrated French architect afterward told me, that one man could not complete the work upon that ceiling in less time than a thousand years. The pavement is of white and black marble. This splendid chapel was designed to be a kingly sepulchre, in which none but the royal should sleep; and the will of the founder has been so far observed, that none have been admitted to burial here who could not trace their descent from some ancient family of kings. But nothing is so universally and justly admired, for its antiquity and fine workmanship, as the magnificent tomb of Henry VII. and his Queen Elizabeth, " the last of the House of York that wore the English crown." This tomb stands in the body of the chapel, enclosed in a curious chantry of cast brass, most admirably designed and executed, and ornamented with statues. Within it are the effigies of the royal pair, in their robes of state, lying close together, carved on a tomb of black marble.

XXX.

HERE at last found rest the remains of the two young princes who were basely murdered by their treacherous uncle, Richard III. The story is faithfully told in a Latin inscription over their grave. We remember that these two boys were confined in the Tower, stifled with pillows, and then privately buried. One hundred and ninety years passed away before their bones were discovered, and then they were found among the rubbish of the stairs leading to the White Tower.

Charles II. removed their remains to this spot, where their ancestors lie. One of these princes was born in the old Sanctuary which once belonged to the Abbey, where his mother had taken refuge during the terrible Civil Wars of the houses of York and Lancaster.

"Two small aisles on each side of this chapel present a touching picture of the equality of the grave, which brings down the oppressor to a level with the oppressed, and mingles the dust of the bitterest enemies together. In one is the sepulchre of the haughty Elizabeth ; in the other is that of her victim, the lovely and unfortunate Mary. Not an hour in the day but some ejaculation of pity is uttered over the fate of the latter, mingled with indignation at her oppressor. The walls of Elizabeth's sepulchre continually echo with sighs of sympathy heaved at the grave of her rival. A peculiar melancholy reigns over the aisle where Mary lies buried. The light struggles dimly through windows darkened by dust. The greater part of the place is in deep shadow, and the walls are stained and tinted by time and weather. A marble figure of Mary is stretched upon the tomb, round which is an iron railing much corroded, bearing her national emblem, the thistle. I was weary with wandering, and sat down to rest myself by the monument, revolving in my mind the checkered and disastrous story of poor Mary."

Time is the great regulator. How sure he is to do justice at last ! Mrs. Jamieson has set this matter in its proper light. Mary Stuart needed no better defender of her fame. After waiting nearly three hundred years, justice was done to her name by the heroic and beautiful biographer of the imperious and hateful Elizabeth.

XXXI.

A GREAT number of the tombs and shrines of the Abbey have been shockingly mutilated and defaced. Even the kings of England, not satisfied with grinding from their living subjects all that oppression could exact, have entered this temple, and robbed the dead of those few choice jewels and treasures which surviving affection had placed in their coffins. But this, perhaps, should pass without censure, as the English Constitution declares the king can do no wrong! The sceptre has been stolen from the mouldered hand of Elizabeth, and there is hardly a royal monument which has not been plundered or mutilated. The grave is a sanctuary for the dead in the peaceful country churchyard; but not so in Westminster Abbey. They who are buried here have found no security against the rapacity and insult of the living.

I pity the man who lives and dies in the hope of being long remembered, who has no more enduring monument than the marble to perpetuate his fame. There are many inscriptions in the Abbey which cannot be read; they have faded away with the names and deeds of those they were intended to commemorate. Nothing ever appears to me so mournful as a gravestone with its epitaph obliterated by time. "Thus man passes away; his name perishes from record and recollection; his history is as a tale that is told, and his very monument becomes a ruin." This is one of those touching morals taught us by Irving, in writing about this hall of death.

One sees in Westminster Abbey almost as much as he would have seen had he lived in England for a thousand years. If a great person has died, or a great deed been done in this island, for centuries, they have brought some memento, and placed it within these walls. Here we read the story of the virtues and the crimes of England's great men; here we find their monuments, their escutcheons, and their ashes. In different ages, and from different scenes of action, England's kings have come to these solemn cloisters at last, to forget in the deep slumber of the grave, the troubles, the follies, and the guilt of the life just ended. No one of them, as he went to his sepulchre, stopped to listen to the clamors that swelled behind him; to the contentions of fierce and eager aspirants to his vacant throne.

Even bluff Harry VIII. goes sturdily to his resting-place, without seeming, in his dying moments, to bestow a thought on his discarded wives or injured daughters.

XXXII.

BUT they are not all of royal or noble blood that rest here. Greater Englishmen than English kings have a name and a grave within these solemn chambers. Bucklers, helmets and broadswords are spread over the tomb of the bold baron; the cross and the crosier mark the sepulchre of some pious bishop; and over this tomb are banners, streamers, and all the insignia of naval triumph, doing honor to some captain of the sea, who is here alike forgetful of the roar of battle and the terrors of the wreck. As you pass along those aisles, whose silence is unbroken save by your own footfall, and read the quaint epitaphs of heroes of olden time, insensibly will the impression steal over the imagination that it was but yesterday that all these dead were alive, and you, a stranger from the far future, have been carried back to the days of ancient chivalry to converse with walking shadows; to think of the present as though it were a prophecy, a dream, or a hope; and of the past as though it were a reality.

And yet, speak to that suit of armor which seems now to threaten as it once did in battle—it returns no answer; the voice is still that once spoke through those iron jaws, and the cold moisture which gathers on its rusted face seems like tears shed over the hero who once wore it.

When the mind is full of thoughts suggested by these relics of antiquity, and the heart full of emotions; when the images of great men who have long flitted around the fancy appear, and we see before us the very sword they once used in battle, and the very banner that once floated over them, there is no room left for other thought; we cannot contemplate modern times or our own existence. While we are lingering in a place where England has preserved all that she could of the great

and the virtuous—a place of which we have read and thought
from childhood, and around which so many bright recollections
cluster—what marvel if hours on hours steal away, ere we
wake from the strong illusion.*

* THOUGHTS ON VISITING WESTMINSTER ABBEY.

OLD structure! Round thy solid form
Have heaved the crowd, and swept the
    storm,
    And centuries roll'd their tide;
Yet still thou standest firmly there,
Thy gray old turrets stern and bare,
    The grave of human pride.

Erect, immovable, sublime,
As when thou soared'st in thy prime,
    On the bold Saxon's sight;
Thou holdest England's proudest dead,
From him who there first laid his head,
    "The royal anchorite,"

To her long call'd the Virgin Queen,
(And oh! what heroes passed between,)
    Who, with a might her own,
The kingdom's sceptre sway'd, and threw
A glory, and a *shadow* too,
    Around her fearful throne.

Mysterious form, thy old gray wall
Has seen successive kingdoms fall,
    And felt the mighty beat
Of time's deep flood, as thrones, and kings,
And crowns, and all earth's proudest
    things,
    It scatter'd at thy feet.

And now, as 'neath this arch I stand,
I seem upon the earth's wide strand,
    And round about me cast,
Upon the dark and silent shore,
The richest freights it ever bore,
    The glory of the past.

Oh! how the pageants rise, and swim,
And vanish round my vision dim!—
    I see the solemn funeral train,
That bears a monarch to his tomb;
The tall plumes waving thro' the gloom,
    The mournful requiem train.

The priest's low chant, the mutter'd
    prayer,
The tread of warriors, all are there;
    And high above, the toll
Of the deep bell, whose heavy knell
Blends with the organ's mighty swell,
    O'er the departed soul.

'Tis gone! and thro' the portals wide
Comes rolling in a living tide;
    And hark! far echoed out,
Whence comes that high and deafen-
    ing peal,
Till e'en these steadfast turrets reel?
    It is a nation's shout.

Oh! how the gorgeous, proud array
Is pressing through the crowded way,
    With drum and trumpet tone!
But who now halts within the door?
A monarch's foot is on the floor,
    His eye upon a throne.

His lip is wreathing in a smile,
As, passing down the foot-worn aisle,
    The banners droop around him;
But oh! his thoughts are not on those
Who hail him as he proudly goes
    To where the lordly crown him.

XXXIII.

THE day had passed away as a night of rich dreams goes by, and we were unconscious how long we had been strolling around the walls, until the evening light began to stream in more and more feebly through the lofty stained windows, and a deeper gloom settled upon every part of the Abbey. And when increasing darkness had spread through all the cloisters, chapels, and passages a more solemn and mysterious gloom, I could not but ask, what is night, deep, dark night—without moon, star or taper—around these silent poets, barons, priests, sages, heroes and kings!

Is never a sigh heard to come forth from these damp tombs?

His heart in this exciting hour,
Doth dream exultingly of power
　　The given crown shall bring;
And triumph sits within that eye,
As, thundering round him, wild and
　　　high,
　　Resounds, " God save the king ! "

'Tis vanish'd ! " like a morning cloud"—
The throne, the king, the shouting
　　crowd,
　　And here I stand alone;
And like the ocean's solemn roar
Upon some distant, desert shore,
　　A low, perpetual moan,

I seem to hear the steady beat
Of century-waves, around my feet,
　　As generations vast
Are borne unto the dim-seen strand
Of that untrodden, silent land,
　　That covers all the past.

I'm with the dead; and at my feet
The graves of two proud queens do
　　meet—

One arch gives ample room
For whom an empire was too small.
Proud rival hearts ! and is this all ?
　　A narrow, silent tomb !

Here, too, are slumbering side by side,
Like brother-warriors true and tried,
　　Two stern and haughty foes:
Their stormy hearts are still—the
　　tongue,
On which enraptured thousands hung,
　　Is hush'd in long repose.

I see the poet's broken lyre.
O'er which were utter'd words of fire ;
　　The hero's shiver'd sword ;
The sage's tomes ; the wreath of fame—
All drifting to the dark inane,
　　And no returning word.

Old Abbey ! on my thoughtful heart,
A lesson that shall ne'er depart,
　　Thy silent walls have left ;
And now. more wise than I have been,
I step into the living stream
　　Again, and onward drift.

a shout from some sleeping warrior ? or an " Ave Maria " from some crusader monk ? If we should stay here until midnight —the hour when spirits haunt these halls of the dead, if they *ever* haunt them—might we not hear the sound of revelry where the ashes of Harry of Monmouth are laid ; and a hollow voice calling out through the stillness of night." Sweet Hal ? " Around the tomb of " Queen Bess," should we not hear the flattery of gallant courtiers, and the preparations of the stage ; the voices of Raleigh, and Burleigh, and Essex, and Leicester, and the notes of the sweet bard of Avon, sounding melodiously over all ; or the plaintive sorrow of poor Mary Stuart ? Might we not hear from some part of the Abbey, a faint voice, as if it came from " the spirit land ? "

Yes!—do these dead ever waken or walk ? The battle-axe has fallen from the strong hand of the Saxon and the Norman, and they rest in stillness together. Genius, which lived in sorrow and died in want, here sleeps as proudly as royalty. All is silence ; but here " silence is greater than speech."

This is the great treasure-house of England. If every record on earth besides were blotted out, and the memory of the living should fade away, the stranger could still in Westminster Abbey write the history of the past ; for England's records are here ; from the rude and bloody escutcheons of the ancient Briton, to the ensigns of Norman chivalry ; and from these to admiralty stars, and civic honors. The changes which civilization has made in its progress through the world, have left their impressions upon these stones and marbles. On the monument where each great man rests, his age has uttered its language ; and among such numbers of the dead, there is the language of many ages. England speaks from its barbarity in the far-off time, before the day-spring of embellishing Art—its revolutions, with their earnest struggles to leave the past and reach the future—while the later shrines breathe the spirit of England's newest civilization.

XXXIV.

EACH generation has laid some of its illustrious ones here ; and it is no wonder that there is not a spot to which an Englishman turns his eye with so much pride, as to Westminster Abbey ; nor a spot the traveler so well loves to visit.

One cannot but feel both gratitude and indignation here : gratitude for every noble effort in behalf of humanity, civilization, liberty and truth, made by these sleepers ; indignation at every base deed, every effort to quench the light of science or destroy freedom of thought ; every outrage inflicted upon man ; and every blow aimed against liberty by the oppressors of the race.

There is not a great author here who did not write for us ; not a man of science who did not investigate truth for us ; we have received advantage from every hour of toil that ever made these good and great men weary. A wanderer from the most distant and barbarous nation on earth, cannot come here without finding the graves of his benefactors. Those who love science and truth, and long for the day when perfect freedom of thought and action shall be the common heritage of man, will feel grateful, as they stand under these arches, for all the struggles, and all the trials to enlighten and emancipate the world, which the great, who here rest from their labors, have so nobly endured.

And, above all, the scholar, who has passed his best years in study, will here find the graves of his Teachers. He has long worshipped their genius ; he has gathered inspiration and truth from their writings ; they have made his solitary hours, which to other men are a dreary waste, like the magical gardens of Armida, " whose enchantments arose amid solitude, and whose solitude was everywhere among those enchantments." The scholar may wish to shed his tears alone, but he cannot stand by the graves of his masters in Westminster Abbey without weeping : they are tears of love and gratitude.

BOOK III.

IRELAND — HER WOES AND STRUGGLES
UNDER ENGLISH OPPRESSION.

"ENGLISH GOVERNMENT IN IRELAND.—During the dreadful period of four hundred years, the laws of the English Government of Ireland did not punish the murder *of one man of Irish blood* as a crime."— *Sir James Macintosh.*

"The stranger shall hear thy lament o'er his plains,
      The sigh of thy harp shall be sent o'er the deep,
  Till thy tyrants themselves, as they rivet thy chains,
      Shall pause o'er the songs of their captives, and weep."

Moore.

"In the mountains of the parish of Cong, when the potatoes fail them, *they bleed their cattle and eat the boiled blood,* sometimes mixed with meal, but often without it."—*O'Connell.*

"Grattan declared that he had watched at the cradle of Ireland, and followed her hearse. He is reckoned among the illustrious dead. *I* live to sound THE TRUMPET FOR HER RESURRECTION."—*O'Connell.*

"The Sans-potatoe Irishman is of the self same stuff as the finest Lord Lieutenant! Not an individual Sans-potatoe human scarecrow, but had a life given to him out of heaven, with eternities depending on it: for once and no second time—with immensity in him, over him, and round him: with feelings that a Shakspeare's speech could not utter: with desires illimitable as the autocrat of all the Russias."—*Carlyle.*

IRELAND—HER WOES AND STRUGGLES UNDER ENGLISH OPPRESSION.

IRELAND cannot be mentioned in connection with England, without striking a sympathetic chord in the heart of every patriot and Christian. Her history is unique. Possessing an indomitable valor, kindling at the first blow of oppression, and striking for freedom in almost every generation, she is still the creature of England's caprices. But bowed and dishonored though she be, she is Ireland still. She has fallen, but not forever. She *can* be, she *will* be regenerated. Her spirit is as untamed and excitable as ever. The apathy and submission of slaves, which chills the hope of freedom, is not on her. Like a brave man, she still struggles manfully with her destiny. She also has an existence as a Nation. She has her universities and her literature. She is still the "Emerald Isle of the Ocean." An air of romance and chivalry is around her. The traditionary tales that live in her literature invest her history with heroic beauty. But she has no need of these. Real heroes —the O'Neills, the O'Briens, and the Emmets, will be remembered as long as self-denying patriotism and unconquerable valor are honored among men. In every department of literature she still takes her place. Where is the wreath her shamrock does not adorn? Where the muse that has not visited her hills? Her harp has ever kindled the soul of the warrior, and soothed the sorrows of the broken-hearted. It has sounded every strain that can move the human heart to greatness or to love. Whatever vices may stain her people, they are free from the crime of voluntary servitude. The Irishman is the man last to be subdued. Possessing an elasticity of character that will rise under the heaviest oppression, he wants only a favorable opportunity, and a single spark, to set him in a-blaze. Distinguished for his inquisitiveness and shrewdness, he is perpetually " talking over things ;" nothing escapes his observation —hence he wants no more intimate knowledge of his condition or rights, or the character of his oppressors :—*Ireland wants only union.* These traits of national character inspire hope ; with an ever active and ardent mind, no people can be effectually subdued—neither does it require so long a training nor so loud an appeal, to arouse them to energetic and successful action.

II.

TO a distant observer, that beautiful Island appears like a city of ruins in the saddened light of evening. Her glory and her strength seem departed for ever. But it is not of the poetry of the past the lover of Ireland must speak. Her bards never sang in strains so mournful and pathetic, as the sad lullaby of the mother over her famishing child. The complaint of poverty and the cry of suffering, are more heart-breaking than her most plaintive melodies. Her woes and her dishonor move not the hearts of her oppressors, but they are noted by the God of the poor.

Before speaking of the present condition of Ireland, it is necessary to refer to some events in her past history. A knowledge of the causes which have reduced her to subjugation, is necessary, in order to know where the right and wrong lie, and what justice now demands should be done. If invasion, spoliation and piracy on the part of one nation against another, provoke retributive justice, and it sinks under the punishment it has justly incurred, it has no right to complain. But if this same violence and robbery, prompted by cupidity alone, reduce an *innocent* people to slavery, the case is widely different. We wish to show by a rapid survey of the past history of Ireland, that she is an invaded and plundered nation—that both her degradation and her servitude are directly chargeable on England—that British cupidity and British pride have been the alpha and omega of Irish suffering.

The earliest history of Ireland is so mixed up with tradition, it is impossible to distinguish the true from the false. In the Sixth and Seventh Centuries, Ireland was distinguished for her piety and her learning. In the Ninth Century, she was invaded and harassed by the Danes. In the Eleventh Century, the people rose against the invaders—deposed the usurper, and placed their own king (O'Brien) on the throne. In an attempt to quell an insurrection, O'Brien was slain ; and though the Irish were victorious, yet being left without a king, they became divided by conflicting animosities and fatal rivalries, and no longer existed as a nation, but remained broken up till the Anglo-Norman invasion. Pope Adrian, himself an Englishman, made a grant of land to Henry the Second, on the condition he should hold it in fee for the Pope. Henry, of course, became suddenly pious ; and wishing to harmonize the conflicting social and political feelings of the country, sent over an army of Norman freebooters, who, with powder and steel, soon succeeded in converting most of the inhabitants.

III.

THIS is the origin of the connection between England and Ireland. Ireland was not, however, wholly subjugated even by the invasion of Richard, Earl of Strigal, surnamed the Strongbow, although she endured enough to have prostrated the energies and broken the spirit of any other people. Through this period of Irish history, the inhabitants exhibited a patriotism and valor deserving of a better reward. But the myrmidons of England, backed by strong military force, proved too strong for them. They were overwhelmed ; the country was put under English deputies, and from that time has been the victim of English oppression. Under the unjust administration of these governors, and through the quarrels of the chiefs themselves, the power of the native princes rapidly declined.

In 1272 Edward II. ascended the English throne. A century had now elapsed since the Norman invasion. Overcome in almost every attempt to regain their freedom, wrecked by successive disasters, the Irish princes gave over the unequal contest, and many of them, especially those who bordered on the English settlements, sought to become British subjects, in order to be protected from outrage and plunder. For their citizenship, they offered Edward a subsidy of a thousand marks. This was opposed by the local aristocracy, who knew if they became British subjects they could no longer be taxed and plundered with the impunity which had before prevailed. The government of England allowed no one but herself to rob her own subjects. This local aristocracy was English ; for it must be remembered, in order to account for the action of the Irish Parliament, that it was always England's policy to keep a certain number of her nobility and citizens in Ireland to preserve the English ascendency.

The people petitioned again and again. It was in vain. British *slaves* they *should* be—British subjects never. Enraged at this unjust refusal, and maddened by the continued tyranny that only mocked their sufferings, they flew to arms. Sir John Wogan was sent over to quell the insurrection. He assembled an Irish Parliament to take into consideration the state of the country. This was the first Parliament ever constitutionally convened in Ireland. It was in 1295. Several just and useful acts were passed, but they availed little to remedy the evils that had taken such deep and widely spread root in the country.

Another cause of evil, was the levying of " coyne and livery" by the great barons to maintain their large retinues. This was another step towards the oppression of the Irish tenantry. Acting on the principle by which aristocrats have always been governed,—that what is wrung from the serf is the clear gain of the lord,—they drove away, by their extortion, the sturdy yeomanry of the land. They forgot, as tyrants always forget, that they reduced the value of their land in the same proportion as they reduced the character of the cultivator. There is a system of compensation in the economy of the Creator, by which good and evil are both made reactive. This exaction was so oppressive, that Baron Finglass declared, "it would destroy hell, if levied in the same."

At the end of the civil war of 1327, the Irish septs again petitioned to be admitted to the rights of freemen. They saw there was no other way to escape insult and outrage. But it was declared that it would injure the *English ascendency*, to convert serfs into freemen—and their prayer was denied. Indignant at this repeated injustice, and every feeling within them roused to action by the unchecked tyranny of those who laughed in their ill-gotten power, at the fruitless struggles of their victims, they again armed their followers, and unhappy Ireland was again drenched in blood. The very priest was slain at the altar, and trampled in the earth with the consecrated elements by his side. But why enter into the sickening details of the butcheries that followed! It is enough to say that England was of course again victorious, and practised with renewed security her former crimes. In war, or in peace, it mattered not—Ireland bled at every pore. England had begun her feast of blood, and grew only the more voracious with every terrific repast.

IV.

IN 1367 the Duke of Clarence, then being Lord Deputy of Ireland, summoned a Parliament which met at Kilkenny. It must be remembered that, in the assembling of Irish Parliaments, it was the English policy always to have a majority favorable to the English interest returned. A fair representation of the people, was the last thing ever contemplated. During the session of this Parliament, the notorious Statute of Kilkenny was passed. Among other things in this diabolical statute, (an offspring, by the way, worthy of its villainous parent,) it was declared, "that if any of English descent should use an Irish name, the Irish language, or observe Irish customs, he should forfeit his estates until security was given for his conformity to English habits ;" and finally it was strictly forbidden " to entertain any native minstrel, or story-teller, or to *admit an Irish horse to graze in the pasture of an English subject.*" In the language of Lord Clare, " This was a declaration of perpetual war, not only against the native Irish, but every person who settled beyond the limits of the pale." None but an English despot has the skill to carry the refinement of tyranny so far.

The attitude of the two nations, as viewed from this point of history, shows their relative position during the entire period of their connection. On the one hand, the wronged and oppressed Irish, finding no relief from other sources, petition England for the poor boon of being treated as her subjects— even offering an exorbitant price for the miserable gift. England, on the other hand, refuses the prayer, and adds to the refusal insult, scorn and greater injustice ; and finally closes the catalogue of her crimes, by a declaration of eternal war against the innocent, because they are helpless.

As we thus trace the progress of British oppression, we seem at every step to have reached the point where retribution would begin. But it has not yet come. In resisting such tyranny, Ireland often exhibited a valor and power that would have stopped the encroachments of the English government, had not the native chiefs been divided among themselves. Jealous of each other's power, and often sore with the memory of old feuds, it required but little skill to keep alive the estrangement of those who should have stood shoulder to shoulder in the strife for common freedom. England was careful that this should never be wanting, and employed every means to keep alive the jealousy and feuds, and thus weaken the power which, united, would have been too strong for her. This has been her policy from first to last ; and its successful application is all that prevents Ireland now, from taking her place among the nations of the earth.

V.

IRELAND now became passive for a while for there were no means of redress : petition and force were alike in vain. She made no more resistance till Henry VIII. attempted, Mahomet-like, to convert her, sword in hand, to the principles of the Reformation. Henry II. had spread slaughter through Ireland, to make her Catholic. Henry VIII. did the same, to make her Protestant. She became the spoil of every monarch.

Henry sent over pastors for the people, but they were a set of adventurers who came only for the booty of extortion, and they drove, by insult and oppression, the common people into tumult. This first civil war of the Reformation, wrongly termed a rebellion, terminated as former ones had done, in favor of the English.

War following on the desolate steps of war, renders the succeeding years a monotonous history of violence and bloodshed. Sometimes, it was baron against baron ; sometimes supported by foreign allies, they made for a while a successful stand against the power that bore so heavily upon them ; but in the end they were overthrown, and might triumphed over the right. Often a great chief, possessed of large estates, was purposely driven by the most flagrant injustice and insults into open rebellion, that he might be branded as a traitor, and his rich possessions revert by confiscation to the English vampyres that so infested the land. Every cruelty and outrage that can dishonor our nature, was perpetrated in those unjust wars by English leaders and English soldiers. Cities were sacked, villages burned, women violated, and the helpless and the young slaughtered by thousands. A record of these scenes of crime and blood *we* cannot furnish. It is written, however, on every foot of Irish soil, and in the still living memories of many an Irish heart. Our meagre outline is scarcely as much as a naked table of the killed and wounded. The suffering we leave undescribed.

The policy of the English government, provoking a war at every turn, is fairly exhibited in its treatment of the Earl of Desmond.

This heroic Irishman happened to be guilty of owning 600,000 acres of land, upon which English cupidity cast an insatiate eye. A dispute arising concerning his lands, he obtained permission to lay his claims before the English throne. On proceeding to London, he was immediately seized, and without any cause being assigned, was committed to the Tower, where he remained a prisoner for several years. This falsehood and crime, together with the murder of O'Neill, another distinguished Irish chief, caused commotions throughout the country. At length the Earl made his escape, and returned to Ireland :—knowing that the government was determined to seize his lands, he took up arms. For this he was branded as a traitor. The war that succeeded, was marked by the most relentless cruelty. Tottering age, and helpless childhood, and pleading maternity, presented no obstacle to the English soldiery. Munster was literally a field of blood.

Overcome—his troops scattered—himself a fugitive—the Earl was at length discovered, and murdered by an English soldier, and his head sent as a present to the queen, who had said of O'Neill, " if he revolted, it would be better for her servants, as there would be estates enough for them all." This single expression of Elizabeth, reveals the entire policy of the English Government towards Ireland. That injured country was the great repast to which every monarch bid his lords sit down and eat. After they had gorged their fill, the remains were left for those who should come after. Tranquillity succeeded these massacres, but it was the tranquillity of the grave-yard. The proud and patriotic Irishmen were folded in the sleep of death, and the silence and repose around their lifeless corpses was called peace.

VI.

> "They made a solitude
> And called it peace."

THEIR treatment of Sir John Perrot, who governed the country in 1589, is ample proof that the Irish were not the discontented rebels their enemies declared them to be. The only upright man England had appointed over the country since Duke Richard, he endeavored to unite jarring interests, to heal, instead of aggravate, old feuds, to conciliate the discontented, and distribute honest justice to all. Notwithstanding the obstructions thrown in his way by the crown and local aristocracy, the generous Irish appreciated his character, and rendered a proper return for his justice and kindness. When he resigned, he told Elizabeth that he could govern her Irish subjects, but that *no power could control her English servants.* As he was about to bid farewell to Ireland, a great multitude assembled to witness his departure, and were melted to tears by his kind words. The wronged and outraged, yet sympathetic Irishmen, pressed on his footsteps as he descended to the shore. For once an English ruler had treated them like men, and striven, however vainly, to render them justice. But now he was leaving them for ever, and the rapacious plunderer would once more desolate their firesides. Tears and lamentations were mingled with the shouts of praise that rose around him. The loved "God bless you" that was wafted over the waters, was the bitterest sentence ever uttered against English oppression. A few such rulers would have saved Ireland, and fastened her as with hooks of steel to the British throne.

The same generous sentiment was exhibited towards the prelates of the Established Church when they ceased to be plunderers, and became shepherds. Later in her history, she exhibited this regard for Bishop Belmore. He sought the spiritual and temporal good of his flock. He strove to win their affections by kindness, instead of exciting their indignation by rav-

aging their folds.   At length, when he came to die, such was
the affection felt for him by Catholic Irishmen, that the soldiers who had no other way of showing him respect, interred
him with military honors, and when the grave closed over him,
all joined in the simple chorus, "*Requiescat in pace, ultimus
Anglorum.*"

These two exhibitions of affection, one towards an English
ruler, and the other towards an English bishop, illustrate most
strikingly, both the cruelty of the English government, and the
generosity of the Irish character.   It shows how cruel and
sanguinary must have been her policy, to deluge, in blood a
nation of such men, how tyrannical the power that must need
continual physical force to keep such men in tranquillity.

The successor of Sir John, renewed the oppressions of his
predecessors, and under a pretence of high treason, had a rich
chieftain arrested and suddenly executed, that he might appropriate his possessions to himself.   Outrages like this on rich
chieftains to get possession of their land, the commission of
crimes for which there was no redress, and the distress and
suffering caused by the oppression of their rulers, roused the
exasperated Irish again to resistance.   But before they commenced hostilities, they drew up a detailed account of their
grievances, and humbly besought redress.   Their petition and
their wrongs were alike disregarded, and war with its deso-
lating flood again swept over the devoted island.   The English
were defeated on every side ; their armies melted away ; victory perched on the Irish standard, and over the dark cloud of
war, the rainbow of freedom was already bending.

Elizabeth became alarmed.   The infatuated rulers who had
driven the inhabitants into rebellion by their cruelty, were
thunderstruck at the terrible elements they had aroused.   Ireland was almost free.   But owing to the arrogance and self-
conceit of the Spaniards, the allies of Ireland, O'Neill, the commander of the native forces, was compelled to hazard an attack
when he foresaw, and foretold a failure.   It came, and Ireland
again was lost—lost in the very arms of victory.   This foolish,

mad, and fatal battle turned the whole current of events, and the British army swept like a sea of fire over the land, burying men, women and children in one indiscriminate slaughter.

England expended in this unjust and murderous war, more than £3,000,000, and lost thousands of soldiers. She reduced the land to a desert, and between famine and war, swept away, at least, one half of the entire population.

When Elizabeth approached her death, and the future, with its fearful retributions, visited her conscience, the ghost of murdered Ireland rose before her, filling her with terrible alarms; so that she immediately ordered that some of the confiscated estates should be restored, and peace be made with O'Neill.

VII.

ON the accession of James I., the system of confiscation recommenced on a more extended scale. In the first place, without a single proof, or attempt at proof, the Earls of Tyrone and of Tyrconnel were declared to be agents in a Catholic conspiracy. Even if it had been true, as they were chiefs, and had the sovereignty, and not the ownership of the land, it could not lawfully be seized by the crown. But seized it was, and six counties, embracing more than 500,000 acres, came into the possession of James. These lands the king wished to settle with English colonists, in order to establish the "English ascendency" in the very heart of the country. To prevent the Irish Parliament in its next session from defeating this plan, he created at once forty boroughs, in order to have a majority in the representation. *This justice in appearance, and dishonesty in action,* has ever been the course of the English government towards her subjects at home and abroad.

His success in this kingly robbery, only whetted his appetite for greater spoils. But what new scheme could he devise by which to wrest from the Irish chieftains their estates, for even a villain's brain will become exhausted of plots! A commission was appointed "for the discovery of defective titles." A set

of men called discoverers, was employed to hunt up defects in
the titles of landholders, who, of course, were rewarded in proportion to their success, or, in other words, a premium was
given to the best informer.   It was not difficult to find defective
titles in a land that had for centuries been afloat on the turbulent waves of civil war, especially when witnesses were sub-
orned for the purpose, and bribes, violence and tortures were
freely employed to wring the Irish estates from their rightful
owners. The annual expense of carrying out this robber scheme,
exceeded by £16,000, or nearly $80,000, the entire revenue of
the kingdom.   We cannot help contrasting a commission like
this, and one, a modern commission, appointed to inquire into
wants of the pauperized people, in order to administer relief
from starvation.

But even this could not satisfy the rapacity of that lion which
seems to take a peculiar pleasure in devouring its own young.
A scheme was set on foot which was designed to throw the
entire province of Connaught into the hands of the crown.
The proprietors of the land in this province, seeing the fate that
awaited them, and knowing they had nothing to expect from
the justice or honor of a venal king, appealed to his cupidity.
They offered him £10,000 to desist from the pillage.   While
the avaricious monarch was hesitating between a small *certain*
sum, and a large *un*certain one, the King of kings summoned
him to a higher tribunal, to answer for his follies and his crimes.

VIII.

THE Irish now became thoroughly alarmed.   Confiscated
ruthlessly in war, and confiscated not less ruthlessly in
time of peace, they beheld their lands rapidly passing over
into the hands of their enemies. On the accession of Charles I.
they held a meeting at Dublin, to take into consideration the
state of the country.   This was in 1628.   They drew up a Bill
of Rights, moderate and just in its demands, and humbly besought the king to grant them—promising if he would, " to

raise a voluntary assessment of £100,000 for the use of the crown.' These articles were called " Graces." In them they asked simply for security of property, deliverance from military exactions, and impartial justice in the courts.

Charles, as villainous as he was weak, *took* the money and then deferred granting the graces, with the secret determination *never* to do it. On the contrary, the Earl of Strafford, the king's minion, endeavored—right in the teeth of the king's promise—to carry out the original plan of James, in the settlement of Connaught. He took with him "500 horsemen as *lookers on.*" He legalized his robberies and extortions by submitting each case to a jury ; but the jurors were picked by himself, and the sheriff secretly ordered to return them. But in one instance, the sheriff returning a true and impartial jury, which of course rendered a verdict against the crown, Strafford in his rage fined him £1000, and bound over the jurors to the Star Chamber, to answer for the flagrant crime of being " good men and true." In one instance, he forced an Irish family to pay £17,000 or over $80,000 to remedy a defect in a title that never existed. In another instance £70,000 was extorted on a similar frivolous excuse. It is strange it never occurred to the monarch and his advisers, to appoint a commissioner to see if there was any defect in *their* titles to these same lands.

Emboldened by success, new acts of oppression were committed, which ended as they always must, in new rebellion ; which in its turn, being crushed by overwhelming physical force, led to new confiscations. In *two days* " bills of indictment for high treason were found against *all* the Catholic nobility and gentry in the' counties of Meath, Wicklow, and Dublin, and three hundred gentlemen in the county of Kildare."

Even Parliament joined in for the sale of 2,500,000 acres, owned by those they pleased to call " rebels." This extensive pillage must of course be sanctioned by an Irish Parliament, which was assembled in Dublin for the purpose, and *sat only three days.* Excluding all who had joined the adversaries of the government, and all who would not take the oath of supremacy, they reduced the number of members to a few servile and unscrupulous creatures of the English government.

In this mere skeleton of facts, in which the years of suffering, the bloody battles, and bloodier victories are wholly omitted, we can partially see the causes of each Irish " rebellion." Persecuted in their religion—abused in the delay of the graces for which they had paid beforehand—made aliens in the land of their fathers, they had nothing left but to fight for it, and even this availed them nothing. It was simply the writhing of the worm under the heel that crushed it.

A treaty was finally entered into ; but before it could be carried out, the head of Charles rolled on the scaffold, and England was without a king—but Ireland was none the better for it, and to this day " the curse of Cromwell " is a form of execration familiar to every peasant in the land.

IX.

CROMWELL, the champion of English liberty, regarded Ireland as the British monarchs had before him,—the exclusive property of England. Every resistance to this claim was called rebellion. Cromwell declared their attachment to the house of Stuart, treason. The unfortunate Irish, do what they would, could not escape the charge, and doom of traitors. Fighting *for* their king or *against* him—for their property or their rights, it mattered not—it was all treason.

It is singular that those distinguished for their love of freedom, and even humanity in other respects, should lose it all when they had any transaction with Ireland. The chivalric Sir Walter Raleigh could coolly butcher the entire garrison of Limerick after they had surrendered, and receive as a reward for the deed forty thousand acres of Irish ground. Even the amorous poet Spenser, who received three thousand acres of land out of the confiscated estates of the Earl of Desmond for his royal flattery, and on which he lived—soberly recommended to government the repetition of those acts which had reduced the Irish peasantry to the state he thus fearfully describes.

He says, " out of every corner of the woods and glynnes they came creeping forth upon their hands, for their legs could not bear them. They looked like anatomies of death—they spake like ghosts crying out of their graves—they eat the dead carrion, happy when they could find them, yea and one another soon after ; insomuch as the very carcases they spared not to scrape out of their graves, and if they found a plot of water cresses, or shamrocks, to these they flocked as to a feast for the time, yet not able to continue there withal, that in a short space there were none almost left, and a most populous and plentiful country suddenly left void of man and beast." Even a poet's heart could refuse sympathy with such suffering, because forsooth, it came from *Irishmen*—nay, recommend a repetition of the cruelties that caused it, for the sake of the ascendency it gave to British power. He would see all Ireland creeping out of the forests they rightfully owned, upon their hands, because their famine - shrunk legs could not support them, staring over the desolated fields they once called their homes—speaking like ghosts out of the sepulchre, and tearing the rotten dead from their graves to appease the ferocity of famine, if by it England could maintain her robber power in peace. The effeminate poet found the reward of his deeds when a just Irish vengeance lighted his castle over his head, and he was compelled to flee for his life.

This vivid picture represents the desolation that followed every invasion of the British : " before them the land was a fruitful field, behind them a barren wilderness."

X.

CROMWELL possessed the feelings of his predecessors, and although armed against oppression, he emulated the tyrant he had just slain, in his dealings with that unhappy country. He invaded Ireland,—and party strifes and fierce factions accomplished for him, what his own forces never could have done—conquered it. We will not attempt to describe the cruelties of this war. It was the custom of Cromwell to offer pardon to every town he approached, if they would immediately surrender; but if compelled to besiege it, he crowned his victory with a massacre. It could hardly be called a war,—it was a slaughter. After it was ended, and before the butchers had time to wipe their blades, confiscation commenced.

The estates thus seized, were settled with English Protestants, who regarded the Irish Catholics as Canaanites, and themselves as the commissioners of God to pursue them with fire and sword. Mercy to the conquered, was rebellion against God. The flower of the country fled into foreign lands, and took refuge in foreign service.

As before, unjust and oppressive laws followed in the path of the sword, to seize what it had left. Among other things, it was decreed, that all who had borne arms against the Parliament, should be banished during the pleasure of the Parliament, and forfeit two-thirds of their estates; also that all papists who had not exhibited constant affection for the commonwealth, should forfeit one-third of their estates; also that all who had not borne arms *for* the Parliament should forfeit one-fifth of theirs. These enactments were certainly broad enough to embrace every Irishman, and the land was effectually divided to the spoilers.

It was also decreed that this land should be settled by English colonists, in order to effect the more complete subjugation of the country. Under this iniquitous settlement, it was found difficult to obtain laborers to cultivate the soil they had seized. In prosecuting this exterminating war, they had massacred the peasantry by thousands; others they had transported as slaves, and multitudes more exiled themselves from the land where they could no longer be free. The few that were left, were converted into slaves to till the soil for the robber and the murderer, and bleed under the iron scourge that was laid on their backs. The Catholic clergy were banished; the performance of Catholic ceremonies was made a capital offence, and blood-hounds were employed to hunt down the priests. *"Priest hunting became a favorite field sport!"* But we pass over these years of unparalleled sufferings, to the Restoration. From Charles II. the Irish justly expected some reward for their services to the royal family,—at least to have their lands restored to them. But one of the first acts of the perfidious monarch, was a decree that the estates disposed of by the Cromwellian settlement, should not be restored. These furious Protestants suddenly became high churchmen in order to come in for a share of the plunder. Besides, "English ascendency" in Ireland was of greater consequence than honor or justice. The executioners of the father, were rewarded by the son—while the faithful vassals who lost their land in defending him, were plundered still more for their faithfulness. The Irish sent in a remonstrance, in which they spoke of their loyalty and distress—the treaty made by his father, and paid for by them—the long and bloody struggle they had maintained for his family,—and urged every motive of honor and humanity to move the heart of Charles ; but in vain. It is true, there was a commission appointed to hear and decide claims, but it never heard them. So there was an after act of "explanation and final arrangement ;" but the result of the whole thing was, that *three thousand* of the noblest Irish families were robbed of their property, and *two-thirds* of the land of Ireland passed from the native Irish,—the true owners—into the hands of English adventurers and English colonists, and a corrupt and perfidious monarch. Such a price did the Irish pay to the son, for their loyalty to the father.

XI.

WE pass over the reign of James II., who being a Catholic monarch, was inclined to be more lenient to Ireland, but still acted on the principle that *English* ascendency was more important than *Catholic* ascendency. At length driven from his throne by William, Prince of Orange, he found refuge in Ireland. That loyal people, though weakened by successive and disastrous wars, and impoverished by confiscations, rallied around him, and would have placed him again on the throne, had not his own cowardice and effeminacy defeated their efforts.

After James had proved himself unworthy to be a king, the Irish would gladly have submitted to William, if he had promised them justice. But knowing that new confiscations awaited their submission, they resisted on ; and but for an apparent interposition of providence, which no one could foresee, would probably have triumphed. This war, which reflects so much credit on the Irish arms, laid the foundation of the British National Debt, which has since gone on accumulating, till it threatens to swallow up the wealth of the empire.

The confiscations of estates by the government of William, turned out of their homes nearly 4,000 families, and robbed them of land to the amount of £3,319,943, or over $16,500,000. This mighty robbery was for high-treason, which high-treason consisted, in defending the British throne against an usurper. The century that succeeded the revolutionary war, is simply a long record of oppressions, crimes and sufferings. Ireland had ceased to struggle, and lay a helpless victim at the feet of its merciless masters. The vulture now plunged his beak into the bleeding form of its prey, and tore away the flesh at its leisure.

The Penal Laws enacted during this period, are a perpetual stain on the English government. These, together with the injustice and tyranny of the local magistracy, the extortions of landlords, and the absence of justice in all trials where an Irishman was concerned, reduced the inhabitants almost to the last step humanity reaches in its downward passage. These laws, which would have disgraced the administration of Nero, imposed a fine on every Catholic who should absent himself from the service of the Established Church on the Sabbath ; deprived them of the means of education, subjecting every Catholic who should open a school, to a fine of £20, or three months' imprisonment ; forbade Protestants to intermarry with

them, and banished the entire Catholic clergy from the land.
If the son of a Catholic became a Protestant, the father could
not dispose of his property by will ; a Catholic could not become the guardian of his own child ; a Catholic could not succeed to the property of any of his Protestant relatives. In
1709, additional acts were passed, and among them a fixed reward offered for the discovery of Catholic priests !

"For discovering an archbishop, bishop, vicar-general, or
other person exercising any foreign ecclesiastical jurisdiction, £50.

"For discovering each regular clergyman, and each secular
clergyman not registered, £20.

"For discovering each popish schoolmaster or usher, £10."

A Catholic could not hold the office of sheriff, or sit on
grand juries ;—hence in all trials between a Catholic and
Protestant, justice was a thing altogether out of the question.
To crown the absurdity and baseness of this Protestant legislation, a bill was actually introduced, and passed both Houses
of Parliament, decreeing that every Catholic priest who came
into the country should be castrated. After its passage, it was
sent to the King, with the earnest request it might be placed
in the Irish statute book. It was, however, rejected by the
English privy council. Nor did the enactment of these absurd
and cruel laws, exhaust the hatred of the enemies of Ireland.
Her commerce and manufactures were restricted, so that her
internal resources could not develope themselves, and her beautiful harbors lay unoccupied along her shores.

In 1727, George II. ascended the throne ; like every other
administration, this also must show its English blood, by plunging the knife a little deeper into dying Ireland. In the outset,
a bill was passed, disfranchising all the Catholics in the nation.
They then constituted *five-sixths* of the entire population : only
one-sixth were left to vote, these being Protestants, and most of
them English. A more tyrannical act could not well have been
conceived ; but the ingenuity of English rulers in devising modes
of oppression seemed sharpened by practice. They appeared

to be experimenting in cruelty and injustice, as if to see how far they could sink humanity in degradation and suffering, and there be no wild waking up of the soul of man—no voice from heaven arresting their career.

These oppressive laws drove the inhabitants in crowds from the land of their birth. After the siege of Limerick, under the reign of William, 14,000 men entered the service of. France, and it is estimated that between this time and the effort of the Pretender, 450,000 entered the service of France alone.

The continued extortions of the Established Church and landholders, reduced the poor at home to starvation and beggary, and forced them into outbreaks and resistance. These were always quelled with the point of the bayonet; and those whose only crime was being born Irishmen, were shot down or hung without even the useless forms of a trial. It was to this gloomy period that Sir James Mackintosh refers, when he says, that for 400 years not a single man was punished for killing an Irishman.

XII.

WE come now to a brief notice of the "Union." In the year 1778, the people of Belfast, finding themselves unprotected while an invasion was threatened from France, petitioned government for a garrison. Being refused, they began to form independent companies for their own self-protection. This example was soon followed in other sections of the country, till they numbered 50,000 men. These were the protection of the country from foreign invasion, and constituted the famous "Volunteers," whose very name thrills every Irish heart with a throb of patriotic remembrance and gratitude.

At the same time, the Irish, seeing their ruin as a nation inevitable, unless the severe restrictions were taken from their commerce; and emboldened by the creation of so great a national army, resolved on a bold movement. About this time also, the long struggle between England and her Ameri can colonies terminated, and America was declared "*free and independent.*"

With a less population, suffering under less oppressions, she had nevertheless resisted and conquered. Her example was contagious. Ireland caught the shout of freedom as it swelled over the Atlantic, and began to bestir herself. Throughout the nation, bands of these "Volunteers" assembled, declaring that the power to legislate for Ireland, rested solely in her own legislature.

In 1782, delegates from 143 companies, augmented at this time to 100,000 men, assembled at Dungannon, and passed resolutions declaring, that the Irish Legislature *ought* to be, and *should* be free and independent, and 100,000 determined men, with nearly 100 pieces of artillery to back them, thus threateningly spoke to England. This demand was almost tantamount to a declaration of war, and the British government would have visited its severest vengeance on the rebellious nation, had it possessed the power. But she was weakened by a long war, and Ireland was fresh and strong with her determined spirit, and her 100,000 organized and armed men.

Besides, England had just lost her American colonies by refusing to grant their reasonable and just requests, and she became alarmed lest she might lose Ireland too. With her exchequer exhausted, her troops worn out and diminished, and fresh from the lesson of the power of a few men nerved with the spirit of liberty, and struggling in a holy cause, she yielded to Ireland what she had repeatedly declared she never would do. Her legislature was declared independent, and Ireland immediately took a *quasi* position among the nations of the earth.

XIII.

THIS revolution, so wonderful and yet so bloodless, conferred one of the greatest blessings on the nation. Ireland could make her own laws, and regulate her own commerce. If at this period the infamous penal code had been repealed, the internal government thrown across the Channel, with the English oligarchy, which still oppressed the people and prevented the healthy action of any legislative scheme, Ireland would now be a free nation—rich in commerce and manufactures—strong in an industrious, educated and happy peasantry, and sending her light and her blessings over the world.   As it was, Ireland attained a prosperity unknown before or since.   An impulse was given to the entire industry of the nation ; her commerce revived, and hope—that world-propelling power—animated the people with the promise of future prosperity and happiness.

But the enthusiasm that at first expected so much, gradually subsided away, and it was found there were evils resting in their own legislature, and obstruction lying at the very threshold to impede their progress.

The extortions of landholders, tithes, taxes, and the rotten frame-work of old oppression still existed, paralyzing the energies of the nation, till her efforts to rise were like those of the fabled giant under the superincumbent mountain.   But Ireland must not cast the entire blame on England for her failure in this important crisis of her history.   It is not once nor twice she has foolishly, madly thrown herself into the clutches of England, from indulging the bitter animosities that divide her councils and associations ; and until they can be noble and patriotic enough to forget their religious differences in a common love for their enslaved country, they never *can be* free—they do not *deserve* to be free.   The " United Irishmen" asked for reform ; the Catholics, for emancipation.   If they all had been " United Irishmen"—united for the welfare of their common country, and had consented to give religious freedom to each, while they demanded national freedom for the whole, she might have staggered up from the degradation centuries of misrule, violence and robbing had heaped upon her.

We cannot here speak of all the causes that led to the rebellion of 1798.   Like every other insurrection, it could be traced directly or indirectly to the English government.   Although its own corrupt legislature, refusing the reforms which justice and good policy both demanded, was the immediate cause ; yet the religious hatred from which it all sprang, can be traced to the unjust settlement of English Protestants on the confiscated estates of the Irish, and the ignorance and degradation which centuries of corrupt government had brought on the people. But like all other insurrections, it was a struggle for freedom. In this attempt, Ireland solicited the aid of France, and a fleet was despatched with 150,000 picked men, which England had no force in the south able to meet. But it again seemed as if heaven fought against Ireland, for the winds and the waves scattered the fleet before it reached the shores.

At the close of the war—distinguished like all the preceding ones, by frightful atrocities on the part of the English—Ireland found herself crippled and helpless. 20,000 royalists and 30,000 insurgents had fallen, and 3,000,000 of property perished. With her Parliament broken down, and virtually annihilated by the efforts of the British minister, and her resources all exhausted, she lay at the mercy of her conqueror.

XIV.

ENGLAND now began to agitate the question of the union of the two Parliaments.

This was quite unnecessary if the Irish legislature had not become independent, for she had always controlled it as completely as if it were her own. James could create forty boroughs in an emergency, all the Catholics could be disfranchised, and the few remaining Protestants sold to the English interest, so that it was very little trouble for England to carry any measure through the Irish legislature.

But after its independence, it was found more difficult, and if the making of the laws, and entire control of the nation could be transferred to the English Parliament, future restrictions, exactions and wrong could be practised without the trouble of calling an Irish legislature together to sanction it. She therefore proposed the "Union."

When this project was first mentioned, it was received with general indignation; and weak and prostrate as Ireland was, and formidable as was an English army of 126,000 men, ready to be precipitated on her defenceless population, yet she would doubtless have taken up arms rather than sanction it, if she had not been duped by false promises. But with all her fair pretensions, England could not have carried the Union without the presence of her immense military force. What could Ireland do? Prostrate from a sanguinary struggle—laid under martial law—the Habeas Corpus Act suspended—no protection to property, liberty, or life—the jails crowded with innocent victims—the scaffold red with the blood of those who had committed no crime—tortures and death on every side,—what could she do? How could she discuss the Union calmly, with more than 100,000 bayonets bristling around her, and pointing at her heart? Yet under all this formidable and merciless force, efforts *were* made to prevent the unholy alliance. A meeting was called in Tipperary, attended by gentlemen of rank and fortune. But the high sheriff had scarcely taken the chair, before a company of English soldiers marched into the Court House, and dispersed the assembly. The same was done in Maryborough. To this fear of physical force were added bribes and corruption. Rotten boroughs were bought up, that those favorable to the English interest might be returned to the legislature. Lord Castlereagh declared in the House of Commons, that "he would carry the Union though it might cost more than half a million in bribes." The price of a single vote on the question was £8,000, or nearly $40,000, or, in its place, an appointment worth $10,000 per annum. More than $6,000,000 were spent in buying up close rotten boroughs; $7,000,000 more in bribes; making in all, in round numbers, *fourteen millions of dollars* distributed to effect the subjugation of Ireland. Yet with her 170,000 bayonets, and $14,000,000, there were 707,000 who petitioned *against* the Union, and only

5,000 *for it.* A very small majority in the legislature finally secured its passage, and that too, when among those styling themselves representatives of the people, there were 116 placemen and officers who did not own an inch of land in Ireland.

But the "Act of Union" passed. In the language of Mr. Sampson, "It was on the first day of January, 1801, at the hour of noon, that the imperial united standard mounted on the Bedford Tower, in Dublin Castle, and the guns of the royal salute battery, in the Phœnix Park, announced to weeping, bleeding, prostrate Ireland, that her independence was no more, and that her guilt-stained parliament had done herself to death."

By a system of violence, theft, falsehood and corruption unparalleled in the history of civilized nations, England forced Ireland into a union that destroyed her independence, ruined her commerce, exhausted her wealth, and left her a helpless victim at the feet of her spoiler. This charge of perfidy, treachery, and infamous theft against the English government, no one who is at all acquainted with this vilest of England's vile transactions, will presume to deny. Said Lord Plunket at the time :—

"I will be bold to say, that licentious and impious France, in all the unrestrained excesses that anarchy and atheism have given birth to, has not committed a more insidious act against her enemy, than is now attempted by the professed champion of civilized Europe against Ireland—a friend and ally in the hour of her calamity and distress. At a moment when our country is filled with British troops—when the Habeas Corpus Act is suspended—whilst trials by court martial are carrying on in different parts of the kingdom—while the people are made to believe that they have no right to meet and deliberate, and whilst the people are palsied by their fears, at the moment when we are distracted by internal dissensions—dissensions kept alive as the pretext of our present subjugation, and the instrument of our future thraldom—such is the time when the Union is proposed."

XV.

IN addition to the iniquitous measures already mentioned, to carry the Union, England made large promises to the Catholics, which she did not fulfil till thirty years after, and then not because she had made them, but to avert the imminent hazard of a civil war. This promise that the elective franchise should be restored to them—so faithlessly kept, was the cause of untold miseries to Ireland. By the terms of the union, she was to have the same system of representation and elective franchise that England possessed. The Exchequers of the two kingdoms were to be kept separate, and Ireland was to collect her own revenues, and pay the interest on her own debt. This part of the contract was also soon broken. There was also to be a future *joint expenditure,* such as would be compatible with the relative ability of the weaker country. This, though unjust, because Ireland had not increased her own debt voluntarily, nor for her own benefit, England finally refused. It was also provided, that when she had a surplus revenue it could be expended to the amount of £5,000,000 in internal improvements, the liquidation of her debt, or any purpose conducive to her own interests. *This* was unnecessary—for England would be sure to prevent any such loss to herself, either by taxation, restrictions on commerce, or in some way—she would turn her revenue so as to make it reach her own, instead of the Irish Exchequer. The whole scheme was an offspring worthy of its infamous father, Lord Castlereagh. He afterwards died by his own hand, and although it seems proper that the same hand that struck Ireland should smite *him,* yet the gallows would have been a more befitting close to a life so stained with every crime.

An act so evidently unconstitutional, and carried by such flagitious means, could not be otherwise than baleful in its effects. Although in its perpetration England was guilty of every perfidious act that can disgrace a nation, she did not scruple, by breaking even the poor promises she had made, to utter her falsehood and shame to the world. This, together with the remembrance of the iniquitous means by which it was effected, awakened the indignation of every Irishman, and makes the cry of REPEAL, now swell like thunder over the land. 'Besides, it is not a union except in name, for there is no common enjoyment of freedom, or equitable laws. It is a union which in its action restricts the commerce of Ireland, and thus compels her to fall behind nations she ought to precede—diminishes, and misapplies her revenue—increases her debt—loads her with taxes—paralyzes her industry, and reduces her inhabitants to starvation and beggary. One of the more immediate effects was the increase of Absenteeism. This has always been the curse of Ireland. The Irish legislature would have soon remedied it, but this union restored the evil to its former magnitude. Out of 12,000,000 acres of land, which embrace the whole surface of the island, over eleven millions and a half changed owners under English government, and some of these estates were confiscated three times in a century. A large portion of these lands came of course into the possession of English gentlemen, who, having no motive to live in a country so reduced and ignorant, increased the evil by residing abroad. Their support was derived from the rental of their lands. Their tenantry is uncared for—they have no interest in the welfare of the nation. In 1801, the amount of rents, etc., thus spent out of the kingdom, was £1,500,000. It is now estimated that ten millions, or nearly fifty millions of dollars are annually drained from the nation. Says the American Editor of O'Connell's reply to Earl Shrewsbury, "Is there any other country on the globe of similar size that can stand this?" No—neither does Ireland stand it. Go look at her squalid huts—her peasantry, that might be the noblest in the world, in rags and filth—listen to the cry of suffering that goes up over the "Emerald Isle," from five millions of people who each day suffer the pangs of unappeased hunger, and you will see how she "stands it." An independent Parliament could remove the burdens that rest so heavily on the people, open up the resources of the country, and introduce laws that should aid, rather than crush, the industry of the land.

XVI.

AGITATION is also a necessary result of the union. Men cannot be satisfied and tranquil while they remember the circumstances under which it was effected, or feel the restraints and misery it creates. But there has been no insurrection since the great rebellion, (as the English term it,) which so nearly secured her freedom, but ended in her complete subjugation, if we except the attempt of Emmet. While men have praised his spirit, they have ridiculed his judgment, in making this abortive effort. But we may not be acquainted with the nature of his plans, nor the means he possessed of accomplishing them. Noble by nature, and rich in endowments, his patriotic soul scorned the fetters of foreign despotism. He had seen his only surviving brother first imprisoned, and afterwards driven from the home of his childhood and land of his love, by English oppressors. He found himself expelled from his university for no crime but that of loving his country, and speaking words of melting tenderness over her sufferings, and words of fire against her destroyers,—he could be silent no longer. He boldly asserted his own and his country's rights. Whether the act was judicious or not, we will not pretend to say.

He said, " till Ireland is free let not my epitaph be written ;" and it shall not be. He offered himself up as a holocaust to liberty. He shouted one battle-cry in the ears of his countrymen, and died. They err much, who suppose he accomplished nothing. A martyr never dies in vain. Every drop of his blood will yet send forth a living man fraught with the fire of his origin. The name of Emmet at this day, stirs every patriot heart in that green isle like the blast of a trumpet. His dying words are remembered and repeated to every generation. He bequeathed his free spirit to his country in sacred trust, looking forward to that day when his emancipated nation should write his epitaph and honor his sacrifice. The flag of freedom shall yet wave over his ashes, and the shout of a ransomed people shake the earth that encloses him.

In speaking of that insurrection, it is but justice to remark that every Irish insurrection, though excited by wrongs, commenced only when those wrongs were inflicted with a brutality and ferocity that could not be borne in silence except by men deservedly slaves. I have not been able to speak in detail of the sufferings of the Irish people, under these long and heavy oppressions. To describe all the torments wrung from the innocent by the rack and torture—to enumerate the robbed and the slain without trial or provocation—and against each sufferer's name write his history—to portray all the burnings and desolation of villages, till the inhabitants, rendered houseless and homeless, reduced to famine, wandered like spectres in the land that gave them birth,—and speak of the tears and groans and shrieks the wronged and helpless have shed and uttered over their friends, or in their own death agony during these long and weary centuries—it would make the most damning record of national crime ever offered to the horror of man, or the justice of God.

XVII.

TO return to the effects of the Union. England expected and sought no result but the subjugation of Ireland, and the increase of her own wealth. We are now brought down to our own century. The Act of the Union was in full operation, but the Catholics were denied the rights of other citizens. Tithes were collected at the point of the bayonet, commerce restricted, and Ireland staggered painfully and wearily on her course.

The Irish debt at the commencement of the French war was only £2,250,000 sterling. By the time the union was effected it amounted to nearly £29,000,000. At the same time the debt of England was more than £420,000,000 sterling. It was this inequality that prevented the consolidation of the exchequers in 1801.

By the Act of the Union, Ireland was to pay one for every £7,500,000 by England for the joint expenditure. But a few years' experiment proved that this proportion was unjust, and that Ireland was unable to pay it. It was then manifestly the duty of England to have a different proportion instituted, which would leave Ireland in the same relative position to her as before, and with equal advantages. Instead of this, and contrary to the express stipulations of the act, England, in 1816, consolidated the two exchequers into one; thus uniting the national debts, without furnishing any equivalent to Ireland, for thus saddling upon her her own enormous debt. When the Scotch and English exchequers were consolidated, England acknowledged an equivalent due to Scotland. An accurate calculation was made of the sum due her for assuming her part of the debt, and paid, to the amount of £1,500,000. Now if the proportion paid by Ireland towards the joint expenditure had been just, and she still fell in the rear, England would have been the last to propose a union of the two exchequers, for she would thus have increased her own liabilities. But seeing that the proportion was unjust, and that if graduated rightly, and Ireland should increase in prosperity, she would soon have a surplus revenue at her own disposal, she by one sweeping act violated her own given word, and consolidated the exchequers without giving Ireland one cent as an equivalent for the burden she thus threw upon her.

It is nonsense in England to pretend that by this act she takes more of the burdens of Ireland on her own shoulders. Any one familiar with her policy, knows she never was guilty of such disinterested benevolence towards that unhappy country.

In 1800, this consolidation was declared impracticable, and Lord Castlereagh himself said in that year, " in respect to past expenses, she, (Ireland,) was to have no concern whatever with the debt of Great Britain, but the two countries were to unite as to future expenses, on a strict measure of relative ability!" The pretence that she had to borrow on Ireland's account, is simply another example of the miserable mendacity at which she never hesitates, to legalize her injustice.

By this act England did charge over to Ireland as a part of the United Kingdom, the debt of £420,000,000 which she then owed. But not to go at length into details, in 1800, at the time of the union, England had to pay a tax of £16,000,000 a year on her debts. In 1836, it was only £5,000,000, being reduced more than two-thirds in thirty-six years after the union. In 1800, the standard of English taxation was far higher than the Irish ; now, it is equal almost universally.

XVIII.

A CCORDING to the finance report of 1835 and 1836, the customs—post office—excise and stamp duties were the same in both countries ; and yet ministers tell us that Ireland is the least taxed, and England the most taxed of all the countries in Europe. Since the year 1814, Ireland has paid the same duties as England, on tea, sugar, coffee, foreign spirits, wine and tobacco. Now these amount to nearly one-third of the entire revenue. It is false that Ireland is the least taxed country. The present rate of taxation in Ireland, if she had only her own debt to meet, would in a few years entirely cancel it. Why ! according to the " act of union," England herself was to pay the annual charge on her debt. This annual charge would have been nearly £17,000,000 while she has paid only £7,000,000, —thus relieving herself by taxing Ireland, of £10,000,000, or nearly $50,000,000, which in five years would amount to $250,-000,000. All this she has deliberately stolen from Ireland, and covered her theft with a lie.

British ministers, and the British press, are never weary of telling us, that the taxes are lower in Ireland than in England, that the whole revenue of Ireland is not sufficient to satisfy her creditors who loaned her money before the union.

If there was not a single available fact to prove this false, it would bear on its own face an ample refutation : for these same individuals will not entertain for a moment the question of repeal. Now if Ireland is such an enormous burden to England, why will she not let her collect her own revenue, and meet her own expenditure—nay, why did she spend so many millions of dollars to secure that union, while it only took money out of her pocket.

Look at facts but a moment. The *whole Irish* expenditure is paid from the Irish revenue. The standing army maintained in Ireland, is paid out of the Irish revenue—even their clothing. The public creditor is paid in full out of Irish taxes. The civil government of Ireland, together with the English foreign pensioners on her list, is supplied from Irish taxes. The enormous charities voted from time to time by the English Parliament for Irish improvements—amounting in all to over £800,000, and on which so many changes have been rung of English kindness were paid entirely out of Irish taxes. England gives back to Ireland a *part* of that she stole from her—but even this *is* extraordinary generosity for England to exhibit towards her weak ally. She *usually* keeps *all* the unrighteous gains she can get. The loan fund amounting to £500,000 called " English gold for Irish uses," is the money of Irishmen.

Instead of Ireland deriving her support from England, England unceasingly draws a steady stream of tribute from Ireland. In the report of the British Parliament, in 1833, " of the balance arising from the remittance of public money to and from the Irish and British exchequers," from 1793 to 1833, the following is the result. The loans received in Great Britain for Ireland, are of course left out in this estimate. The whole amount remitted from the British to the Irish exchequer during that period, was £8,256,274 8s. 4½d. The whole amount remitted from the Irish to the British exchequer, for the same period, was £19,640,453 8s. 3d. leaving a balance of £11,384,-178 19s. 10½d. in the British exchequer above the amount she had paid to the Irish. This sum was left *over and above all her expenditures.* The report then goes on to give the expenditure of that year. After taking out over £1,000,000, for *interest and management* of public debt, over £1,000,000 for the army and other charges, it leaves after all, £600,000, or nearly $3,000,-000, remaining in British exchequer. Nor is this all. In this balance in favor of Ireland the duties on tea, refined sugar, hops, paper and glass, were not reckoned ; these being all collected in England, and never included in the Irish revenue. These together with the remittances to absentees, would swell the sum to many millions more ; and yet England supports Ireland! Yes, she "supports" her with one hand, while she robs her with the other. Her boasted charities are like those of the hypocrite ; with one hand she puts a penny in the urn of poverty, and with the other, takes a shilling out.

The loans to Ireland left out in the above estimate, were to meet the contributions made for a war in which Ireland had no part nor advantage. If Ireland had been blotted from existence the same expense would have occurred. Yet, on this pretense, England keeps the gold yearly remitted by Ireland to her exchequer. £1,500,000 sterling, or nearly $7,500,000, expended by the English government in bribes to carry the Act of Union, *has been charged over to Ireland.* The *interest on this* also comes out of *Irish remittance.* England hired robbers to plunder Ireland, and now forces Ireland to pay the robbers for their crime. Ireland "supported" by England! The government that can stoop to such baseness to gratify her cupidity is capable of any perfidy. England knows she utters a falsehood when she says Ireland is an expense to her over and above her remittances. She knows that for every shilling sent to that country, she receives directly or indirectly its double in return, and it ever has been so.

If Ireland was forced to pay only her portion of the consolidated debt, she would have a surplus revenue every year under all her disadvantages. So much for the Act of the Union, made still worse by the Act of Consolidation.

XIX.

THIS Union, so called, and by England declared to be the
safety of Ireland, is the union of anything but friendship.
There is a communication between the two nations, but it is the
communication of a robber with his victim.   It is a channel
through which England can exhaust with more ease and safety,
every vein of Ireland.

But this iniquitous Union is yet destined to be severed again.
In the fierce agitation in both kingdoms on the repeal 20 years
ago, it was stated on one side that Ireland had been rapidly improving since the Union, and on the other, that she was as rapidly retrograding.   We are not inclined to agree entirely with
either statement.   That Ireland has advanced, we think is certain, and for two reasons.   First, some of the unjust restrictions
have been removed, and more freedom given to her energies,
if the little so ungraciously bestowed, can be dignified with
the name of freedom.   Secondly, she did increase in population,
and from the very position she occupies, must feel to a greater
or less degree, the impulse to which the whole civilized world
is moving.   But it is equally true that her advancement was
slow, and bore no proportion to the growth of her population,
or the march of improvement around her.   It is also true,
that her prosperity was checked by the Union, and that if she
had been left to pursue her own policy, she would now have
stood side by side with Scotland.   The Union reduced the
linen trade at a single blow, four-fifths.   The revenue is a sure
test of the nation's prosperity.   In one of the Reports on this
subject, it is shown that the difference between the gross
revenue for Ireland for three years previous to the Union, and
three years after, (from 1833 to 1835,) when it was in full operation, was only a little over £1,500,000, while in the *same
years*, England had gained in her revenue, £46,000,000.
Though her revenue has latterly increased, it has been in a
diminished ratio to those of the nations around her.   Had she
been fairly treated, she would now doubtless throw £15,000,000

yearly into the exchequer instead of a little more than half that sum. It should be remarked here, that this increased property, small though it be, has affected only the land-owners and the Established clergy. The tenantry and the millions of poor do not feel it.

The Emancipation Bill, removing all civil disabilities from the Catholics, was passed. The Reform Bill likewise achieved something for Ireland, though its benefits have been slight compared with its promises. In the first place, (see the letter of O'Connell, to the Earl of Shrewsbury, for these calculations,) it did not give Ireland a fair representation in Parliament, allowing her only 105 out of 658 members. According to Castlereagh, himself, this is not enough. Says O'Connell, "I now come to the year 1831. The population returns of that year give England, in round numbers, a population of 13,000,-000, and Ireland of 8,000,000.

The following is a correct abstract of the revenue produced by both countries in that year.

Revenue credited to Great Britain, ...	£48,325,215
Deduct teas consumed in Ireland, ...	500,000
Deduct for all other customable articles consumed in Ireland, ...	1,000,000
Real revenue of Great Britain, ...	£46,825,215
Revenue credited to Ireland, ...	4,560,897
Add the above, ...	1,500,000
Actual Irish Revenue, ...	£6,060,897

"Now to avoid all cavil whatsoever, I will take the Irish revenue as only one-tenth of the English, and even at this most disadvantageous mode of making the calculation, the right of Ireland to increased representation did, at the time of passing the Reform Act, stand thus.

Members.

Ireland for population—8 to 13 in 500, gives, ... 207

" 　　Revenue—1 to 10 in 500 gives, ... 50

Total, ... 257

The mean on those two being one-half, entitled Ireland to 178 members."

In speaking of the invidious distinction between the two countries in this respect, he says : "Every county in England, with more than 50,000 inhabitants, got an increase of one member. Every county in England, with more than 100,000 inhabitants, got an increase of *two* members. There is but *one* *county* in Ireland, with so few as 100,000 inhabitants; yet no Irish county got any increase to the representation." He goes on to state that the population of Gloucestershire in 1831, was 211,-356, and the Reform Bill gave them two additional representatives, making in all four members for Parliament. Galway had 381,407, and got no addition, having now only two members.

Leicestershire had two members added, with a population of only 197,276, making in all, four; while Tipperary, with a population of 380,598, has only two. Northamptonshire, with a population of 279,276, got two additional representatives, making in all four ; while the county of Down, in Ireland, with the greater population, 307,571, got no addition, and has only two members. Cumberland, with 126,681 inhabitants, got two additional members, making in all four ; while Cork, with nearly six times its population, got no addition, and hence, has half the number of representatives. And this is the fraternal union of two sister kingdoms !

XX.

THE municipal reform, although a gain for Ireland, still treats her with great injustice. In England, every citizen that pays the poor and borough rate, is entitled to vote in all municipal elections. In Ireland it is different. Says O'Connell : "no man in Dublin, is entitled to the burgess franchise, unless he be rated at ten pounds a year." "In Liverpool, or Bristol, the resident Englishman is entitled to be a burgess upon paying one tax, while in Dublin, he must first "pay nine taxes." The consequence is, as he states, that in Dublin, 22,000 persons are rated to the poor rate. If these persons were in Liverpool, 20,000 of them could vote. So much for the elective franchise, both in the counties and municipalities. In England, a little over twenty-five per cent of the adult population, enjoy the elective franchise, while in Ireland, not over two per cent possess it.

In the county of Hertford, with a population of 95,977, there are only 5,013 voters. In Galway, with 381,564, only 3,061 voters, and so on. These are O'Connell's figures.

The next reform is, the commutation of tithes. "Irishmen now pay no tithes," is bandied about, till men really believe that England has, in this respect, at last granted Ireland justice.

She could take to herself no credit in this thing, even if it were true. But the fact is, she could no longer collect the tithes, even with the point of the bayonet. Finding the folly of resisting an armed force, the people allowed their goods and their cattle to be taken—but alas, there were no buyers. The cattle had to be carried across the channel to find a market. England was losing her tithes. The cost of collecting, eat them up. What then should she do? Give up the revenue which supported her fat bishops and sinecure rectors ? Oh, no. But they were no longer collectable ; the injustice was too manifest, and Irishmen would no longer submit to it. She removed the tithe from the tenant to the landlord. The landlord pays it, and then deducts it out of the man's wages. It is the first thing the landlord makes the tenant pay. So that the boasted magnanimity of England in removing the tithes, amounts to this—she gets the landholder to collect for her, that which she could no longer collect herself. It is true, the poor Irishman's only cow can no longer be driven to the pound, because the few shillings due for tithes cannot be paid. The last quilt can no longer be taken from his bed when the tithe is due, but he is compelled to pay the same amount in another, and not less oppressive form to the land-holder. The tithe is now taken from the mouth, instead of the back. He can no longer eat his third rate potatoe in peace and shut his eyes to the future. Coming out of his rent, he must reduce his living to meet it and the rent, or lose his land ; so that the present mode of collecting it, presses harder on the people, and creates more starvation and suffering, than the former. The evil is not so apparent, because there is no gathering of the crowd clamoring against the soldiery—no bristling of bayonets in front of the widow's wretched hut, under the double command of the constable and the minister of Christ. Silently, resistlessly, it is removed and the effects are seen only by him who looks into the hut, and beholds a scantier table, or rather, fewer of those third rate potatoes, which constitute all his food—or the more loathsome rags that cover him. To us, it is a matter of wonder that England did not sooner think of this plan—so certain, so noiseless, and so cheap. It formerly cost the Government more than $5,-000,000 to keep sufficient soldiers in Ireland to oversee this " collection for the saints." The police cost nearly $1,000,000 more, not to mention the law-suits between the people and clergy on account of tithes, which swelled this sum to $7,000,-000, the mere cost of collecting. During the three years, ending 1821, 100,000 prosecutions were made by the clergy, to collect from the hungry and impoverished people, this unjust revenue of the Church. Nearly one-twelfth of the entire surface of Ireland is owned by the Church of England. The income from this land and the tithes, etc., is more than $10,-000,000, annually. All this comes out of 6,000,000 people, not one-tenth of whom are Protestants, while the remainder—that is, the nation, on the contrary, deem the service of the Church they support, sacrilege and blasphemy. These $10,000,000 go into the pockets of four archbishops, eight bishops and a thousand and two or three hundred clergy. Of the latter, nearly half never see their parishes. These bishops and archbishops receive their hundreds of thousands of dollars annually, while several million Irishmen have not even sufficient third rate potatoes all the year. There has been no real reformation in the Church. Government has changed only the mode of its exactions.

XXI.

MANUFACTURES generally, have declined since the union. The woolen trade, the refining of sugar, glass manufacture, and other minor manufactures, have not only decreased, but have been almost entirely destroyed. O'Connell thus takes from the reports on Irish trade and manufactures in 1834–1840 : " It is ascertained from authentic documents and returns, that in 1800 there were in Dublin ninety-one master manufacturers in the woolen trade, employing 4,938 persons. In 1840, there were only twelve master manufacturers, and only 682 persons employed in this trade. In Limerick, at the union, there were 1,000 woolen weavers, there are not now seventy. It is ascertained that the 1,000 had, in the year 1823, declined to 400, in 1826, to 300, in 1827 to 200, in 1828 to 150, in 1830 to 100, and in 1832, to 30—and in two years afterward, there was not a vestige of this formerly important and remunerative branch of industry." These are only examples of the general decrease in trade and manufacture. He makes it out, that at the time of the union, there were over a hundred and fifty thousand out of a population of 4,000,000, engaged in woolen, cotton, and silk manufactures, while in the year 1840, out of 8,000,000, there were only eight thousand engaged in the same occupation. We know that some manufactures may decline, while others rise, and still the country be on the increase. But linen has suffered the same diminution, and with no certainty of its permanent increase. Besides, the agricultural interests of the country have not increased in proportion to the decrease of manufactures. It may be said, indeed, there has been a diminution of taxes ; true, but this slight relief has been more than compensated by the act of assimilation, in 1823, by which all the custom duties were raised to the British standard, and afterwards the assimilation of post office paper, and glass duties, etc. The truth is, take Ireland throughout, and the little progress she has made, has been gained in spite of England, and not by her assistance. As a general rule, it may be laid down, that England has granted Ireland nothing she has dared to retain, unless it manifestly was for her own pecuniary interest to do it ; and that in nearly, if not quite all the petty reforms she has permitted, she has only changed the *mode*, not the *character* of her oppressions.

England no longer gives a bounty for the head of an Irish priest, but she rewards his oppressors on a grander scale. The estates of Irish lords are not confiscated, and the peasantry shot in pastime ; but how long is it since soldiers were quartered upon the people—exciting their deadliest hatred, and fanning the coals of rebellion, which would bring a recurrence of those calamities. The bards and songs are not destroyed as formerly, lest they should animate the people to strike again for liberty ; but how long is it since the freedom of the press has been restricted—nay, in some instances, invaded and scattered, by a ruthless soldiery, for speaking too freely of the abuses which stained and maddened the people ?

Read over the acts passed to prevent rebellion—forbidding communication between societies : look at the exactions of military law—the efforts to repress petition—the open and shameless dishonesty in her pecuniary and church relations—the injustice of her representative system ; and you will find that England has never retreated from the high ground she first took, and that Ireland is still bound, hand and foot, as far as the government dare carry its despotism.

XXII.

BUT let us return to a summary view of the late and present sufferings of Ireland. The oppressive character of the government, and the extent of its plunder, are developed with more terrific clearness in the actual destitution, and almost incredible sufferings of the Irish people. The restrictions on Irish commerce, and indirect ruin of her manufactures by England, prevent the employment of Irish industry in mills. The Established Church, and a few gentlemen, owning almost the entire surface of the island, the inhabitants cannot fall back on the land and become independent agriculturists. What little they earn as tenants and laborers, becomes so reduced by Church and governmental taxes, as to leave them but a fraction of the pittance their industry may bring them. The money of the nation, through the demands of the British exchequer, by non-resident clergy and absentees, almost entirely disappears over the Channel. But this is not all. After the Church and government have taken, not only their pound of flesh apiece, but all the flesh, the land-holders pick the bones. After passing through the clutches of a government, destitute of even the appearance of justice, and of a heartless, merciless Church, the poor Irishman, instead of finding sympathy from his landlord, is seized by him with the same spirit, and cruelly beaten and trampled into deeper poverty and suffering. Many late acts of Parliament have tended directly to give the rich greater power over the poor. The alteration of the constitutional law, raising the qualifications to vote from 10s. to £10, injured, in more respects than one, the lower classes. When it was 10s., the landlord sub-divided his land, in order to secure more voters. But now he consolidates his farms in order to have £10 tenants, and in doing it drives from their homes the small farmers and cottagers to seek employment in a far away land. So also when a Protestant comes in possession of land once owned by a Catholic, he has the power, soon as the lease of their land expires, to turn the tenants loose on the world. One man in the parishes of Hacketstown and Clonmore, coming thus into possession of property, ejected, in four years, ninety-three families, amounting in all to one hundred and seventy-three individuals. Several of these were widows, most of whom soon died from want and neglect. The more immediate cause of this immense suffering is the *high price* of bread and *low price* of wages, to which is superadded scarcity of work. I need not say that these are to be attributed entirely to the iniquitous oppression of the government.

The highest average of wages, and that for only a portion of the year, is but 8*d*. a day. If this were the average the year round, it would amount to only $50. Out of this take only $10 for house rent, and the meagre sum of $20 a year for the clothing of his entire family, and $10 more for fuel, and the poor man has left only $10 with which to buy food for himself and family, in a land where a curse is put on life. Remember, this is the *bright* side of the picture. Wages do not average so high the year through. There are hundreds of thousands who would rejoice as over a sudden fortune, could they be assured of receiving regularly 8*d*. a day for their labor. Is it strange, then, that almost the entire population hunger in hovels, and are clothed in rags?

XXIII.

SAYS Raumer, the German, in writing from Ireland : "My mind is filled with one thought—I can entertain no other— it is that of the inexpressible wretchedness of so many thousands. No words can express the frightful truth which everywhere meets the eye. To form an idea of it, you must see these houses—not houses but huts—not huts but hovels, mostly without windows or apertures ; the same entrance, the same narrow space for men and hogs—the latter lively, sleek, and well fed, the former covered with rags, or rather hung with fragments of rags, in a manner which it is *impossible* to con-

ceive. If I except the respectable people in the towns, I did not see upon thousands of Irish a *whole coat,* a *whole shirt,* a *whole cloak, but all in tatters,* and *tatters* such as are no where else to be seen.

"The ruins of ancient castles were pointed out to me; but how could I take any pleasure in them, while the desolate ruined huts surrounded me, and testified the distress of the present times, more loudly than the others did of the grandeur of the past? Other huts were half fallen down, but the occupants crept into the remaining half, which was not larger than a coffin for the wretched family. I have read, and written much on the sufferings of different ages and nations, and wrote with sympathy; but it is a far different thing to see them—to see them in their gigantic forms in our highly extolled times—*denied* and extenuated—nay, acknowledged and justified by those who, like the French, fancy they are at the head of all human civilization. No wonder if the native Irish, like the prophet of old by the waters of Babylon, sit down and weep, if I, a stranger, am compelled to reckon the few days I passed among them as the most melancholy of my life."

These are the outlines of a picture, which we must fill up from the Report of the Poor Law Commissioners appointed to examine the condition of the laboring classes of Ireland, and made up from testimony taken on the spot where the circumstances occurred. To see these scenes as the Commissioners saw them, we have but to look on a collection of Irish huts along the lines of our railroads and canals, half turf and half boards, without floors or windows, one apartment sufficing for the whole family; and then imagine them standing in groups over the whole surface of Ireland, presenting gloomy spots on its fair bosom, silent records of a people's woes. But, no, this would not be a fair representation, for I remember these huts that arrest the eye of the American traveler, and awaken his sympathy, are comfortable tenements compared to the hovels of Ireland; an improvement in civilization, for the owner receives his dollar a day or more, and pays no rent.

Hunger, at least, is not one of their inmates. Reduce these rude huts to ruin, dilapidate that which seems to be beyond dilapidation, and instead of the well-dressed laborer, with his meat and potatoes, gather in them half-naked, half-starved wretches, and scatter such wrecks of barbarism and humanity over one of the sweetest isles the ocean ever murmured around and you will have a more correct picture of the reality.

XXIV.

BUT to return to the Report, and the condition of Ireland twenty-five years ago, before we come down to 1866. From the counties of Galway, Meath, Clare, Kildare, Cork, Donegal, and Tipperary, there is but one answer returned, starvation and death! In Mayo, say they, in the parish of Long, in the mountains, "when the potatoes fail them, they *bleed their cattle, and eat the boiled blood*, sometimes mixed with meal, but often without it. The same beast has been known to bleed *three times in one season.*" A witness says, he knew a family to have, during three days, but one substantial meal of potatoes—they kept life in them by picking up shell-fish on the strand. In the county of Longford, it states that the peasantry "go through the fields and gather wild weeds, and boil them with salt, and live on them *without even a potato to eat along with them.*" Others "remained in bed all day to *stifle hunger.*" Says another witness : "I declare to my God, I know several men who never tasted food for forty-eight hours— and many is the man who thinks himself well off with one meal a day."

But to enter more into detail. The Report says, one witness testified that "he, his wife, and five children, have often lived three or four days on weeds alone, without a potato ; I have not had a shoe or stocking these six or seven years (it is easy to count all the shoes I ever bought, two or three pair, I be-lieve) ; I have not bought a new coat for four years, nor trousers for five ; I was three weeks in the house ; I could not go out for want of clothes ; my sister's son gave me these old breeches ; I have no hat of my own, good or bad." And yet the Report says, that there was not in the parish a better workman than this man, who adds—" I have one pair of blankets ; the whole family (seven in number) lie under them on one bed, lying heads and points ; they are worn and spent now, and are the only pair I have had since I was married, seventeen years ago."

Another says : " That he, his wife, and children, were compelled to sleep in the open air, with nothing to cover them but one blanket ; that he never had any employment since he came to the town where he was, though he often looked for it."

One witness says : " I have not a stitch of clothes but what I wear now, shivering and famishing as you now see me ; yet when I can get fivepence a day, I am glad to stand out in the cold wind and rain, every blast and dash of it driving to the heart of me ; we live in a deserted house ; we have to shift our bed from one side to the other as the wind changes, and if it were not in that state, sure I would not be left there, for sure I can pay no rent ; our bed is a shake down of straw, as we have but one blanket, not four pounds in weight, among us all, and even that my wife has round her when she is begging ; we had not one spark of fire in our cabin last night, and I was up at day-dawn this morning to purchase a load of turf out of the fivepence that I received out of my day's hire late yesterday evening, and there we were about the fire-place to-day, I striving to spare the sods, and the children driving and pulling one another to see who could get nearest the coze."

Another says : " I am counted a good laborer, and while there is employment to be had for any fair proportion of laborers, I am seldom idle in the whole year. I am idle for three months on an average. In the beginning of this summer I was idle for about three weeks ; one day after another I had no provisions ; I sold every article in my house rather than let my wife out ; you may be sure we ate the price of them but sparingly ; at last I sold the pot I had to boil my potatoes ; I walked out of the door, my wife, myself, and six children. *I went off where we were not known, and begged."*

Another witness says : " I hold land for which I pay 30*s.* a year ; I am also a cooper ; I may be employed for three months in the year ; I can earn 2*s.* every day I am employed, and am therefore better off than most people." In answer to question, ' Does your family use milk with their potatoes ?' this witness says : ' Milk, sir ! I declare solemnly before my neighbors here, that know whether I speak the truth, for eight weeks that I have been lying in my bed, having blister after blister on me, I did not drink a quart of milk, but ate potatoes and salt herring ; had no drink but water. *A great many of us would pray to the Almighty to take us off ; it would be better for us, than live on in our poverty and need.'"*

Another witness says : " During the laŝt summer, I had not enough, nor anything like enough potatoes for my family ; we lived principally on herbs gathered in the fields, and shell fish from the shores ; bad as I was last summer, I will be worse next ; my potatoe crop has failed this year ; the cause was, that I had no money to buy proper seed, and no means of earning it, and was obliged to use the refuse of what others planted, paying for it by labor."

Another witness says : " I was thirteen weeks without employment, and often went to bed without any meal in the day at all—so much did it work upon my mind that I fell sick ; I would willingly turn to any part of the land that I would get employment ; but this moment I do not know what or where to turn for employment, and often if a penny would get a dinner for my wife and children, I could not get it. From the anxiety of mind, many is the night when I do not get a wink of sleep."

One witness inquires : " Can any hardship be greater than to get up in the morning, as I have done, hear your children crying for food, and not having any to give them ; to look at myself, a man able and willing to work, obliged to send the eldest of my children out to beg food to feed the young ones."

Another witness showed to the Commissioners the following account, as it stood between him and his landlord at the end of the year :

Rent of cabin, ...	£1 10 0
Rent of ¼ acre of manured land, ...	1 15 0
Rent of ¼ acre of unmanured land, ...	0 10 0
Half a barrel of potatoes, ...	0 10 0
Milk, ...	0 7 0
	£4 12 0
Deduct 195 days' wages at 4*d.* a day, ...	3 5 0
Balance due to farmer, ...	£1 7 0

" He said—' I owed him £1. 7*s.*; I am trying to work it off ; I did not take any manured land this year ; for that reason I shall be obliged to take twice, three times as much potatoes on time next year ; I do not know how I will be able to pay for them, *unless I get away from the master I have now, to one who will be more kind, and give me indulgence.*' "

Others declare they " go half-naked," lying on rotten straw upon the floor or ground, but one blanket to the whole family —that they would be willing to work all winter for bare food. One says that " he, his wife, and three children, lie upon straw —that they have *no bed-clothes,* but throw over them at night the clothes they wear by day." *This was not a famine year !*

XXV.

THUS far we have taken from the Report the testimony relating to the *working-classes alone.* If able-bodied men, willing to work—if the healthy peasantry of the land are in this deplorable condition, what new forms of wretchedness should we expect to find around the huts and couches of the widow, the orphan, and the infirm? Female labor in no country can compete with male labor ; hence we find the widows of Ireland, not only wasted by poverty and reduced by famine, but actually dying under the accumulated load of their misfortunes. The Report, in speaking of this class, unfolds a tale of suffering that wrings the heart of the reader, and awakens the keenest indignation against the cupidity and inhumanity that inflict it.

Says one witness, a widow with five children around her: "I sleep on the ground, which is almost constantly wet, and often have not as much straw to lie on as would fill a hat. On a wet night I must go to a neighbor's house with my infant child, born after my husband's death ; I have *but a single fold of a blanket to cover my whole family ; I have had it for eight years ;* my children are almost naked."

Three widows testify that they often live on *one meal a day,* and that composed of dry *potatoes.* If any of them are fortunate enough to rent a little piece of land, the proprietor, unless payment in full is made, often takes every thing for the rent, except a single blanket, not worth the seizing. One witness says : "I saw myself and six or seven poor women turn their faces to the wall, and eat the *cabbage stumps* the pigs had picked."

Some conception of the destitution and famine under which this class silently suffer, may be had from the fact, that when the cholera prevailed in Cork, three widows dissembled sickness, that they might be taken into the hospital to escape the horrors of famine.

Dr. Longheed, one of the witnesses cited in this report, says : "As for the widow with young children, she certainly has no resource whatever besides that of begging. He knows of no instance of a widow being provided for by the landlord under whom her husband lived. The landlord seldom loses any time in getting them off his ground as fast as he can."

In answer to the inquiry, if any had died of actual destitution for the last three years, one witness says : "Many poor creatures have pined away for want of sufficient sustenance, and have died or pined away in fever, in consequence of want and destitution."

Another, the Rev. Mr. Roche, says : " A great many have died from exhaustion consequent on distress."

From three parishes, Castletown, Delvin and Westmeath, the Report says : " From absolute destitution, from twenty-five to thirty—from disease incurred by extreme want, from sixty to seventy." Making in all from eighty-five to a hundred, in three parishes, perishing through lack of bread, while the single tax levied on those parishes to support a corrupt church, would doubtless have supplied not only *their* wants, but those of many more, doomed to the same melancholy fate.

Says another witness, Rev. Peter Ward, of Aughena : " In the year 1841, six persons died of actual want ; since that period I take upon myself to say, that of every five persons who have died, *three* always die of *inanition*, brought on by bad food, bad clothing, and bad or no bedding."

Another says . " Last December, a poor woman, who was ill of the fever, lay for three nights under a hedge for want of a house. The laborer cannot lay any thing by for sickness, and the small farmers and cotters are even worse off."

The ruin which the oppressive system of England fastens on Ireland, reaches not only the laborer, but *every* one *below* the rich landed proprietor.

Says another witness : " The state of some of the sick is beyond any thing wretched. I have met cases where, being unable to procure straw, they had a sort of hard knotted fern for bedding, and I have frequently found this, as well as grass, wet under them."

Another : " According to the census which I made two years ago, there were then in this parish 751 men who had no shoes, and were unable to procure them ; and of a population of 9,000—3,135, male and female, had not within five years purchased any important article of clothing, such as a coat, a gown, or so forth."

A physician stated that, " A few sticks placed against a mud wall, and covered with furze or clods, have sometimes formed the only protection of a man in fever."

Says another witness, Rev. Andrew Phelan, respecting the number of those ejected from estates : " Within the last five or six years, 190 families have been ejected from the estates of the landed proprietors in the barony of East Idrone, amounting in the whole to 626, of whom 152 are widows and orphans. I recollect in one instance, of ten or eleven families who were driven off of one town land—three or four persons perished in the most melancholy manner."

XXVI.

THUS we might go on extracting from the Report—but this is sufficient. We might also insert, *ad infinitum,* cases that have come under our personal knowledge ; but we have preferred facts before published, because they are official, so that those disposed to be incredulous and retreat behind the charge of exaggeration, should be compelled to believe. It is no picture wrought out by fancy and colored for effect. These are facts of the Nineteenth Century—fruits of English benevolence— the results of English philanthropy ;—neither are these isolated facts. The Report of the Commissioners is dark with them. These huts, with these burlesques on humanity shivering around them, meet you at every turn. Yes, twenty years ago, out of 8,000,000 of people, every third person, during thirty out of the fifty-two weeks of the year, did not have a sufficiency of even third rate potatoes.

Says another Commission, appointed by parliament to inquire into the condition of the hand-loom weavers :

" In Belfast I found the cotton-weavers and others living, to a great extent, upon a diet which in England would only be used as hog's wash. It is a liquid called ' sowens,' made in the process of manufacturing starch. I went with Mr. Muggeridge (our assistant commissioner) to visit a starch manufactory belonging to Mr. Emerson, for the sake of learning the nature of sowens, and inquiring into the fact of its being used as an article of food.

"In manufacturing starch, a quantity of wheaten meal is put into a large vat, with water, where it lies fermenting and souring for about three weeks. It is then taken out and passed through basket sieves to separate the bran; afterwards it is put into another large vat, and suffered to stand some days; in this vat the starch, being the heaviest substance, sinks to the bottom; the remaining particles of the bran and other light substances rise to the top, and form a scum, and the milky-looking water, between the starch and the scum, is the sowens. The surface is then skimmed, and the sowens drawn off, the starch remaining behind in a thick pudding-like state, requiring only to be made into square blocks and dried.

"The sowens is sold to the poor at the rate of a half-penny a measure, a measure containing nearly a gallon. It is boiled and used by them chiefly as a broth, or soup, for breakfast and supper. Several persons came for it while we were present, and we saw it ladled out to them. We were informed that some who had attempted to live wholly upon it, had found it fatal to their health. The quantity sold in this manner by Mr. Emerson amounted to £6 per week, from which it would appear that upwards of 400 persons are supplied with sowens for food from this establishment alone, allowing seven gallons a week to each individual. A little flour held by the water in solution after the starch has been extracted, is the share of wheat, and a poor share it is, which these 400 persons obtain by our present protective system."

Into this fearful sketch enter only the figures which look silently down on us—the beating heart is out of sight. We know they sigh and weep, but we do not hear or see them. We know they suffer, for they tell us so, but we do not watch the victim through all the separate stages of poverty, scarcity, famine and death. The Eternal God alone knows it all, and in the even scales of His everlasting truth and justice ever weighs the suffering and the wrong together. We cannot but contrast Ireland as she is, with her state before civilization dawned upon Northern Europe: and as we behold her barbarian tribes wan-

dering over that beautiful island, with enough to eat, enjoying
the light of heaven without paying a tax for it, we cannot but
inquire, "What has English civilization, or English philanthropy, done for Ireland?" and the answer is returned by a
ragged, wretched, and perishing population—"It has done this
for us." We wonder not that Raumer felt the few days he
passed there "the most melancholy of his life." The mere
copying of the description of those scenes he witnessed, has
made us share his sadness. Poor Ireland! What a sad picture
she presents! Her castles are in ruins—her princes gone—her
harbors neglected—her manufactories silent—her habitations
are hovels, and her inhabitants beggars. We wonder the sparkling wit of the people is not extinguished, and her joyous harp
shivered for ever. We wonder they have not the spirit as well
as the degradation of slavery; no other nation could have
borne up under such accumulated wrongs; no other nation
could have suffered so much, and yet retained such nobleness
and independence of feeling. But her woes are not yet ended.
The shadow of a gloomy throne is still over her. The hand
of cruelty is yet on her heart, and the iron still enters her soul.

XXVII.

BUT an end must come to all this. It is natural that the Irish
should seek relief from such sufferings. If there are impossibilities in the way, so that Ireland cannot become like
Scotland, or other nations; if her people must starve, and it is
her fate to be left utterly desolate, then effort is fruitless. But
if there are no impossibilities; if with proper government, she
can become a commercial, agricultural, and wealthy nation, it
is proper she should seek to obtain that government. But there
are only two possible ways by which this object can be secured.
Either the English government must entirely change its legislation towards Ireland, or Ireland be allowed to legislate for
herself. The resources of a country must be expended on itself
or it will grow poorer still. England now draws them all to

herself. To reform her legislation so as to benefit Ireland, would be to give her the control of her own taxation, commerce and revenue. But England wants the money of the Irish; hence she will never reform to this extent, unless by compulsion. Besides, shall Ireland die by rapid consumption in waiting and petitioning for this reform? Has she not tried every argument with her unjust ally? She has entrusted her interests to the English government long enough; let her now try the experiment of self government, and see if she cannot rise from the deep abyss into which she is plunged. This is all she asked in the demand for Repeal of the legislative Union. Many Irishmen did not desire or expect an entire separation from England. They wished a legislature of their own to regulate her internal affairs. One thing is certain, she cannot be worse off than she is by the experiment. Besides, when she had her own legislature, her prosperity was greater than it has ever been since. Her representation in parliament is of no avail. They may declaim, they may vote; England understands it all beforehand, and is resolved that neither argument nor justice shall induce her to change her policy. Now, give Ireland a legislature that shall control her commerce and manufactures; keep her own revenue at home; make the tenure by which land is held more fixed and just; stop absenteeism, which is annually draining her of millions; abolish the whole system of church oppression, and pitch the bishops over the Channel; give the people the elective franchise, and let them do their own taxing; and it will be strange, indeed, if with her resources and intelligence, she cannot be kept from her present starvation and beggary. The insecurity of tenure is one great cause of Irish suffering. The landlord now can put what price he pleases on his land, and the poor tenant must consent to it, or do worse. When the year comes round, he is unable to pay the rent, and is immediately turned out to starve, and his beds and clothing, (if he have any) taken for the debt. It is under these circumstances that the wronged tenant sometimes takes such " wild justice" as the outraged often seek. However ignorant the lower classes may be of the intricate and ever-changing policy of the English government by which they are crushed, *this* evil they all perfectly understand.   Hence, it is made one of the grounds for seeking an independent national legislature.   Thus we found in 1840 the Repeal manifesto scattered like leaves over the length and breadth of the land, saying :

" That the sufferings of the people from insecurity of tenure have increased, and are so great ; and that none but an Irish Parliament will give fixed holdings to the Irish people, is so certain, that we have, in these two facts alone, a greater force for combining the people into one body, constitutionally determined to obtain nationality, than the men of '82 had.   That the organization of the people in every parish in Ireland into associates, members, and volunteers, so as to give them one will and one voice, is the only means of bringing their power and opportunities to bear constitutionally for the accomplishment of repeal, and that such organization can be most rapidly carried on by the repeal wardens, with the influence and co-operation of the Irish clergy, upon whom the success of the cause mainly depends.   That, further, you are requested to take every opportunity of pressing upon the peasantry the nature and importance of the tenure question ; that repeal alone çan settle it. And, once Ireland is organized, be who will in office, she will be in a condition to demand legislative independence."

The intelligent man who sympathizes least with Ireland in her sufferings and demands, cannot but admit that she has three legitimate grounds of complaint.

First. The exclusion of the great body of the Irish Catholic population from the right of suffrage.

Second. Compelling the Irish Catholic population, and their nonconformist brethren, the Presbyterians, Methodists, Baptists, etc., to violate the rights of conscience, by forcing them to contribute large sums of money for the support of a Church whose doctrines they reject, and whose members are less than a tenth of the people of Ireland.

Third. By permitting a tenant law, by which the peasantry

are enabled to lease farms only from year to year, liable to eviction by the landlord, and receiving no compensation for any improvements they may have made upon the place. The Scotch tenant system should be introduced into Ireland, by which the lease should last fifteen years, and the tenant, at the expiration of the lease, should be allowed the value, at a fair appraisement, of all improvements he may have made upon the property.

XXVIII.

BUT lest I should be accused of describing a state of things which no longer exists, I shall trace the condition of Ireland down to the present 1866, and show, that with all the alleged relief she has experienced from English legislation—from five years of famine, and her enormous emigration, which have together reduced her population two millions during the last fifteen years—she is *now* in a more deplorable condition than ever; and that unless she finds relief, in justice from England, the Irish race will soon cease to exist in the home of their fathers.

Let us, however, glance first at Ireland as she is, or rather what God made her, before our final survey of the ruin England has wrought. "Ireland," says Jean de Paris, one of the ablest writers in France—*La Question Irelandaise*, 1860—" like Sicily, is one of the most richly endowed lands of this earth. A soil eminently fertile, a temperate climate, a situation peculiarly adapted for commerce, abundant mineral resources, a brave and intelligent people, naturally honest, affable and benevolent in manners, enterprising by character, gifted with a lively imagination, a witty, cheerful and expansive gaiety—these are the prominent features of the country and character of the people of that Ireland, whose name, by some fatal error of fate, has become synonymous with Famine-Land !"

XXIX.

IRELAND is the first country touched or sighted, by vessels coming from the great western world, America. It offers them spacious harbors, safer and more convenient than those of England, for neither London nor Liverpool could compete with the Irish ports, already famed in the time of Tacitus. If Man had been as just towards Ireland, as Nature has been prodigal, what ships from all parts of the world, what active commerce, would fill with life her numerous harbors! What splendid sights would be the bays of Dublin, Bantry, Galway, Waterford, Belfast, Cork—the natural point of communication with Australia! What traffic on the canals, and on so many lovely rivers! What activity, what industry, what life, in all those villages, silent and in ruins to-day! What riches would be extracted from the soil; what manufactures, raised up by the national capital, would attest the genius and the energy of that unfortunate race, prosperous in every land to which the blast of misery carries them—prosperous everywhere, in fact, except in their own unhappy country!

"Of the different branches of commerce and manufacture which contribute to England's prosperity, which are those that Ireland would not possess? We could name some in which the Irish, by their peculiar faculties, by their natural taste and imagination, and by their artistic talent, assuredly excel. How different would be, in fine, *that* Ireland from the one now known to us only by its misfortunes! What animation would then ring everywhere; what joy would resound on those shores, where tears only are shed to-day—on those mountains where people perish of hunger! What gladsome scenes would be reflected on the bosom of the lovely lakes of free and prosperous Ireland!

"Perhaps we shall be reproached with indulging in poetical fancies. Let it be remembered that the bright dawn of prosperity *was* seen during the short period of Irish independence, from 1782 to 1798, when Ireland possessed only the mere shadow of a National Parliament. But leaving aside the dream of the past, or ambitious views for the future, let us return to the realities of the present."

The following are figures and facts of the present time :

" Ireland has a greater extent of territory, has a more numerous population, and gives the State a larger income, than many of the second-rate powers of Europe. Before the great famines of 1846–51, in spite of those of 1817, 1823, 1831, 1837, and we may say in spite of the *permanent* famine which reigns since 1800 (the date of the definite union with England), Ireland had *over eight millions of inhabitants.* We shall prove that it is not by *her* fault that there remain to-day *less than six millions.* While the famine was raging, in that one year—1847—Ireland lost, by hunger or by the typhus fever, five hundred thousand of her children, while two hundred thousand others fled from her shores. Yet the agricultural produce of Ireland was computed at nearly forty-four millions sterling. So that in that very year, Ireland, reduced to starvation, actually produced enough to feed and clothe double the number of its inhabitants. Economists have calculated that, if well cultivated, the country would easily supply the wants of a population of twenty-five millions."[*]

XXX.

THE established rule of Irish landlords now, is to *drive out men, and turn in cattle.* This is a *régime*, not resorted to occasionally, but carried out almost everywhere. If this broad statement be a fact, it is a horrible one. It is a resort to barbarism. It is robbing civilized men of the natural right to live on the soil ; it is going back to the primitive state in which

---

[*] We read, even in a work considered as official authority, *The Parliamentary Gazetteer of Ireland:* " The annual value of the agricultural produce of Ireland seems to be pronounced by nearly all parties only one-half, some say a fifth part, of what it is capabab'e of giving."—*Introduction*, p. 69.

beasts, and not men, possess the earth. If it can be shown, that this frightful condition of things exists, it will abundantly account for the fact, that Ireland has never suffered so much during any quarter of a century of her history, as she has *during the last twenty-five years*. Never have so many of her people died of disease and famine. Never has her population been so decimated by pestilence, or the shedding of blood; never such a people left to such an alternative—total extermination or exile. This compulsory choice is fast leaving to Victoria, what Elizabeth had in the same island—*little but corpses and ashes to rule over*.

XXXI.

LET us look at the position of the Irish peasant *under English law, as we find it actually working.*

M. Jean de Paris asks if the odious legislation which condemned to death a whole people on the very land which was taken from their ancestors, be still in vigor.* If the proprie-

---

* On the 23d of June last year, 1865, the House of Commons ordered the Report of the Select Committee on the "Tenure and Improvement of Land Act (Ireland)" to be printed.

This question, of such vital interest to the Irish nation, had been often crowded, as we have shown, upon the attention of the British Parliament, and investigating committees had been appointed. But in every case it ended in proving what the *Dublin Review* so conclusively shows to have been, "merely a mechanism for shuffling aside the consideration of the great question of state and of law, and a question of a very high order of administration." That Review says, that the night before Sir Robert Peel met with the accident that caused his death, in walking homewards from the House of Commons, his mind seemed to be very anxious. To one of his favorite disciples he said: "It is impossible this ministry can hold office for many months. I must, despite myself, be Premier again very soon. I wonder how people will take my policy? I mean to bring in sweeping measures in regard to Ireland!" "What! to abolish the Established Church?" asked his companion. "Certainly not," replied Sir Robert; "no one cares very much about the settlements of the Church in Ireland at present. It is the Encumbered Estates Court that must be enlarged. Some way must be found, at whatever cost, of fastening the people to the glebe: the system of wholesale evictions must be put an end to." In

tor of the land in Ireland is not always *forced* by law to press
into extinction a conquered race, as he was at former periods,
it is nevertheless certain, that he *may* evict his tenant at will;
and the fact is, that Ireland counts to-day *an army of* 20,000
men constantly employed to evict, or drive out all tenants whom
the landlord does not wish to retain. The tenant holds nothing—not even the house, or the hut he himself built, and from
which he can be driven at any moment, without receiving any
compensation. He may have made the most costly improvements—spent on the buildings and land, not only his labor but

Hansard's Debates (vol. 97, page 1010), Sir Robert Peel, in speaking of the
wholesale ejectments of the Irish tenantry, remarked, "That these ejectments
were illegal, is expressly stated in the Report. But the law is powerless in
procuring redress." Again, (Hansard, vol. 105, page 1287) "I must say that I
do not think the records of any country, civil or barbarous, present materials
for such a picture . . . . the recitals of them are heard with an expression of
the deepest abhorrence." But not a single one of the measures which Peel advised with such solemnity, has ever been introduced; and at the close of the
last Parliament, (1865) Mr. Cardwell informed the Irish people, through the
House of Commons, on the great question of the Tenure of Land, "Her Majesty's Government were determined to make no concession whatsoever."

The whole drift of the Report of these Committees on Ireland have gone to
show, that agriculture in that island is in a very backward state. There is no
adequate capital expended on permanent improvements, either by landlord or
tenant; and on the tenants alone, all the reliance is to be placed. This creates a
feeling of discontent, for every tenant knows, that at the will of his landlord
the value of every improvement he makes will go to men who have contributed
to them nothing at all. Compensation for such improvement is a thing unheard
of in Ireland; the majority of tenants now hold as tenants from year to year,
and the number of leases is diminishing daily. Mr. Macarthy Dunning's evidence before the Select Committee appointed to inquire into the alteration of the
act 23 and 24, Vict. c. 153, on the Tenure and Improvement of Land in Ireland,
says: "Since the last day of last April, I saw myself 12 or 14 houses unroofed,
and the whole of the population turned out on the road-side: their ancestors,
as I understood, had been on that land for upwards of a hundred years."

The Bishop of Cloyne stated, "That during the last 60 or 70 years, no one
acquainted with the history of Ireland, I believe, would deny that all the improvements made, were made by the tenants, . . comparatively very few tenants in Ireland have leases; the landlords up to the present date, have had the
benefit of making no compensation, and whatever improvements are made, they
have had exclusively the advantage of them." He continues: "I firmly be-

his savings—all he had in the world—still be forced, without any notice, to quit at any moment, to abandon everything without being repaid a single penny! By virtue of law, the landlord alone profits by all the improvements. There is no redress whatever for the man who has expended his toil, his savings, and even the sweat of his wife and little children, during their lifetime.

It has been proved a thousand times, that the serfs of the middle ages, and the millions of serfs lately emancipated in Russia,

lieve, without any exaggeration at all, that at this moment there is ground for as much useful and remunerative employment as would employ all the idle hands in Ireland, and many more: and that this useful employment could raise from the soil several millions annually of which the country is deprived, and impart a stimulating and healthy influence to the prosperity of all classes."

The act of Mr. Cardwell was proved by all the witnesses before the Select Committee, to have been a dead letter. The Bishop of Cloyne especially declared, " It had not offered any inducement to the tenants to improve, and there could not be a better proof of that, than the fact, that *nothing whatever had been done under the act.*" Mr. Dillman stated, that " It had done no practical good to Ireland." Lord Dufferin said : " The act has been inoperative as far as it concerns the case of any tenant on my estate."

The able Dublin Reviewer sees " only two honest alternatives before those who have on their consciences the responsibility of advising the public conduct of the Irish people. Either they must take higher ground in the argument of this case, and compel the attention of Ministers and Parliament to it by every constitutional process capable of employment, or else advise the people to abandon their country, and go where it is possible for them to live according to the ordinary conditions of manhood. Being as they are, an exclusively agricultural people, if it be impossible for them at home to acquire any property in the results of their peculiar industry ; if in relation to their landlords they can only remain in a condition, which, now that Negro slavery and Russian serfdom have been abolished, is the lowest actually existing in any civilized society : if Parliament absolutely will not remedy this state of things at all, then, in the name of the law, let the country be emptied of men and filled with cattle. In America, or Australia, an Irish farmer can become a landed proprietor for half the expenditure of sweat and money that it costs him merely to furnish temptation to his landlord's rapacity at home. The millions of property that have been added to the value of the country by the improvements which have been made exclusively by the tenants themselves, are utterly unsecured by law, and systematically appropriated by the landlords with the protection of the law."

In closing an able discussion of this question, the writer quotes the delib-

were treated infinitely better, than the Irish peasants. At the worst, the serf is only *attached* to the glebe—it must feed him —he is not exposed to death by hunger, while the land he tills can grow a crop. But in Ireland, there is not a single legal duty which the landlord fulfils towards his tenant. He is, himself, the magistrate in the case—he is, to all intents and purposes, clothed with the power of condemning to death, the peasant and his family ; for they must get to the seaside, begging their way, and with money got from some quarter, to emi-

erate opinion of certainly "the highest authority upon political economy that has arisen in England since Adam Smith—we mean the honorable member for Westminster, Mr. Stuart Mill, whose powerful support the advocates of the tenants' cause in Parliament will doubtless endeavor to enlist when their case is introduced next session. In his chapter on Property in Land, Mr. Mill says : ' *Whenever in any country the proprietor, generally speaking,* ceases to be the improver, political economy has nothing to say in defence of landed property as there established . . . . landed property in England, is thus very far from completely fulfilling the conditions which render *its existence economically justifiable.* But if insufficiently realized even in England, *in Ireland these conditions are not complied with at all.* . . . Returning nothing to the soil, the landlords consume its whole produce, *minus* the potatoes strictly necessary to keep the inhabitants from dying of famine ; and when they have any purpose of improvement, the preparatory step usually consists in not leaving even this pittance, but turning out the people to beggary, if not to starvation. WHEN LANDED PROPERTY HAS PLACED ITSELF UPON THIS FOOTING, IT CEASES TO BE DEFENSIBLE, and the time has come for making some new arrangement of the matter.' "

The Reviewer expects, whenever the principles of Mr. Mill shall be brought into Parliament by him, as member for Westminster, an outcry will be made about *Communism.* No statesman has ever advocated the monstrous doctrine, that there was anything sacred in the rights of landlords to real estate, wherever their rights stood in the way of the public good ; and the Reviewer inquires, " Who has ever seriously censured the revolution effected by Stein and Hardenberg, in Prussia, or the various settlements of land tenure made by the British government in India, or the arbitrary arrangements of property made by Austria and Russia in connection with the abolition of serfdom and villenage ?"

In this great question, as in others of similar moment, the statesmen of England must be prepared to meet the coming crisis with political courage, energy and independence, or meet the consequences.

Perhaps Stuart Mill may introduce some sweeping measure—but to be just, it must change the whole system by which most estates are held in Ireland to-day.

grate, or die on the roadside, as thousands have, during the last fifteen years ; or indeed, in the last extremity, these pilgrims from famine may receive some pittance—relief in a *workhouse*, where they have reserved for them a more lingering, but absolutely far more humiliating, mournful, and dreadful death.

XXXII.

WHATEVER may have been the crimes of African slavery in the United States, or in any other part of the world, the systematic starvation of whole masses of slaves, has never been known. The condition of the Irish peasant, therefore, is without an example on the face of the globe. Is it any wonder, under such a system as this, that we should hear so much about the lack of proper agriculture in Ireland? The Irishman is often reproached in England, with laziness, idleness, unwillingness to work. All men display these attributes to a certain extent, when all motives to exertion are taken away. But the Irishman, be it said, is characterized by two things in an eminent degree ; the first is a disposition to be busy, which we perceive all over the United States among Irish emigrants— the first move they make on landing, is to dash for a job. The second characteristic, is patient perseverance—steady, continued labor, all through life. Show me a single instance on this continent, of an Irishman who has ceased to work, or relapsed into ease and luxury, even after having become rich. Yes, the Irish peasant, the worst fed, the worst clad, the worst used in Europe ; the man who, in his own country, was crushed down into powerless degradation—see him transformed when he touches the soil of a *free* country, after he has fled from the land of his oppression. He left in rags, insulted and despised, aided perhaps, as has been done in tens of thousands of instances, by some friend in America, who remitted him the money. It has been ascertained by careful figures, that during the last twenty years, from five to twenty-five millions of dollars annually, have been sent to Ireland, for the purpose of aiding emigration.

Large sums are also sent for that purpose from the British Provinces, particularly those in North America, and the whole Australian world. In the British Colonies, the Irishman betters his condition ; but his natural and political paradise is in this Republic. It is the very Canaan of his oppressed people ; and oh! how gladly they plant their feet upon this, to them, holy soil—holy to them by adoption and freedom, as the spot that gave them birth ; for the one has few lasting associations except those which cling tenderly and sadly to the strings of the heart ; and strong as these may have grown, only a few unbidden tears burst from the springs of memory, bedewing the cheek of the Irish emigrant.

XXXIII.

WE have shown how British legislation first impaired, and then exterminated the Irish manufactures. Laws with this sole object in view, were constantly being enacted, from 1699 to 1782. The industrial prosperity of England, reposes to a great extent, upon that stupendous iniquity practised towards Ireland ; and, even now, were the British hand of government taken off from the shoulders of Irish industry, how poor would be the chance, without capital, without social standing, without the power of social organization, for the protection and encouragement of labor, for anything like a rivalry with her ancient foe. Those who have not visited Ireland, and gone over it for themselves, or read, with great care, reliable accounts of the physical and moral condition of the population, will have a very lean idea of the proportions of this misery. The county of Ulster is often pointed at, as being in the enjoyment of commercial prosperity. This is easily accounted for. When the English Parliament in the time of William III. required the destruction of woolen manufactures in Ireland, the linen trade was allowed to be continued there, because the climate was favorable to the growth of flax ; and England wanted Irish linen for her use on the one side, and to exclude the linen fabrics of

Holland on the other. The emigration of Protestants into Ireland, after the Revocation of the edict of Nantes, was encouraged by some concessions in Ulster ; and Protestant Scotch farmers, under special privileges, established themselves ; and finding no formidable rivalry with the Irish around them, who had no privileges or immunities, the Scotch became owners of farms, and took precedence of the Irish in all things. But facts show, that even in the county of Ulster, laborers, artisans, and the mass of the people, are wretchedly poor. Nearly all the great landlords are either habitually, or occasionally, absentees ; and not one-fourth of the rents of Ulster are spent at home. Even the linen trade of Ulster, with all the fostering of class legislation and administrative favor, has never reached one-tenth the importance it might have done. Even in Ulster, the Irish peasant finds it almost impossible, except at exorbitant rates, to get possession of a piece of ground with a hut—this being the height of his ambition in his own country—where, rather than not have something of the consciousness of having a home, even if it be but temporary, he will share his single apartment with his companion, the pig. If he can grow potatoes enough, to keep him and his family, he dares hardly hope for more ; and even in this laudable endeavor, he is often interrupted by an order of eviction.

XXXIV.

IN this process of eviction, as I have said, all the law is on the side of the landlord. More than this : he is furnished with officials to execute his orders ; and on the appointed day, women, old men, children and the sick, must abandon the cabin which the destroyers are preparing to raze ; for the police-constables are on hand, with iron crowbars, to help these drivers of human beings from their homes. Popular indignation has given a name to this whole force throughout Ireland— they are called " *The Crowbar Brigade.*" The official statistics of the British government before me state, that, during ten years, from 1841 to 1851, they destroyed *two hundred and sixty-nine thousand, two hundred and fifty-three* dwellings, or cabins ; and in 1849, they evicted fifty thousand families.

XXXV.

THE horror with which these statements are received implies the question—"Has nothing been done to modify the barbarity of such proceedings?" There are on record eighteen attempts to this effect. The last was made by the enactment of a law pretending to be more thorough than the Commission of 1844 ; for, although that Commission was charged by the British government to make inquiry into the relations existing between landlord and tenant, it was composed of landlords ; and, although it established the existence of great misery and abuses, the Commission reported that there would be danger for the just rights of property to grant "Tenant Right" in full. They recommended the fusion of small farms as "absolutely necessary ;" but, since this plan would necessitate the expulsion of over 190,000 families—at least a million of people—they seriously recommended emigration as the most reliable remedy.

In 1847, a Special Committee of the House of Lords on this same subject, after covering the whole ground, reached the fundamental conclusion that it was necessary, in some way or other, to reduce the population. The great famine began in 1846, and it is a fact that should never be forgotten, that, during the whole period of this famine, which was prolonged five years, Ireland produced enough to feed and clothe double the number of its inhabitants. Had not the breadstuffs and provisions raised in Ireland been carried off to enrich bloated proprietors, and stolen by the Established Church, the word "*famine*" would never have been spoken on the island during that period. But the Royal Commission decided that it was better to send a million of Irishmen to other parts of the world than to stop robbing them of bread. What the government, however, failed to achieve by any remedy whatever, was partly done by terrible necessity. Hundreds of thousands of the wretched peasants rushed in crowds on board rotten ships, and set sail for eternal exile.*   Many of them were rotten coffin-

---

* To show, on pretty high authority, what was the condition of Ireland, even in February of the year 1865, Mr. Maguire, an Irish member of the House of Commons, in the debate on the Queen's Speech, said : " He could not concur in that portion of the Speech which declared that Ireland partook of the general prosperity of the country.   What was the fact at present as regarded emigration ?   They had one hundred and twenty thousand people crossing the ocean last year, despite the bad trade that interrupted commerce by the war which raged on the continent to which they turned their steps.   Must there not be something wrong to account for this, and was it not the duty of the government to endeavor to remove it ?   If the government took the question up as they ought, he believed they could stop the tide of emigration, which was sweeping away not only the bone and sinew of the country, but a good deal of the strength of the empire.   If leases were given to the tenant farmers, or if the law stepped in and gave a liberal measure of compensation for improvements, it would stop the tide of emigration, and the people of Ireland would be happy and contented, instead of what he knew them to be, and was sorry to be obliged to say they were, deeply discontented ; and he was ready to say, with the honorable member for Cork (Mr. V. Scully), deeply disaffected.   He solemnly and sincerely declared that there was in Ireland discontent and disaffection, which nothing under heaven but just laws could change.   The Lord Lieutenant, a few days ago, expressed his deep regret that the people were leaving the country in such numbers, and carried with them a feeling of hostility to the British government.   Let them look at the case straight in the face, and not shrink from a consideration of the question.   The feeling carried to America by Irishmen would have an influence upon the policy of American statesmen.   The Irish emigrants, and their children born in the United States, outnumbered the population of Ireland.   They were active and energetic, and many of them commanded the press and the platform.   They were animated by hatred of England ; and he asked them into what calamities might they not precipitate the two countries.   He hoped that the government, instead of troubling themselves about complications in distant parts of Europe, would endeavor to heal the sore that existed in the heart of the empire.   Royal visits would not meet the wants of Ireland.   They would only be as courtplaster over a deep seated ulcer.   The Irish people would be glad to see her Majesty, or any member of her family ; but the starving people who saw the utter hopelessness of any effort for which there was no reward, did not want the sunshine of royalty, or the glitter of pageantry ; what they wanted was just laws, that would liberate their arms, and give them a field for their exertions."

ships, which were never seen again. The British government thus got rid, for a time, of those who survived or escaped starvation, English law coming to the assistance of famine, and famine to the assistance of English law.

At the end of these five famine years, it was found that there were two millions of Irishmen less—a million and a half having died of hunger and plague, and half a million having emigrated. No other instance is known in history parallel to this, except in the East Indies, where, as a rule, millions starve in the midst of abundance.

If Ireland were independent, she would be armed, and not garrisoned by foreign troops. She would not be exposed to be placed, as has so often been the case, under martial law, all of whose rigors are inflamed by upwards of thirty different Coercion Acts, passed during the present century. Once independent, Ireland would almost entirely cease to emigrate. As it is, the thing promises to be so thoroughly overdone, and real estate will become of so little value in Ireland, that cupidity can grasp no more.

XXXVI.

YES, exile is the last vicissitude of martyred Ireland. *Jean de Paris* finely says : " Placed high in rank among the most enlightened nations of Europe, she left, in early times, a luminous track in the history of Christian civilization. Suddenly violence, aided by treason, made her the slave of the stranger. Since then, her virtues became the cause of her misfortunes. Faithful to the creed of her fathers, she is persecuted by an apostate people. Faithful to the loyalist cause, her people were massacred, her plains devastated by the regicide troops of Cromwell, and, still later, her generous blood was shed for the ungrateful Catholic Stuarts. It is no longer possible for a nation to enjoy at the same time, the benefits of oppression, and the advantages of a reputation for liberality. The complaints of her people are heard to-day from one end of the earth to the other. Neither the loftiest mountains, nor the murmurs of two oceans, can prevent the cry of anguish arising from trampled nationalities, in reaching ears that sympathize with her sufferings." Lord Macaulay said that Ireland and Poland were universally considered as two sisters in misfortune. Great Britain may in vain throw between Ireland and us her majestic shadow, and trouble the air with her powerful voice; but the moans of Ireland are heard in every farmhouse, in every home in North America. When England took the liberty of inspecting the dungeons of the late infamous tyrant of Naples, he told her to turn back and see the soil of Ireland, strewed with the bleaching bones of thousands of human creatures who had died of hunger, the victims of artificial famine. When England asks for privileges for Christians in a Mahometan country, for Protestant missionaries and preachers in Rome, the Pope or the Grand Turk can say: ' Go back to Ireland and behold that monstrous intolerance— an Anglican clergy richly supported by money extorted from poor Catholic Ireland." When Englishmen blame Austria for not restoring liberal institutions to Hungary, Cæsar can say: " Give back to Ireland her independence, and her parliament;" and yet we learn that the Grand Turk has struck a blow against the supremacy of the hierarchy of his empire; and the Emperor of Austria has restored to Hungary her parliament.

No; Ireland does not willingly surrender her harvests to England. England robs them. Having no industry, Ireland must pay her rent to England in produce. Her political, industrial and social life centre in England. Nine-tenths of the landlords of Ireland reside on English soil. In England, the produce of Irish harvests is spent—luxury for England, poverty for Ireland. England is the only market Ireland has. England gives nothing, and takes all; Ireland gives all, and receives nothing. Of course, British cupidity must leave something, in order that starvation may not become universal and complete; and the man who cultivates for the foreigner, the land of his ancestors, has a sort of acknowledged right to—

potatoes. To show how universally true all this is, the demonstration is at hand. A horrible famine spreads its black shadow of death over a whole country, through the first failure of the potato crop. No other nation ever existed where a famine was caused by the failure of so inconsiderable an article of human diet.

I thought I would print here a living picture of these five terrible famine years ; but I have not the heart to do it. We all know that people died literally by thousands at the roadsides, and in their cabins. Whole families perished. Multitudes remained without burial. The parishes had no funds to pay for coffins. The poor-houses became hospitals, where the dying man lay struggling in the agonies of death by the side of a cold corpse. In the county of Mayo, the most fortunate victims fed on their asses and horses.

And yet this was not a famine which means, in the proper sense of that term, a calamity sent by the Almighty upon the fruits of the earth. It was all legal assassination—foulest of all murder—cruelest of exile by enforced emigration. Would not a coroner's jury of Americans, sitting at an inquest over such dead, be compelled by their oaths as honest men, to render a verdict of wilful murder against the Queen of England ?

All remember the horror which struck through the Christian and heathen world after news of the first six months of the famine had been winged to other nations. The peoples of Europe sent alms—the Turks opened their hearts and hands ; while ship after ship, freighted generously from the American shores, in sailing into Irish harbors, passed fleets of English vessels carrying away from a dying people the fruits of their own labor. God in heaven ! Ireland, with all the sweat of her manly brow; Ireland, crushed so long, and so deeply, by such heartless foreign masters ; Ireland, who had given her riches, her labor, her life—such an Ireland as this to be compelled, in the last agonies of hunger, to accept charity from democrats on the one side, and the worshippers of a false prophet on the other !

But all this may be disposed of by statesmanship with a single wave of the hand—" there are reasons of state for all this—public economy—to sustain the revenues and rank of the empire—to maintain the pomp and splendor of the nation," which, *par excellence*, claims to be file-leader of civilization ! God send the world as little more such civilization as He possibly can ! If such be Christian civilization, better, in Heaven's name, to have none.

But no man who professes to be a Christian, not to say a meek and lowly follower of the Man of Nazareth—no man who recognizes the revealed Religion of Jesus Christ as the standard of morality and virtue among men and nations, will pretend to say, that the teachers of the gospel, the "successors of the Apostles," have any right to eat the bread of famine and tears, much less to roll voluptuously along their golden track of this world's splendor, at such terrible cost to so many millions of quivering human hearts.

XXXVII.

THIS brings us to the Established Church of England in Ireland, for which we have space only for a few glances. The outrage of forcing an ALIEN CHURCH *on an unwilling people !** This has always been denounced by enlightened men, and particularly by British statesmen, as one of the grossest acts of oppression of which government can be guilty. In an Article on the Irish Church Establishment, published a year ago—January, 1865—we find an array of facts, the authenticity of which will not be disputed. Sir Robert Peel said, that Catholic Emancipation was granted, "neither as an act of jus-

---

* " All persecution directed against the persons or property of men, is on our principle obviously indefensible. For the protection of the persons and property of men being the primary end of government, and religious instruction only a secondary end, to secure the people from heresy, by making their lives, their limbs, or their estates insecure, would be to sacrifice the primary end. . . All civil disabilities on account of religious opinions, are indefensible. For all such disabilities make government less efficient for its main end."—*Macaulay's Review of Gladstone.*

tice, nor as an act of favor ; but because it could not any longer, on account of the numbers and power of the Catholics in this kingdom, be safely refused !" Sir Robert said, " It was imperatively necessary to avert from the Church, and from the interests of institutions connected with the Church, an imminent and increasing danger."—Instead therefore of being a free concession, it was the unwilling sacrifice of a part of what had been unjustly withheld, in order, if possible, to make safe the unjust withholding of the remainder. When Catholics were told, in the time of Charles James Fox, to be content with the sop thrown to them, his reply was : " I am told that the Catholics have got so much that they ought not to ask for more. My principle is directly the reverse of this. Until men obtain *all* they have a right to ask for, they have comparatively obtained nothing." " The question, in fact, simply is, whether Irishmen are to be admitted to an equality with Englishmen and Scotchmen. If so, the Irish Established Church cannot remain as it is."—Much of Ireland's trouble has arisen from " the insane attempt to establish and maintain a Protestant church in the midst of a Catholic people."—It is " an abiding social grievance." " Nobody pretends that this Protestantizes Irish Catholics." " The sword and the Protestant Church entered Ireland together. . . . Ireland was persecuted, impoverished and embittered for the sake of the Established Church."

An *alien Church* has been forced on Ireland. " If the fact be at this moment, that the Irish element in America tends in any degree to intensify the animosity of Americans against England, any unpleasant results accruing from this antipathy may well be regarded as in some measure retributive for the wrongs heretofore inflicted by England on her Irish subjects." " Let England deal with Ireland as an integral part of the United Kingdom, as it does with Australia, with Canada, with the Mauritius, even with Malta, or with India. Why should Ireland be treated worse than the inhabitants of any of these colonies or possessions—worse even than Mahometans or Pagans ?"

Mr. Burke exclaimed (of the Irish Establishment), "Don't talk to me of its being a Church! It is a wholesale robbery."

XXXVIII.

LORD BROUGHAM, in 1838, called it "an anomaly of so gross a kind, that it outrages every principle of common sense. Such an establishment kept up for such a purpose, kept up by such means, and upheld by such a system, is a thing wholly peculiar to Ireland, and could be tolerated nowhere else. That such a system should go on in the 19th century—that such a thing should go on while all the arts are in a forward and onward course—while all the sciences are progressing—while all morals and religion too—for there was more religion and morality than is now pretended in all parts of the country—that this gross abuse—the most outrageous of all, should be allowed to continue, is really astonishing. It cannot be upheld unless the tide of knowledge should turn back."

Disraeli said most eloquently, in 1844 : "That dense population in extreme distress, inhabited an island, where there was *an Established Church which was not their Church*, and a territorial aristocracy, the richest of whom lived in distant capitals. Thus, they had a starving population and *an alien Church*, and in addition, the weakest executive in the world. That was the Irish Question. Well, what would honorable gentlemen say, if they were reading of a country in that position ? They would say at once—the remedy is revolution. But the Irish could not have a revolution ; and, why ? Because Ireland was connected with another, and more powerful country. Then what was the consequence? *The connection with England thus became the cause of the present state of Ireland.* If the connection with England prevented a revolution, and a revolution were the only remedy, *England, logically, was in the odious position of being the cause of all the misery of Ireland.* What then was the duty of an English minister ?

*To effect by his policy, all those changes which a revolution
would do by force.* That was the Irish Question, in its integrity. The moment they had a strong executive, a just administration, and *ecclesiastical equality*, they would have order in
Ireland, and the improvement of the physical condition of the
people would follow." Disraeli thus sums up my argument—
and I could cite no higher authority on such a subject.

The present Sir Robert Peel, in a letter to the *Times*,
April 15, 1862, says that his father distinctly stated, " that in
passing Catholic Emancipation, he acted on a deep conviction that the measure was not only conducive to the general
welfare, but imperatively necessary *to avert from the Church*,
and from the interests of institutions connected with the Church,
an imminent and increasing danger, so that in truth, emancipation was granted *in order to save the Irish Church.*"

In 1782 and 1793, England did relax somewhat of its despotic rule over Ireland. The attitude of the Irish volunteers
frightened England into the first alleviations of the penal laws ;
and in 1793, the elective franchise was granted to Irish Catholics
—but under circumstances disgraceful to England, and insulting to Ireland—this will appear by consulting " Newenham's
View"—a Protestant, and therefore, not a partial authority
in this case. " There is not a fault or deficiency in either the
people or the country which may not, in a great measure, be
traced to the misgovernment of England." The late noble Dr.
Doyle said to his countrymen : " These are your vices—the
faults of long and grinding oppression, which render many so
base and vile, that the rights of man are denied to you, and less
regard paid to your wants and wishes, than to the wants and
wishes of any other people on the earth." Says Review : " If
Irishmen are accused of idleness, what in the ordinary course
of nature can be expected when industry and improvement
have been systematically discouraged? Often have we, as an
English traveler, asked the Irish peasant, why he neglects such
and such an improvement, on his land ? The answer uniformly
has been, " If I did it, my rent would be raised."

XXXIX.

LET the *Reviewer* find the convincing commentary on his words, in the herculean achievements of Irish *labor* under the genial influences of free Institutions in the United States. No man ever saw an Irish workman in America, who was not ready for a job. To show that the policy of England has always been to discourage enterprise in Ireland, I could quote a score or more of discriminating writers. Davenant, long ago illustrated the truth on this point. He argued, that England ought to give " to the planters of Ireland, all encouragement *that can possibly consist with the wellfare of England*, for it is an outwork of the seat of empire, here."

Sir William Temple, certainly a very able political writer, says : " Had it not been for circumstances, prejudicial to the increase of trade and riches, in a country which seems natural, or at least, to have *ever been incident to the Government of Ireland*, the native fertility of the Irish soil and seas in so many rich commodities, improved by a multitude of people, and industry, with the advantage of so many excellent havens, and a situation so commanding for foreign trade, must needs have rendered this kingdom (Ireland) one of the richest in Europe, and made a mighty increase, both of strength and revenue, to the crown of England."

XL.

IS it not strange then, that there should be less crime in Ireland, *pro rata*, than in England, while the crimes of dishonesty and fraud, I find in the Criminal Returns for 1854, to stand thus ? Convictions for 1854—

	In England and Wales.	In Ireland.
Larceny from the person,	1,570	389
Simple larceny,	12,562	3,329
Frauds and attempt to defraud,	676	62
Forgery,	149	4
Uttering, and having in possession, false coin,	674	4
Larceny by servants,	2,143	44

In March 30, 1835, Earl Grey said "that the Established Church had not only failed to propagate the Protestant religion amongst the Catholics of Ireland, but that it had been most injurious to the true interests of religion, amongst the Protestants themselves." Macaulay said of Pitt, that "he was the first English minister who entertained a really sanguine intention of benefiting Ireland, upon a footing of equal laws, equal rights, and equal liberties." But he failed. In his speech in 1785, on introducing the first commercial relaxations, he said that, "the species of policy which had been exercised by the government of England, in regard to Ireland, had for its object, to debar the latter from the enjoyment of its own resources, and to make her completely subservient to the opulence and interests of England ; that she had not been suffered to share in the bounties of nature, or the industry of her citizens, and that she was shut out from every species of commerce, and restrained from sending the produce of her own soil to foreign markets."

"Where," said Sir Charles Wood, "could they find any country, under any system of Church establishment, be they Catholic or Protestant, where a rich Church, with a small congregation, was maintained at the expense of an overwhelming majority, belonging to a different persuasion ? . . . Why should they not at once strike at the root of the evil, and determine upon a different appropriation of the revenues of the Irish Church ? "

"The principle laid down by Lord John Russel was, that Church property was appreciable to all such purposes of general utility, as Parliament in its wisdom might determine." And yet it has not been done.

XLI.

I CANNOT better, perhaps, bring this long Book to a close, than by paying my tribute to the greatest Irishman of his age—a man whom I knew and loved so well. I extract from

my Private Diary an account of his death and funeral obsequies, at the old city of Genoa, where I had the honor at the
time to represent the United States in an official capacity :

On the evening of the 6th, on his way to Rome to spend the winter,
Daniel O'Connell landed at Genoa, to pass but a single day. At any period,
he would have been received in Italy with every demonstration of respect,
for he was there regarded as the protector and advocate of eight millions
of oppressed Catholics, in a distant and beautiful island, which has been
sanctified by the faith, and made dear by the sufferings, the poetry, and
the wit of its people. But at that time, many unusual circumstances
conspired to give to his journey through Italy all the splendors of a
great triumphal progress. During the previous six months, the journals
of Italy had been filled with the sufferings of Ireland; and when the
name of that devoted country was heard by an Italian, he lifted his eyes
to Heaven, and thanked his patron saint that he was not born under
British sway. To be a British subject was once, in their estimation, to
be born to rule, to conquer, and to be free; now, to be a Briton, is to die
by the lingering tortures of famine. Sad indeed must be the state of
Ireland, when an Italian thanks God, or even a saint, that he is not born
there. Besides, O'Connell was dying on the eve of a great day for Italy
and for the Irish people. While his soul was passing to the future state,
the bells of all the churches of Italy were sounding their holy chimes, to
call the pious and the humane to their altars, at the command of Pius
IX., to offer their prayers and their alms for the relief of that distant, suffering people. In Genoa, it was known that the great Catholic Liberator
was dying; and when the population streamed up in dense masses to
the churches, in obedience to the command of the Pontiff of Rome, they
seemed like solemn processions for the souls of the departed.

XLII.

O'CONNELL'S health had felt the first shock a year before. (I received
all my information from his youngest son, who was with his father
on his journey, and closed his eyes when he was dead.) In the early part
of winter he began to fail so rapidly, that his friends were alarmed, and
they prevailed on him to visit Italy; believing that, in a serener climate,
he would again recover, in some measure, his former vigor. Attended by
his youngest son, his family physician, his Irish confessor, and his most
confidential servants, he set out for Italy. But the journey was deferred
too long. He was taken down in Lyons, and it was feared he would not
be able again to leave his bed. But through the aid of a skillful French

surgeon, he recovered partially, after a long illness. It was now thought best for him to return to Ireland; but he had set his face toward the south, and he said he wished to see Rome; and if he must die away from home, to die in the capital of Christendom, where Pius IX. had renewed the mild pure sway of the early successors of the Apostles. He went to Marseilles, and embarked on a steamer for Genoa. His son thought him again too feeble to risk the fatigues of the voyage; but O'Connell hoped at least to be able to see the dome of St. Peter, and he would go on. There is something touching and almost sublime in this same desire, which so many great men have expressed when they felt themselves dying. In those last days of life, when everything else external grows dim, how often has the wish arisen to die in sight of that gorgeous temple, which fancy brought so near to the soul! With O'Connell, who felt that life was coming to a hurried close, it was a natural feeling. He knew that he could not live to reach Ireland again; and when the scenes of this life began to fade from his vision, his heart turned toward the Eternal City which, to a true Catholic like O'Connell, is, after the Hill of Calvary, the most holy spot on earth.

XLIII.

HE was rapidly failing when the steamer arrived at Genoa. It was necessary for him to get repose, and he was taken to the Hotel Feder, which stands near the water. It was known that he was coming, and an immense crowd gathered to welcome him with acclamations. But when they caught a sight of his pale cheek, as he was borne along in the arms of his attendants, the crowd received him in respectful silence, and every head was uncovered. He passed a comfortable night at the hotel: the vessel waited to take him on to Rome, and it was his intention to go. I had had the fortune to know O'Connell many years before; I had been honored by his confidence and kindness, and I ventured to call at his hotel, but with little expectation of seeing him. I sent up my card and inquired after his health. He sent back a message that he would be glad to see me in a few moments. He entered the room into which I had been shown, dressed for going on board the steamer. He was leaning infirmly on the top of a large cane: his step was feeble, and his form was wasted away. Familiar as his countenance had once been to me, I could recognize little but the eye of the man I had known before. But he still stood erect. He extended to me his emaciated hand for a moment, and said a few kind words. I left the room with a sad feeling, which I can hardly describe. I saw the lines of death clearly written on his face. It was evident that his *body* was dead; but his indomitable spirit still held a feeble sway over the lifeless form it had ruled so long. As I joined the friend I had left in the hall below, I told him, "O'Connell never will see Rome." In an hour or two he began to fail rapidly; but everything was prepared for going on: the steamer was waiting: it was still hoped he would revive. But he had rallied for the last time. For more than seventy years his heroic spirit had never yielded; but the time had at last come for body and spirit to give way. He laid himself down on his bed, saying:

"Well, it is God's will I shall never see Rome! I thought I should live to get there. I am disappointed; but I feel ready to die. It is all right."

XLIV.

AT ten o'clock that night, the steamer, which had hoped for the honor of carrying the great Irishman to Rome, was told he could not go, and she went on her way. In a day or two it became certain that his life was drawing rapidly to an end. He seemed (I was freely admitted to his bedside) to suffer from no particular disease: it was a gradual sinking—a slow giving way of strength. Consequently he suffered very little pain; while his consciousness, and even the brilliancy of his intellect, continued undimmed to the very last moment. He conversed with perfect calmness about all the members of his absent family; his children, his grand-children, and his friends; about suffering Ireland, and the life to come. He not only expressed his fullest conviction of the truth of the Christian religion, but conversed with luminous and cheerful serenity of the principles of Christianity; and often repeated, in a variety of forms, his unshaken confidence of salvation through the merits of Christ. He was deeply affected in thinking and speaking of the call of the Pontiff, on all the Catholics of the Christian world, to present their prayers and offerings for Ireland during this period of her calamity; and the fact that this noble call had gone forth from Pius IX., was one of the reasons why he had felt so earnest a desire to reach Rome.

He was constantly attended by his two physicians, the vicar of the church of the parish, and his own bishop. No office that medical skill could suggest, nor consolation that religion could lend, was wanting to the dying man. He lingered till the night of the fifteenth, when he seemed to be rapidly sinking. The last offices of the Church were then administered. While the prayers were being read, he clearly uttered the responses; and as those solemn rites ended, he closed his eyes serenely with a half smile. Those of us who stood by his bed, and gazed on his countenance, did not know he was dead till the surgeon announced it.

And just at that moment, from more than a hundred thousand domes and spires, were pealing solemn chimes in answer to the summons of Pius IX., and from unnumbered altars was going up to Heaven a vast cloud of incense for the afflicted and stricken country of that heroic spirit which was passing away.

XLV.

HIS body was at once embalmed, and laid in the magnificent church *Delle Vigne*, where preparations were made for celebrating his obsequies. The invitations issued were limited to foreign consuls, for whom seats were prepared in an area around the coffin. The British Consul had refused to offer his services on this occasion, or even his attentions to O'Connell, while he was dying in a strange land; although such proffers came in from several royal princes and men of the greatest distinction then in Genoa. It was consequently my good fortune to occupy the post he was expected to do, and I was proud of the honor of showing, as far as this act could do, the respect of my nation for the illustrious man. All Europe, however, (except England) and indeed I may say, *the world*, was represented at the funeral, for I believe every other foreign consul was there. The coffin was raised on a platform fifteen feet high, thirty feet in front of the main altar. It was covered with a vast pall of black velvet, to which was attached a large cross of crimson, embroidered in gold. Around this pile were gleaming forty massive wax tapers. Forty other tapers were burning on the main altar, and the twelve altars of the twelve chapels of the church, were also illuminated. The church was dressed in mourning, and the seats of the altar around the coffin were spread with velvet and damask, embroidered in fine gold. The vast edifice was crowded by a silent and solemn multitude. The bell struck the meridian, (the 20th of May) and the obsequies began with the introduction, on the organ, of that sublime service with which the imposing ceremonies of the Catholic Church dismiss the souls of believers to the eternal world. The altar was surrounded with a numerous company of priests and prelates, adorned in their richest robes. Forty singers, attached to the church, were also ranged round the altar, and behind it stood some of the best vocal and instrumental *artistes* in Italy. The soft deep notes of the organ, touched by the hands of a master, rolled down the pillared aisles, and broke in solemn reverberations among the lofty frescoed arches. As the different parts came in, the bass, the tenor and the soprano, the effect was electrical; but when at last the chorus commenced, with every voice in that great company of singers, and the heavy bass of the organ blended the sounds together, even the congregation, accustomed as they were to such scenes, swelled the familiar strains; and it hardly required the aid of fancy to imagine that the death-anthem must have awoke the soul of the mighty sleeper.

XLVI.

THE service lasted about an hour. No eulogium was pronounced on the Great Liberator, and none was needed. For half a century he had himself been uttering words of fire. He had mingled in the strife of all the elements of a nation's life and progress; he had been the soul of all her struggles for freedom; above all, of her struggles for the holy rights of conscience. And now, when the champion of "freedom to worship God" had finished his labors, he was borne to one of the most gorgeous temples of the Church he had battled for, in the land where her proudest trophies are gathered, to receive all the magnificence of her divine honors. He had during a long life warred for that Church, in a distant island; for a suffering and a poor people, against haughty and oppressive foes and prelates, who scorned his faith and derided his religion; undismayed by numbers, untimidated by power, with a heart beating for liberty and his country, and his eye turned toward the dim, distant dome of St. Peter. Does it seem strange, then, while the sleeper lay there in the midst of this scene of triumph, and the glorious strains of his death-anthem, sung by the prelates of that mighty Rome who watched his heroic struggles from her golden See, were rolling through the arches above him, that this triumphant pæan should have stirred the dust of the sleeper? Could O'Connell himself have cast his eye down into futurity, from the beginning of the vista of life, would even *his* ambition have demanded a prouder triumph.

Such were the honors offered to the dust of O'Connell; such the tribute which a distant but generous nation rendered to greatness and to truth. The vast crowd which had choked the piazza before the church, and every avenue leading to it, slowly dispersed. For a long time they stood gazing silently and solemnly upon the gorgeous pile which sustained his coffin. As the shadows of evening gathered around the city, and wrapped the temple in darkness and silence, save that far up the aisle the great lamp, that is forever kept burning before the image of the Virgin, sent its tiny star-light through the gloom, a company of priests bore the coffin into a private chapel; and there the great Agitator rested after his labors. On the return of his son from Rome, whither he had gone to deposit his father's heart in the tomb of St. Peter, he proceeded by sea to England with the ashes, and committed them to the keeping of his expecting, weeping and grateful countrymen.

BOOK IV.

SOCIETY IN ENGLAND.

We think it would be a vast advantage to the public in general, if ingenious opticians would turn their attention to a remedy for that long sighted benevolence which sweeps the distant horizon for objects of compassion, but is blind as a bat to the wretchedness and destitution abounding at their own doors.—*Blackwood.*

I cannot however believe that the Creator made man to leave him in an endless struggle with the intellectual miseries that surround us: God destines a calmer and more certain future to the communities of Europe. It appears to me beyond a doubt, that sooner or later we shall (in Europe) arrive like the Americans at an almost complete equality of conditions. —*De Tocqueville.*

We appeal to all competent observers, whether all the moral elements of an American state of society are not most rapidly growing up among us.—*Edinb. Review.*

The result of the long struggle between the Patricians and Plebians of Rome was their perfect equality; and incontestibly this is the tendency of modern Europe.—*Raumer.*

SOCIETY IN ENGLAND.

I.

THE World's Convention, in London, in 1840, was one of the most important assemblages of our times, and was destined to have greater influence on the fortunes of the United States, than the proceedings of any other body of men in Great Britain, since the passage of the Stamp Act by the British Parliament. The English abolitionists had invited all nations to send delegates to London, to discuss the question of slavery, wherever it existed, and devise ways and means for its abolition, all over the earth. Nearly all of the illustrious men of Great Britain, and many of the most eloquent and learned men of other countries, were present.

The venerable Thomas Clarkson, in his eighty-first year, had come from his home in Ipswich, to preside over the Convention. Freemason's Hall, on that day, held a most dignified and imposing assembly.

The name of Clarkson called forth loud applause. We were requested, in consideration of his age and infirmities, to refrain from any manifestation of our feelings when he should enter the Hall. The whole assembly was silent, and every eye was turned towards the door. The scene which followed, surpassed anything I ever witnessed.

This venerable patriarch of liberty had left his quiet home in his old age, to meet the representatives of the different nations of the earth; to devise means for the " Emancipation of man, everywhere, from the thraldom of man," and then go back to his peaceful retreat, and await his summons to heaven. As he entered the Hall, the Convention rose and received him in silence. He seemed bowed down with age, and his hair was perfectly white. He was deeply affected by his reception ; and when he was proposed as chairman, there was a general murmur of approbation which could not be suppressed. He took his seat and held his handkerchief to his face.

We felt a veneration for the aged Chieftain, which words could not express. We saw before us the man whose name had been associated, for more than half a century, with almost every great enterprise for the advancement of human liberty ; the originator, and now the only surviving member of the first Committee ever instituted for the abolition of the slave trade. Hoare, Smith, Dilwyn, Harrison, Phillips, and Wilberforce, were all dead. This was probably the last great assembly in whose deliberations he would mingle ; and feeling that his time on earth was short, and under the impulse of freedom's fires, which burned on the altar of his heart as brightly as ever, he had brought his little grandson, Thomas Clarkson, into the Convention—the only representative of his family and name, left on earth,—to lay the beautiful boy in consecration upon freedom's altar, on this, his ninth birth-day. It was a beautiful offering to the genius of Liberty : a nobler dedication than when his father brought the young Hannibal to the altar, and made him swear eternal hostility to the enemies of Carthage.

The gentleman who introduced the boy to the assembly, laid his hand upon his head, and prayed that the blessing of heaven might rest upon him, and that, with the descending mantle of his venerated ancestor, he might catch a double portion of his spirit. " I am sure," said he, " that this prayer will find a response in every bosom in this assembly (cries of amen), as well as the earnest hope, that when some of us shall be removed to that bourne where the wicked cease from troubling, and where all distinctions of clime and color will be swept forever away, he may live to see the day when the divine blessing shall so eminently have crowned this great cause of justice and mercy, we have this day assembled to promote, that the sun shall cease to rise upon a tyrant, or set upon a slave."

Clarkson then rose, and delivered a most affecting and eloquent address. Some parts of it were sublime. In alluding to himself, he said, " I can say with truth I think, that although my body is fast going to decay, my heart beats as warmly in this sacred cause now, in the eighty-first year of my age, as it did at the age of twenty-four, when I first took it up. And I can say further, with truth, that if I had another life given me to live, I would ask no better fortune, than to devote it all with firmer resolution and warmer zeal, to the same glorious work of redeeming humanity from oppression."

He closed with a benediction upon the assembly, and upon all the friends of human liberty, throughout the world. When he sat down, I believe there was not a heart in the Convention that was not deeply moved, nor an eye that was not filled with tears.

II.

DANIEL O'CONNELL was called for. He rose and said: " This was a Convention, the most important that ever assembled. To it, came men from hundreds and thousands of miles distant; not with a selfish motive, not even alone for the pride and pleasure of participating in the great and ennobling work, but from sincere philanthropy to the human race—and it included delegates from all parts of the world, even from America; certainly from all parts of the British Empire, and none ought to be exempt from coöperation. In the chair he was happy to see the patriarch of liberty. He was glad that the venerable gentleman had lived to see the brightening of a day, the dawn of which the fervor of his youth could scarcely have hoped to see. His was the purest of all fame—that of doing good. They were not met here only to talk, or display talent; that would be insufficient; they must direct their minds to some practical movement: Forward must be the word. They must speedily adopt practical means for establishing correspondence, and cooperating societies all over the world. It was a gratifying thing to hear that Massachussetts had declared the first clause of American independence to be utterly inconsistent with slavery, and on that ground alone it should be abolished. At present, it was only in the East Indies that slavery, under British rule, existed. *There, not only the laborers were slaves, but the great mass of the population were serfs, completely under the sway of the East India Company, to be ground down by the 'land-rents' exactions, at its will.* There should be a glorious combination of anti-slavery societies all over the world, and no motives should be allowed to mar the disinterested sincerity of their efforts. He was rejoiced to see their chairman among them. He was happy to find himself in a Convention, to the members of which no selfish motives could by any possibility be attributed. Let them persevere in their efforts, and they would raise the entire of the human race from a state of slavery and degradation, to that liberty which was the best preparative for receiving the truths of Christianity, and the blessings of civilization."

At the close of O'Connell's speech the chairman was obliged to retire. The whole Convention rose, and as he left the Hall, leaning upon the arm of the Irish Orator, the feelings of the assembly were expressed by the most enthusiastic applause.*

* I was introduced to the celebrated Mrs. Amelia Opie, who was enjoying a green old age. She lived in Norwich, about 120 miles east of London, but, like everybody else, was spending "the season" in town. She had, long before, adopted the simple faith, and plain, rich costume of the Society of Friends, and suppressed several of her fictitious works, from conscientious scruples in regard to their influence. But she showed unbounded cheerfulness, and was certainly a delightful woman. I did not know her age, but she must have been over seventy, I think, although her cheek still wore the rich bloom of earlier years.

"It is very painful," she said, "to think that your great and free Republic should be desecrated by slavery. It is very lamentable. It is like some odious blemish on a beautiful painting; the eye *would* contemplate the beauties of the picture, but it cannot: the blemish fills the vision. Oh! I hope I shall live to see the day when there will not be a slave in all your beautiful land. It has been the home of freedom; there is no such land on earth; and this makes it so indescriably painful to think that it is a land of slaves."

"You have never visited our country, I think, madam?"

"No, I have not; but there is no part of the world I so much desire to see.

III.

THIS World's Convention *had a deeper meaning than any of the men or women present dreamed of then*, unless it may have been the instigators and abettors of a deep and well-laid scheme on the part of politicians, to create trouble for the United States.

Let us glance for a while at the course England took towards us twenty years later, after her statesmen and nobles had raised the " negro indignation" against the United States.

We Americans cheated ourselves most egregiously when we thought England—once the head of the slave-trade, and only a few years ago the front of the abolitionism of the world—would turn her slavery-hating back on the only organized band of slavery propagandism on the earth!

Poor fools we! Just as though the *British aristocracy*—(the true name for the *British Government*)—meant anything but interference and trouble for us, when her Grace the Duchess of Sutherland chaperoned the gifted Harriet Beecher Stowe through the court of her Majesty, simply because Mrs.

It is a great pleasure to meet so many Americans here on this grand occasion. I never looked forward to a public meeting with so much hope. I well remember, many years ago, when the first efforts were made by the friends of liberty for the suppression of the slave-trade. It was a dark day then for the world; and, although philanthropists are quite apt to be too sanguine, yet who in this assembly ever expected to see such a day as this? It is a very sublime spectacle to see this representation of the philanthropy and piety of the world. What can be more grand than to contemplate the object which has called this Convention together? And that idea of O'Connell's was so fine—that we would elevate the whole human race to the possession of liberty—it is an affecting thought.

" But you will come and see me, I trust; I want to converse with you about America, your authors, your scenery, your great men. I shall be most happy to see you at any time you can make it convenient to call. Do not think that age has quite frozen up my heart. Indeed, if it had, I think this Convention would make it green as spring-time again."

I did see her again—often; and her grand and symmetrical character became to me more and more sublime and beautiful.

Stowe, by writing a great dramatic novel against slavery, could be made a cat's-paw for pulling the chestnuts of the British aristocracy out of the fire !

Yes, abolitionism suited the purposes of the British aristocracy just *then ;* and lords and ladies swarmed at negro-emancipation gatherings at Exeter Hall. On all such occasions three standing jokes were played off, to the infinite amusement of dukes and duchesses,—duchesses. more particularly.

First. There *must* be a live American negro,—the blacker the better, sometimes ; but they generally got one as *little* black as possible, and an octoroon threw them into the highest state of subdued frenzy admissible in the upper classes. The aforesaid negro must have escaped from the indescribable horrors and barbarities of slavery in the Southern States,—gashed, manacled—(if he showed the manacles, so much the better)—a sample of American barbarism, and a burning shame on the otherwise fair cheek of the goddess of American Liberty.

" Oh, yes," said my Lord Brougham ; " nothing stands in your way now but negro slavery. Abolish that, and every heart in England is with you."

Second. At these Exeter Hall meetings they *must* have a live American abolitionist,—once a slaveholder who had emancipated his slaves. Here they found their man in the noble Judge Birney, as in the *first* they found a splendid specimen of a runaway octoroon in Frederick Douglass, Esq.,— the black Douglass,—and who, by-the-by made a better speech by far than any aristocrat in England.

Third, and last of all, some ecclesiastical gentleman bestowed upon the proceedings " the benediction."

This would have been well enough,—certainly so far as the benediction was concerned,— had not future events proved beyond a doubt, that, at the very moment these curious things were occurring, the whole *prestige* of the British empire was invoked to sanctify and adorn a secret spirit of hostility to the Government of the United States, and that the solemnities of our holy religion were also invoked in the same cause.

But to my unpractised eye it looked at the time very much as later events have shown it,—a thorough hatred of America by the ruling classes of England.

IV.

AT one time Lord Brougham presided ; again, O'Connell ; and again, the venerable Thomas Clarkson : they even got his Royal Highness Prince Albert to do it once, on a somewhat narrower scale,—where even tender young duchesses could attend with impunity (the American negro always being present), and being fortified with a supply of highly-perfumed kerchiefs, the young duchesses managed generally to live it through, and revive after reaching the open air !

These farces were played off all through the British Islands; and the poor British people—who, from long habit, I suppose, go where " their betters" go, when allowed to—joined in the movement, and "*American* anti-slavery societies" were everywhere established. Even chambermaids and factory girls contributed to raise a fund to send " English missionaries" over here " to enlighten the *North* about the duty of the *South* to abolish slavery."

Some of these scenes were sufficiently vulgar ; but they were occasionally got up in fine taste. One occasion I recal with the highest pleasure, which, although ostensibly an anti-slavery dinner, was limited chiefly in its company to the literary men of London.*

* Among the good things of that evening was a short poem, written for the occasion, by William Beattie, M. D., the gifted and well-known author of *Scotland Illustrated*, etc. I do not know if it has been published. I remember a few of the stanzas. It is an address from " England's Poets to the Poets of America."

Your Garrison has fann'd the flame,
  Child, Chapman, Pierpont, caught the fire;
And, roused at Freedom's hallowed name,
  Hark ! Bryant, Whittier, strike the lyre;

While here, hearts myriad trumpet-toned
  Montgomery, Cowper, Campbell, Moore,
To Freedom's glorious cause respond.
  In sounds which thrill through every core.

v.

IT was a noble enthusiasm among the people; but it was (anybody could see through it, for it was the veriest gauze) all an aristocratic sham. It did not mean anything for human freedom. It meant hostility to the United States. *It was got up by British politicians.* Sir Robert Peel and the Duke of Wellington had no part or parcel in it, unless it were through sheer courtesy to the men of their class.

This English crusade against the United States, was got up by the British aristocracy in sheer animosity against our Government,—not so much, perhaps, against our people, chiefly because they cared nothing about them. It was our *system of government they hated,* because it was a standing, growing, and luminous reproof of the blighting and degrading system of England, which starves the masses of her people in order that the privileged few may die of surfeit.

Blackwood's Magazine, an authority not likely to be charged with hostility towards the British oligarchy, nor with favoritism towards our Republic, said, in speaking on this same subject in the same year (1840)—

" It were well if some ingenious optician could invent an

Their voice has conjured up a power,
　No fears can daunt, no foes arrest,
Which gathers strength with every hour
　And strikes a chord in every breast,—

A power that soon o'er every land—
　On Europe's shore, on ocean's flood—
Shall smite the oppressors of mankind
　And blast the traffickers in blood.

Oh, where should Freedom's hope abide,
　Save in the bosom of the free?
Where should the wretched negro hide,
　Save in the shade of Freedom's tree?

Oh, by those songs your children sing,
　The lays that soothe your winter fires,

The hopes, the hearths, to which you cling,
　The sacred ashes of your sires,—

By all the joys that crown the free,—
　Love, honor, fame, the hope of heaven,—
Wake in your might, that earth may see
　God's gifts have not been vainly given.

Bards of Freedom's favor'd land,
　Strike at last your loftiest key;
Peal the watchword through the land,
　Shout till every slave be free.

Long has he drained the bitter cup,
　Long borne the burden, clank'd the chain;
But now the strength of Europe's up,—
　A strength that ne'er shall sleep again.

All England was ablaze about American slavery and its abolition.

instrument, which would remedy the defects of that long-sighted benevolence which sweeps the field for distant objects of compassion, while it is as blind as a bat to the misery around its own doors."

Well said! I saw and felt it all when I went through the streets, and lanes, and cellars of Manchester, where fifty thousand blanched skeleton-men, women, and children, were slowly or rapidly dying of starvation. In that city, also, vast anti-slavery meetings were got up to induce the North to put down slavery in the South. These assemblages were invariably under the auspices of the aristocracy, and they were held where the police were stationed at the doorways to drive off the famishing, lest their plaint of hunger might salute the ears of their bloated task-masters.

There was no lack of cotton in Manchester then. There was something worse than that. It was the same old complaint you will find in any part of England,—the poor over-worked and under-fed, to make the rich richer, and the poor poorer.

I went up to Paisley, where more than half the population were being fed from soup-kettles,—and pretty poor soup at that. There, too, the abolition of American slavery seemed to be the only thing which drew forth the sympathies, or reached the charity of the aristocratic classes. So everywhere in England, it was " that long-sighted benevolence, sweeping the distant horizon for objects of compassion, but blind as a bat to the misery at the door."

It was not so in 1840 alone. I have been in England several times since, but I never saw a good year for the poor of that oppressive empire.

To show that this was all the poorest of shams, and that England owes us no good will, let us step from 1840 to 1861.

We see all things the same in England to this day, except in the " negro business." Here all is changed. British sympathy is now shifted from the slave, and lavished on his master ; from " moral pocket-handkerchiefs, and religious fine-tooth combs" to the overseer's lash and the unleashed blood-hound ; from the maintenance of free institutions to their overthrow ;   from civilization to barbarism ; from liberty to bondage.

VI.

MR. STEPHENSON, our Virginia slave-breeding ambassa-dor near the Court of St. James, in 1840, became so odious that no chance to snub or insult him was lost by the British government.

Now, Mr. Adams, holding that same post, and embellishing it with all the great and noble qualities of illuminated talents and Christian philanthropy, is treated with far more neglect and far less cordiality by the same class which despised Stephenson, and fêted Harriet Beecher Stowe.

Then, England complained of our remissness or shirking in not doing our share towards putting down the slave-trade. Now, all her sympathies are with the supporters of slavery itself, which is the only support of slavery on the earth ; and her ship-yards and arsenals are taxed to their utmost to build fleets of the strongest and swiftest steam-pirates to help the slave-driving Confederacy sweep our peaceful commerce from the sea, and once more inaugurate the traffic in flesh and blood.

The British Government knew, when the Alabama's keel was laid, that she was to become a pirate ; and our minister protested against it in vain.   Three hundred of the rich merchants of England, in broad daylight, boasted of their pur-pose, and exulted over its successful execution.

The British government gave the earliest and heartiest encouragement to the rebellion, by recognizing it as a bellige-rent power the moment its task-masters reached London.   It allowed all the materials and munitions of war the rebels called for to be furnished ; and it has, from the first hour, given to the rebellion all the aid and comfort it dared to furnish our enemies in their atrocious attempt to immolate liberty and enthrone slavery in the Western world !*

* It has amazed those who are familiar with Lord John Russell's public history, that he should have trifled so heartlessly with the great issues of civilization and free government at stake in this rebellion. The shuffling has cost him the confidence of the great middle-class in England, and the respect of the world. If the following letter addressed to him may seem to be unlike letters usually written to titled men, I consider it quite respectful enough to the man who has struck hands with pirates and become pimp to the propagandists of negro slavery. Although written nearly four years ago, I see no occasion for retracting a syllable or cancelling a word of it :

" MY LORD,—We have a habit you are not much accustomed to,—of straight talk and honest dealing : so you need not be amazed if we speak very plainly in this despatch.

" You have all your life been a place-seeker or a place-holder. To get power and money, you have always turned your back on your friends and let your Reform measures go to the dogs. Whenever you have been an ' out,' and any American question came up, you were a warm advocate of our Republic. When you were an ' in,' you changed your tone. When Liberty was at stake in a foreign nation, or at home, you have been its noisiest champion, if an ' out.' If an ' in,' you have done your best to crush it, in Ireland, Hungary, Italy, Spain and Poland. It was with a pang that you saw even old Greece become free. For half a century, if an ' out,' you have brawled for Freedom and Free Government; if an ' in,' you have resorted to the very last trick to keep there. You have, if an ' out,' always paraded your friendship for the United States, and virulently assailed any Tory or Conservative ministry. ' In' again, you first veered, then hesitated, then tacked, and then attacked us, our Government, and all American things. You know our Republic has never had any fair play from any ministry except the Tories or Conservatives. All Americans involuntarily say of British politicians of your stripe, ' Save us from our friends, and we will take care of our enemies.' But you have reserved the meanest and most bare-faced tergiversation of your public life till you were pressing the verge of your mortal existence. After pointing a thousand times with exultation to our great and prosperous nation, and deploring the two wars England waged against us, you are now gloating over the prospect (as you deem it) of our speedy disruption and downfall. After hobnobbing with every abolitionist, and fêting every run-away American negro who managed to reach England, and imploring Britons no longer to use slave-grown cotton and sugar, you now take sides with the ' nigger-driving' secessionis s of the rebel States, who are trying to break down freedom in America, extend the area of that accursed institution and sanctify the revival of the African slave-trade. You are threatening war against the United States, unless we will surrender two intercepted traitors on their way to your abolition arms and sympathies, the chiefest emissaries

No jurist will pretend to say that in all this she has not violated the spirit, if not the letter, of her own laws of neutrality, and the laws of nations.   No intelligent man will deny that by these acts she has prolonged and inflamed this accursed war.   No man in his senses supposes for a moment that England would have ventured on such a course of hostility and inhumanity at any other period of our history since the Peace of 1815.

No other thoughts can suggest themselves to impartial men now, while we are going through a domestic trouble,—a *great* trouble, which has filled every true heart in America, or elsewhere, with a sadness which has dragged us " down to the depths of the earth."

That England should choose such a moment of our national

which the slavery you have always pretended to hate could send to your shores.

" O, John Russell ! how unworthy is all this of the descendant of your great ancestor, who sealed with his blood, on the scaffold, his life-long devotion to the cause of justice and human freedom !   Why must you, just as you are ending your career, rob your proud name of that ancient halo which has gathered around it, by expending your last efforts in trying to blot out Free Government, for which the founder of your race so nobly died, and perpetuating on our virgin soil African slavery, which the world is clamoring to see blotted out ?

" My lord, do you plead that the necessity of slave-grown cotton calls for so dastardly a betrayal by yourself of all the *souvenirs* of your life ?   And will you, to accomplish this purpose, trample on all the canons of international law, and become public robber, and go and steal this cotton ?   If you attempt it, will you succeed ?   How much cotton would you get before your ministry went down ? before you lost a market for your commerce with twenty-three millions freemen ? before our breadstuffs, which are now keeping the wolf away from British doors, would reach your shores ? before bread-riots would occur throughout the British Islands which would make you turn pale ? before all seas would swarm with our privateers, now twentyfold more numerous than in 1812, when you found them too fleet and too strong for you ? before you encountered, in addition to two millions of our native soldiers and sailors, half a million of adopted citizens, able-bodied men, *formerly British subjects,* and burning to avenge the wrongs of centuries inflicted on their devoted island ?

" My lord, do you plead that the exigencies of statesmanship demand that you should turn the arms of the earth against you ?   Do you suppose that Napoleon would lose such a chance for avenging Waterloo ? or Russia for taking

adversity, such as she has so often passed through, of *vindicating the supremacy of government, to save civilization*—a moment when she saw what she fondly deemed a fatal blow levelled at our prosperity, if not our very existence—such a moment to join our foes, to make our destruction sure!

Thank God! she was the only nation that contemplated with satisfaction our impending doom. Thank God! she will never live to see it. We have been punished for our national sins already, till the blood has burst from every pore; and the cup of trembling may be pressed still harder to our lips hereafter. But we shall not *die*. In the Doomsday-Book of Nations, many a leaf must be turned after England's record has been passed, before ours can be reached. *Nations never die in the morning*

Constantinople? or all despotisms for crushing your supremacy? or all the peoples of Europe for crushing monarchy?

"It would seem that England should be willing, at least, to let us manage our domestic affairs, since she has incurred a quarter of her national debt in interfering with them; that she should not now take to her arms 'the foul corpse of African slavery on our soil,' when it cost her *so many millions of dollars* to get rid of it in her own territories! Should not the Founder of Modern Liberty be glad to see how prosperously the brood of her young eagles had founded an empire-home in the New World's forests, and not writhe, and chafe, and bark at, and hawk at our nest, till she could come here and tear it to pieces?

"The time had gone by, we hoped, when England, our *own mother*, would try to become *our step-mother!* Why could she not have been proud in the pride of her daughter, and let her wear the jewels she had herself so nobly won? And yet malicious people say that England acts like some old dame, who, after parting with the title to a daughter's estate, feels that she has still some *reserved right* left to interfere in what no longer concerns her, and casts now and then an envious glance at beauty yet unshrivelled, and conquests forever beyond her reach.

"Can it be, my lord, that such unworthy feelings as these can now enter your heart as an English statesman? We cannot believe it. Can you desire to put one more great trouble on the heart of your beloved, widowed queen? We cannot believe it.

"My lord, you should be engaged in doing some good to the people of your own empire, for God knows they need it badly enough, rather than in trying to hurt a great, a kindred, and a friendly nation.

C. EDWARDS LESTER."

of life. They are chastised in their youth, that they may grow up in wisdom and righteousness. But when they have grown hoary in crime, and chastisement will no longer end in reformation, they must go to their graves, unwept, unrepented, unforgiven.

VII.

GRATEFUL it always is to turn away from the contemplation of British unfriendliness to our Government, and, crossing that narrow channel, greet the sight of the vine-clad hills of France. Once on that genial soil, the American feels at home. He may not speak its language, he may not understand its simplest expressions ; but he feels among friends. France may be growing restive under the reign of Louis Philippe, and the fever of an approaching revolution may be felt in the heated air ; or that great nation may have grown wild in the delicious delirium of a Lamartine republic ; the *coup d'etat* of the 2d of December may have just fallen ; or he may find all France calm, prosperous and happy, under the strong but beneficent sway of the Emperor of her choice.

It is still France to the American. So true is that saying of Rousseau : "It is possible to love friends better than kindred."

This sentiment is nothing new in our times. Under all forms of government, and at all periods of our political existence, the two nations have been friends. This friendship has been broken up by no war ; it has been disturbed by no revolution. Nor is it at all likely to be, unless the aggression of the present Emperor, on American soil, shall awake a new feeling of animosity against all forms of monarchy, or imperialism. The reasons are plain. Under no possible circumstances can France love England. Under no possible circumstances can England like France. France did not willingly resign her empire in North America ; and the moment our Declaration of Independence was made, she became our national ally, and helped us to wrest the Thirteen Colonies from the grasp of her ancient foe. She, again, for a miserable pittance, sold us the vast territory of Louisiana—*first*, to strengthen our Government, and *second*, to keep it out of the hands of England. It is safe to say, that if we had not held the mouth of the Mississippi, we should have had a very different history.

VIII.

BUT this is by no means all we owe to France. We are indebted far more to her efforts for the civilization of America, than we are even to her friendship, since we became a people.

A glance or two at the past will make this clear.

Most of the continent, lying within the limits of the forty-ninth and twenty-ninth parallels of latitude, belonged originally to France ; and all along its great shores and rivers she set up the light-houses of civilization. She explored all the great lines of communication which the trade and commerce of the continent follow to-day.

Beginning with the mouth of the great river St. Lawrence, she penetrated the unknown bosom of North America. Arrested only for a day before Niagara—that eternal miracle of the physical creation—the explorers pushed on over inland seas, till, without the stars to guide them, they would have been hopelessly lost, on the waving prairies of the Far West.

Those early explorers were the Jesuit missionaries of France. They were the first pathfinders of our empire ; they first carried the torch of Christianity and science into those unexplored regions.

Two centuries have gone by ; but their monuments still remain. They can be traced from Arcadia to St. Anthony's Falls. The magic shores of Champlain and Lake George still hold the echoes of the shouts of the chivalry of France. They planted the *fleur-de-lis*, and it grows there still. The names of Montcalm and Champlain still ring around those mountains ;

and among the few stricken descendants of Indian tribes who still haunt those neighborhoods, these names are household words.

The French left their language among the children of the forest, and it is preserved. The Iroquois still remember, with tenderness and love, the souvenirs left them by the humanity, the science, the genius and superb manners of the Jesuit fathers, and the brave cavaliers of the age of Louis XIV.

Sailing up the other great continental river from the Gulf of Mexico, the French explorers reached the westernmost point their St. Lawrence brothers had made, till they met and held council on one of those anticlinal ridges, where, if a drop of water be spilt on a sharp edge, half of it finds its way to the ocean through the St. Lawrence, the other going to mingle with the warm Gulf Stream.

And so everywhere, in following the path of these explorers, we find evidences of the efforts of the French to introduce civilization. They founded cities ; they established missions ; they explored regions utterly unknown ; and they left in their writings imperishable monuments to their fame.

France came to America to give light, knowledge, science, religion, liberty. For no other purpose did she ever set foot on this continent, till a Quixotic expedition landed in Mexico.

England never came but for robbery, conquest, or to establish negro slavery. She never tried to civilize the American Indian. She never helped establish a colony on this continent, unless it may have been to reward a court favorite with a monopoly, or to make sinecures for her nobility.

New England owes her no thanks ; for it was settled by the Puritans, after she had hunted them out of her kingdom like wild beasts. Miles Standish, Roger Williams, Lord Baltimore, William Penn, Oglethorpe : what did the British government ever do for any of these men, or their colonies?

True, England was ready enough to claim such colonies as her *property*, and such colonists as her *subjects*, as soon as they were important enough to tempt her cupidity. But what help did the British government ever give these colonies ? It was claimed in the House of Commons during the debate on the Stamp Act, that we had been planted by its care, and nurtured by its protection. " Planted by your care ? " exclaimed the indignant Colonel Barré. " No ! your oppressions planted them in America. Nourished by your indulgence ? They grew up by your neglect."

IX.

LEAVING, however, all old wrongs in oblivion, and forgetting even the insults which followed them in later years, a new generation had come prepared to look with friendly eyes on what was once called in America, *our fatherland*. The two nations seemed coming together and clasping hands in a lasting alliance. A cable was laid on the floor of the ocean that rolled between us ; and *once*, at least, it sent a message of amity, and it was heartily responded to. Here, the amity seemed to end. The cable could go no further. *Was it ominous?* It seems up-hill work to lay another, particularly with both termini on British soil ! Yes ! to flash by submarine lightning new aid and comfort to the murderers of our republic—advising them, that a new steam war-pirate for their service has just passed the grain-ship Griswold in the Mersey—the one to destroy the commerce and the lives of loyal American citizens, the other freighted with bread, to save the lives of the starving operatives of Lancashire !

Most English statesmen seemed, during our Rebellion, to be laboring under a strange infatuation. They appeared to forget from what sources this nation sprang, and the elements of strength and endurance we had aggregated in our progress ; that we are not *one* people, but *all* peoples, since all have mingled to aggregate one Republic ; that these new combinations have resulted in a new form of national existence ; *that none of of us propose to surrender this system of political life ;* that any other system must, at least for a long time to come, be an impossibility here ; and that it is the fixed and unalterable determination of the great body of the American people, to maintain their institutions forever.

If, in taking this course, we are to encounter the opposition of other nations, we are prepared to do it. We have done nothing to provoke it, as far as we know, nor is it likely that we shall. We wish to avoid it, if we can. But it would be going too far to say that we would purchase immunity from foreign intervention, at any price whatever.

x.

ROYAL *Literary Fund Dinner at Freemasons' Hall* in the spring of 1848, was the most imposing and brilliant assembly I have ever seen. Being the only American present, I was called on to reply to a broad and generous sentiment. I extract the following from the official report of the meeting :

REAR ADMIRAL SIR AUGUSTUS CLIFFORD.—My Lord Duke and Gentlemen, I have been requested to propose the health of "Mr. Charles Edwards Lester, and the Literary and Scientific Men of Foreign Countries."

MR. LESTER.—My Lord Duke, My Lords and Gentlemen, That so humble a person as myself should respond to so great and humane a sentiment as the one which closed the eloquent speech of the hon. and gallant baronet who has just sat down, needs some explanation. When I came into the room, I had no idea of saying a word ; I had only congratulated myself on being admitted to the presence of the gifted writers of England ; and could I, from all the world, have chosen the place where I would pass the evening, I would have chosen this Hall, where the great, the good, and the noble, have assembled to-night to sympathize with the struggles and the sufferings of the children of genius in every part of the world (cheers). And even now that I find myself on my feet, my better judgment tells me that I should have no right to attempt to speak the gratitude of the Literary and Scientific men of Foreign Countries for the honor done them here, if there were any one of them present who would respond to so touching and generous a sentiment. A little while ago I was pressed so earnestly to speak, that I felt I could not with courtesy refuse. In thinking what I should say, it occurred to me that I might make a hit, as it is called, with one observation. But the noble and learned Lord opposite to me (Lord Campbell) has run off with my idea, although I still claim the credit of it (and this is no trick of speaking).

I was going to say something about the stability of the Commonwealth of Letters (hear) : for in times like these, when all things human, and, if we may believe what the *Times* newspaper of to-day says of Rome, everything that has been called divine, seems to be sliding from its foundations (laughter and cheers) ; when fugitive princes are chasing each other over the continent ; and governments, and even society itself, are dissolving at the touch of a world-wide revolution, it is a matter of satisfaction to us, and to the learned men of all countries, who will hear of your proceedings where they dwell (cheers), that there is one Republic that is safe (loud cheering) ; the first that was ever founded in the world, and the last that will ever be destroyed (cheers) ; a republic in which have been numbered all the great and good men to whom the world has been indebted, from the early patriarchs of literature, Moses and Job, and Confucius and Plato, down to Hallam and James (loud cheering), and all the gifted men who have poured the light of their genius over England, and are now rallying to save her from destruction (loud cheers). I need not say that I allude to the great, the indivisible, the eternal Commonwealth of Learning (cheers) ; a Republic which has never disputed about the form of its government (cheers) ; which has never raised a question of succession (cheers) ; which has never quarrelled about legislation (cheers) ; which never had an interregnum, nor even a Provisional Government or a Committee of Public Safety to quell its disturbances or administer its affairs (cheers and laughter). It has been engaged in better business. This Commonwealth has always cared more for substance than forms. It has always been united on essential points, points so clear and grand that there's no one of its members that does not see them, and love them, and act on them (cheers). That the scholar's mission is to diffuse among mankind the light of liberty and truth—to inspire veneration for the God of the universe, and love for all his creatures—and amidst the toil and bustle of a working and a suffering life, to point the eye of his humbler brother to a better life to come (applause). Such have been, and such will be, the objects our Commonwealth keeps in view, and therefore it must be immortal (cheers). It seems improper and unbecoming for so obscure and unworthy a cultivator of letters to be a *speaker* in this assembly. (No! No!)

I was told that the distinguished ambassador of the country of which I have the honor to be a citizen, would be here this evening ; and I am sure that an historian who has so ably illustrated the annals of his own country, and been so useful a contributor to the early colonial history of Britain, would have met here the warmest reception, and represented not only the learning, but the heart of his countrymen (cheers). Lest it should be thought I have taken upon me *voluntarily* this office, let me say, that I have been obliged to yield to the importunity of your Secretary, whom I never saw but once before, and that a thousand miles off, in consenting to represent one feeling, one fraternal feeling, among the authors of America for the authors of Great Britain (cheers). If I could call up before you any one of five-and-twenty writers I might name, who dwell beyond the blue sea that divides us, to tell you how we feel towards the land of our fathers (cheers), how Americans feel towards this Institution, in whose beneficence some of them, I have every reason to believe, have participated, some words of fire should be struck off to-night that would make this fine old Hall echo to the shout of a literary brotherhood that must one day bind all our hearts together (prolonged and enthusiastic cheering). The object contemplated by your Institution is one of the purest and noblest man ever conceived—to relieve the sufferings of those gifted men into whose hearts the God of Light has breathed the inspiration that belongs to a higher order of intelligence, but who, in the devoted work of redeeming the lost millions of earth, have been left, like the Son of Man, with no place to lay their heads (cheers). On such a mission what angel would not have been proud to go (cheers)? Literature is a very precarious profession at best; from the early days of the earth's history, when blind old Homer, to get his bread, went singing scraps of the Iliad (under less comfortable circumstances than our friends have done to-night) under the walls of half a score of cities which afterwards fought for the honor of having given him birth, down to the garrets of Chatterton and honest Tom Steele (cheers), authors have been a marvelously hungry and destitute set of men (cheers and laughter).

Now, it seems to me, that an Institution whose object is to compensate for the lack of that ordinary prudence which more calculating men abound in, is a Society which attempts in some humble manner to emulate the beneficence of Heaven, whose inspiring light goes softly and kindly stealing into every cornfield of Europe and jungle of India, that warms the slopes of the Rocky Mountains, and visits with healing influence every broken heart (cheers). The delicacy with which you send your bread to feed the solitary scholar on the desert of life, like all true benevolence, is attended by no flourish of trumpets (cheers). The world knows not what you do; but the suffering scholar knows it, and his beneficent Father in heaven knows it,—and that is enough (loud cheers). It is very late, gentlemen, and I think we ought not to waste any of our time in clapping (cheers). It don't disturb me, but it uses up the time, and this seems to me bad economy (cheers and laughter). Yes, I feel that in saying a few words in reply to the toast proposed, I am doing a wrong to the authors of all countries, but particularly of America, whom I honor and love, and who could more worthily represent that Republic to which I have the honor to belong in a very humble capacity.

But there is another consideration which oppresses me still more. I was surprised in coming here this evening—I might have anticipated it all, but with the thoughtlessness that belongs to some authors, I forgot it —that I should be brought into the presence, not only of some of the most learned of the nobles of England, whom I honor for the great deeds of their fathers and for their devotion to letters, but into the presence of some of those writers whom I have worshipped from afar over the sea, as my fathers and teachers when I was a boy (cheers). For in college days I was, despite all present evidence to the contrary, carefully drilled through the Rhetoric and Logic of the Right Rev. Archbishop who sits opposite me (cheers and laughter); and had I then been told that at a future day I should have been admitted, even as a stranger, into his presence, it would have inspired me with an enthusiasm for his name over those dry pages—dry as I *then* thought them, but not since—which as a boy I learned by heart, only to discover their meaning too late to make me good at anything which requires either reason or eloquence (cheers). There was another name I learned to utter with that of Shakspere and Scott, and afterwards to love almost if not quite as well. Like others who have paid some attention to letters, I had groped blindly through the Mediæval age, till Hallam had shed over it the light of his genius (cheers). But with that great work in my hands, I went as confidently through the labyrinths of the Dark Ages, as I followed a father-guide through the trackless forests of my native land. So did I cling to the skirts of Hallam (loud cheers) ; and while I have been attempting, for six years, to decipher on the spot the inscriptions engraven on the ruins of Italy, I have found him my best guide. He has written about them with the heart of a lover, and the head of a sage (cheers). And I now thank God in the earnestness of my heart—and this you will not call a trick of speaking, you would insult the genuineness of my feelings if you did—that I am permitted to come and lay the tribute of my gratitude at the feet of my historical father (loud and long cheers). In rambling through the caves of Carrara, where Michael Angelo saw the statue of David in a rejected block of marble, it was evident that his mission lay in showing what genius could create out of stone. It seemed to me too, that the mission-of the great historian, so beautifully illustrated in this case, was to show what genius could create out of darkness (cheers).

For though the Dark Ages before that book was written, an Italian critic said, "A flood of light has streamed so broad and clear on our Mediæval history, from the pen of Hallam's genius, that ever after we may call that hitherto chaotic period the *light* ages." He has conducted the student of history through the dark ages, as Galileo led future astronomers through the untravelled passages of the skies, which the Almighty had never before opened to the telescope (cheers).

But I have already spoken too long, although I have not yet said what I rose to uttter (Go on, go on). I will, and stop too as quick as I can well manage to do it, for the warm hospitality with which I have been received has quite put every idea of a speech out of my head, and left me nothing but my heart to give you (cheers). You must excuse me for talking as I would if I were at the banquet board of a company of old friends whom I had just rejoined after a long separation—for in no assembly and in no home of England have I ever been able to feel like a stranger (loud cheers). It has been with no little surprise that I have heard so many speakers this evening allude to that "10th of April" (laughter). No future historian will be likely to say much about it, I fancy. In the midst of the convulsions that are shaking other thrones to dust, England is safe! The world can never dispense with her agency in civilizing mankind; her commerce and her literature are instruments God himself has appointed for emancipating the world. All that is true, and just, and generous in these islands will live. Those appalling changes that have taken place on the continent were inevitable, for neither governments nor legislations marched with the progress of society. The wave that swept away the institutions of France, dashed against putrid masses of corruption—it found French human nature there; here it found Anglo-Saxon human nature—and I take it there is a considerable distinction between them (cheers and laughter). There is one conservative principle which lies at the bottom of Anglo-Saxon character, which has always saved England—it is still able to do it—it is reverence for law and order, because nothing but law and order can prove any effectual safeguard to liberty of person and liberty of conscience. This principle has animated her literature in every age. Here the Press is not only free, but, for the most part, it is under the control of scholars—of men who believe in progress—who fix no limits to future civilization, and whose hearts are with the coming age. They will guide England through the future as they have led her through the past (cheers):—yes, in their hands England is safe (loud cheers).

His Grace the Archbishop of Dublin intimated—and I will not try to quote his words, for fear I might dim their lustre—that such was the spirit of the British nation, that even the long-descended nobles of England were not content to repose on the laurels of their ancestors. It was a great satisfaction for me to feel its truth, and to know that nothing commands so much veneration in England as genius and virtue, in whatever rank they may be found. A nobility that enters the common field of achievement, and deserves the thanks of its country—that leads the way in all that contributes to the glory and prosperity of a great people, has something to repose on that can withstand any shock—such men are "the *natural* nobility of earth" (loud cheers). Something of that kind I seem to see here, where nobles are authors and authors are nobles (loud cheers). But before I sit down I have a request to make of your Grace. It should be your Grace's *pardon* for having so long abused your courtesy in listening to my desultory remarks. But hoping this may be granted without a formal petition (cheers), I beg to be allowed to do something that may bring the authors of America nearer home to your hearts and your sympathies—to forward on my return—for I am on this island only as a bird of passage flying over it—an offering—I will not say how large it will be, but it shall be a hearty one—from some of the literary men of America for this Institution (loud cheers). I trust your Grace shall be satisfied that, however I may have misrepresented the eloquence of American authors (cheers), I have done but feeble justice to their feelings when I assure you that they feel, that in anything that is great and noble and good in England, they have a right to share as brethren (cheers). And after all, who was Shakspere? Our ancestors were all living together then, and together they went to see his plays (cheers). Until our history begins in America, it belongs to England, and England's to us, as well as you (cheers). And no man worthy of being born in either country will ever clap the torch to that beautiful temple of harmony between the two countries that God intended to raise, and that man ought never to defile (cheers). What British or American writer would ape the Ephesian wretch who made himself immortal by laying such a holy fabric in ashes? (Loud cheering). Threadbare penny-a-liners, reduced ladies of quality, needy adventurers, and *id genus omne*, have long enough been supposed to represent the feelings of the mother and the child (laughter). Let us represent ourselves (hear, hear). Let us know each other better, and who can say we may not some day come to like each other better than we expected (laughter and applause). Nothing sanctifies all our better feelings so much as doing good together (cheers). What humble agency I have, will be heartily extended towards such a consummation; and with the permission of your Grace, and those you are proud to call your friends around this festive board, I pledge myself, with the blessing of God, to forward from some of the friends of literature in America, during the year, an offering—such as it may be—

to show that in everything England does, that's above reproach and above praise, we do feel that we have a claim to be admitted as your younger brothers (great applause).

XI.

NOTE BOOK.—During one of my many visits to London, I find the following :

A few evenings since, after being present at a musical soirée at Lord ——'s, as I was passing through King street, St. James, I heard two gentlemen conversing about the last ball at Almack's. I had often heard of Almack's, but I knew very little about it. Since then I have, from various sources, gathered the following information concerning this "Temple of Fashion :"

It is a place where "the very soul of enlightened society centres ;" where the most splendid and noble of the noblest aristocracy of the noblest and most enlightened nation of the earth assemble ; where the spirituelle and ineffable quintessence of the sublimate of fashion, refined from the clarified essence of wealth and rank, "is collected in one hot and luminous focus." It is, in fact, to London what London is to England, what England is to the civilized world : a place, in short, to which the most ancient and honorable nobility look with reverence ; nobility whose ancestry can be traced back in one bright chain of fox-hunters to the Norman Conquest, or the times of the Saxon Heptarchy ; for this is an establishment to which age and old time must do honor ; the very temple, and, as it were, the most holy place of fashion.

How many robes of passing splendor have swept over the threshold of this sacred tabernacle, none but the recording angel can tell. For nearly a century now its halls have been illustrated year after year, and month after month, with all that England could crowd together of brilliancy and rank. Nothing low or vulgar has ever approached the hallowed verge of its consecrated precincts : *Procul, O procul este profani !*

There are mysteries here not to be gazed on by common eyes : a few starred Sibyls (looking marvelously like English females with the yellow hair of Saxony yet on their brows) have established certain unearthly rites and ceremonies in King street, St. James, to the full understanding of which none but the titled elect are admitted ; and who are required to live sublimely apart from the rest of the world, from which they are separated by a barrier as broad and impassable as the Sahara Desert. The happy few, the priestesses of the temple, exercise an absolute authority over all its affairs, and are unbending in the execution of their decrees. The proudest titles cannot avail against them; for they, too, have received their authority from prescription. Their favor is worth more than all other honors, for it comprehends these, and unspeakably more. To be admitted to Almack's is to be above all solicitude for character or titles; for admission here presupposes all this, and, moreover, is of itself so vast an elevation in public consideration, that all others may at once be lost sight of and forgotten.

XII.

THE Ladies-Patronesses are themselves beyond the reach of envy, and hold their authority by a tenure which can neither be disputed nor dissolved. They are the divinities to be propitiated by all who would meet with success or consideration in the fashionable world. Their power is suspended over the heads of all, and they can in one moment strike from the galaxy of fashion the brightest and loftiest luminary there; and even this, all but the fallen will approve, for it serves only to purify and refine the circle whence they have been taken.

When once precipitated from this eminence, nothing they have can avail them in their disgrace; the trappings and stars of ancient nobility have lost their lustre, and reflect but a flickering ray, compared with the brilliant light and éclat issuing from the salons of Almack's. These female divinities, who hold the scissors, and sometimes the thread of fate, designate those who are to succeed them in their sacred function; and as one of their number is fading away from existence, they look for some happy mortal to take the sublime seat she is just about to exchange for the "narrow house." In short, when one of the six elderly duchesses, countesses, or marchionesses, happens to die, the remaining five fill up the void; and thus the priesthood, or, rather, the priesshood, lives on in a sort of corporate immortality; and the long life of the establishment is made up of the odd fragments of the lives of divers ancient females, who, in the course of Providence, or by electioneering artifices, have been elevated to preside over this University of West-Endism.

It cannot be said, indeed, that these appointments are always made without contention, rivalry and heart-burnings: this would be too much to expect, even of the divinities of Almack's enchanted halls; since the honor is so high that none but the tamest and most ignoble spirits would be wanting in ambition to aspire to it. Where the fate of the present, and, perhaps, a succeeding generation of fair ladies and dashing beaux is made subject to, and dependent on, the favor of a Synod of six Ladies-

Patronesses, who would not wish to be a sharer in such fullness of power, and thus be placed beyond all the evils of life?

XIII.

WHEN a seat becomes vacant by death, a struggle worthy of so great a prize commences; and among the remaining five, bitterness and reviling do sometimes make their unholy way. One cannot give up the suit of a "very dear friend," whose face she has long hoped to see in effulgence and honor, at "the Board of Red Cloth." Another has formed fond anticipations of seeing the companion of her early life raised to the sacred office, which she herself now fills, and doing honor to the associates with whom she would then mingle.

In short, each one has her antipathies and preferences, and is anxious to secure for her *protégée* the vacant seat: whence originate suspicions and jealousies, rivalships and back-bitings; whence come artifice and intrigue, and the marshalling of every motive of fear, interest, love, resentment, and ambition, that can possibly weigh upon the suffrages of those who are to decide. It would be unfair to regard their deportment on these momentous occasions as indicating their general character. What though words of dark and dubious meaning do sometimes escape from their lips; and what though epithets which would better become the brawls of the streets, and the bandyings of kitchen heroines, should, in moments of trial, be liberally applied to the characters of these staid and haughty regents; yet such are but occasional outpourings, and doubtless only introduced to fill up the vacancies and interstices of sublimer contemplations.

Of course, they who would insinuate that such contentions and rivalships do always secretly exist, but are never visible except on these great occasions, do so of their own unadvised foolhardiness and malice aforethought. These Guardians of the sacredness of fashion's circle have enough to do in keeping perpetual vigils, that none invade their halls who have not passed the purifying ordeal. To them is committed the keeping of the Golden Fleece; and they are to guard it with a wakefulness which no power of herbs can ever lull. Those gifted with such small accomplishments as nature can bestow, apply in vain for admission here, unless they have some more powerful talisman to enforce their claims; there must be titled rank, and rank untarnished by poverty.

This, you—my shoddy friend—with wife and daughters used to Bowery life and City Assembly balls, will say, is all delicious! It is, indeed. It does your Republican heart good, I doubt not, to think there is one

place where the favored few are above the reach of those low vulgarities
which infest the dead levels of Democracy.

XIV.

AND what think you, dear sir, is done within the precincts of so much
exclusiveness? Why here the great, or, rather, the favored ones,
become accustomed to each other's society; and there being no other
enterprise on earth worthy the attention of the English Aristocracy, they,
like wise men, have created this object of ambition to prevent their
noble faculties from rusting out in the coarse and trivial pursuits of
ordinary life. They must have something to do; for even noblemen
and kings have not yet succeeded in taking out a patent for a *happy*
do-nothing profession. So they busy themselves first in gaining admit-
tance to Almack's, and then in luxuriating upon their hard-won honors.

After days, and nights, and weeks, and months of management and
anxiety, with trembling hands and fainting hearts, they send up to the
awful scrutiny of the *Judgesses* their respectful supplication. I think
you cannot but envy the delectable state of their feelings—the flutter-
ings of hope and fear they now experience.

The oracle is not long silent; the responses, inscribed on triangular
billets, are scattered, like Sibyls' leaves, among those whose fate they are
to decide; and then there are smiles, and self-gratulation, and rejoicings,
and exultation with some; and frowns, and tears, and disappointment,
and rage, with others.

Dear sir, can you conceive how it is possible to live after being
rejected? It is very certain that ordinary eating, and drinking, and
sleeping, and breathing, are not the true essentials to life; for the smiles
of the rich and the Almack-favored are worth more than all these for
the purposes of living, at least good living, to the applicants at this
ineffable Court. To the young and ambitious among the gay and opulent of London, rejection comes like a sentence of banishment from the
very light of life. All other places of fashionable resort are regarded
only as faint and wretched imitations of this sublime original. More
than one instance has been known of such rejection producing death, by
the rupture of a blood-vessel in some exquisite young lady's bosom (perfectly horrible, you will say); or a fate little less painful has awaited the
angelic-disappointed, of fading away by the slow poison of chagrin
and gloom.

Young gentlemen, when overtaken by this dreadful calamity, generally blow out what brains they have with a pistol, or, in failure of this,

devote them to the less romantic end of writing poetry. Ah! sir, it is quite gratifying to me to know, while writing these paragraphs, that they will excite in your sensitive heart high and generous emotions, suited to so touching a theme.

XV.

IN a spacious *salon*, with all the unostentatious elegance which wealth, rank and taste can bestow, is assembled, beneath brilliant lamps, and reclining on voluptuous sofas, the cream of all the beauty and gallantry of England. Precious stones are flashing in the light; and bright eyes sparkling, and flushed cheeks glowing on every side. Here a whisper of musical voices is heard in the soft murmur of confidence; and there words of gallantry, and flattery, and gentleness, insensibly melt into sighs.

Forms of chiseled gracefulness are gliding about; and when the sound of music begins to creep over the scene, swelling, and dying away like the breath of evening, light footsteps are heard just audibly to rustle, and fairy fingers floating on the waves of the mazy dance, beat softly to the pulse of melody.

The young and blushing countess is fluttering by the side of the dashing captain; and ever and anon, as her white hand touching his, a thrill of delight passes over her form. There, a boy, who would be esteemed awkward if he had not lately come to a dukedom, is blundering and swelling before a proud beauty, whose heart rebels against maternal injunctions, and spurns with contempt the clumsy attentions of her vain admirer; and by their side a graceful *Premier* is moving gallantly to the voluptuous waltz of a high-born youthful duchess. Yonder is a *prudent* mother, whose schemes in providing her daughter with an advantageous settlement have all been frustrated, and in whose guarded countenance jealousy and chagrin are but half concealed. Here glances by the form of a young marchioness—and such a form! swelling with exultation and triumph as she bears away from her tearful rival a young and gallant fortune.

In this place is never heard the sound of loud mirth and hilarity; all is gentle and regulated; every emotion is subdued; and whatever it be, it is expressed on the countenance only by a smile. Here every one is bent upon conquest; and every avenue to the heart is guarded with unrelenting severity. I scarce need tell one so familiar with the gay world as yourself, that all this is *necessary.*

XVI.

BUT still, there are scenes here occasionally, which in other assemblies would excite something more than a smile. Around the dancing arena, a rope is drawn for the purpose of preventing encroachments upon those within, not very unlike what you may have seen in your plebeian days at a menagerie ; and the " perfumed courtiers " lead their exquisite partners into the ring, as in the afore-mentioned days you may have observed the Shetland pony led in by Dandy Jack. It sometimes happens in the flush and excitement of the *gallopade* (for the gallopade and waltz are now the only things danced at Almack's, though Lord Byron, whose moral tastes have never been condemned for their purity, thought the waltz should be banished from virtuous society), that cases are not unfrequent, in the full tide of the dance, of the more spirited beaux dashing themselves carelessly against the rope, and by the rebound being thrown prostrate upon the floor.

This, of itself, would be but a slight misfortune ; but it is often followed by others of a more serious nature. Those nearest the fallen dancer are not always able to stop themselves at once upon the polished floor, and frequently numbers of young ladies are either dragged down by their companions (for it is proverbial that a sinking man will hold fast to a *trifle*), or stumble over those already fallen.

Here, then, is a delightful scene for the staid gravity of the assembly : duchesses, marchionesses, captains, dukes, and premiers, all huddled together in one grand promiscuous pile of—rank and beauty. Slight screams are heard ; and blushes, and smiles, and tears, are seen confusedly mingling in the faces of the scrambling unfortunates. Some hitherto slighted rival exults in the sudden shame of her tormentor ; while the fallen ones retire from the ring in the deepest mortification and chagrin. The music, arrested for a moment by the confusion, now breaks forth again in voluptuous softness, and the rustle of flying feet begins again to steal upon the ear.

Such scenes as this are at times witnessed in these famous *salons*, where the severity of elegance has banished all ostentation of wealth. The simplicity of its entertainments excludes all idea of luxury, and almost of comfort. Of course, gaudiness is not tolerated here, for that is something which those who have no other recommendation than mere gold (a vulgar thing) can put on. But it is not the society, or the intercourse, which gives value to an admission to this circle : the very *fact of admission* is all that is prized, as this is a tacit award of eminence in the world of fashion. It is a sort of test to try the purity of nobility, whether it be the unalloyed ancient metal, or only a showy compound of modern times. It separates the former from the latter by a broad and plain line of distinction. The young and the sanguine are here brought together, and matrimonial alliances are rarely formed out of the exclusive circle in which they move. Thus is an aristocracy refined and perpetuated, which has but little sympathy with the rest of the world.

XVII.

LIKE all establishments claiming for themselves peculiar superiority, Almack's has been many times violently assailed. It exercises, in fact, an authority really more oppressive and unjust than any the throne ever dares assume. It shuts out hundreds and thousands from the standing and consideration to which they are justly entitled in society; and so omnipotent is the tyranny of aristocratic opinion, that its seal of disapprobation once fixed upon the name of an ambitious aspirant, disgraces and obscures him in public estimation forever. Of course, all the jealousy and rancour of disappointed ambition are arrayed against it; for such as can never share in its honors are deeply stung by its contempt.

So deeply have certain persons felt this galling yoke, that a combination has even been contemplated, for the purpose of breaking its power by parliamentary interference.

But do not suppose, dear sir, that this indicates any advancement of the coarse principles of Democracy among *these* parliamentary reformers. Oh, no! it proceeds from quite another motive than this; they wish to rend, because they cannot rule the halls of Almack's. Besides, it was soon discovered that the Imperial Parliament was itself one of the chief supporters of Almack's; and felt that any innovation upon so venerable an institution was an invasion of the time-honored prerogatives of the English aristocracy.

The power of legislation is sometimes directed to sad purposes; and although in this instance the evil is doubtless enormous, yet we can hardly suppress a smile when we hear legislators talking seriously about turning the supreme power of a mighty nation into a regulator of fashions and master of ceremonies. Destroy Almack's! The fair ladies who are so happy as to resort there have woven their charm for too many noble lords and right honorable members of the House of Commons, ever to be disturbed by "an act entitled an act to abolish the right of certain distinguished families to associate, waltz, gallopade, and tumble in the ring with whomsoever they please."

Indeed, it is an institution which addresses itself to a strong principle of the human heart—the *vanity* of man; and although it may make thousands wretched, thousands more will hope on for its favor and the flattery it brings. It can never be abolished until Englishmen shall lose their reverence for rank, and scorn the idea that a few distinguished ladies should hold in their hands all the means of human enjoyment; until they shall learn to esteem other consequences than such as ease, titles and idleness bestow, and to honor only those who add something to the stock of human intelligence, and make the world better by their influence; OR, until a quarrel, which cannot be hushed, shall involve the whole establishment in ruin.

Woman was the last and most perfect work of God. But if she came from the hand of the Creator the sweetest, she is also capable of *becoming* the *sourest* of all beings. It happily is not often we find her in such *imperfect* state, and for this we should be thankful. But should the lovely divinities of Almack's enchanted halls ever have the peace of their "Board of Red Cloth" broken by a serious contention, this gorgeous temple of fashion will come down with a crash that will be a warning to the exquisites of all future generations. If Almack's ever falls, "great will be the fall thereof."

XVIII.

WHEN I left Lord ——'s, it was twelve o'clock. I hurried on through Hyde Park, and found an omnibus standing before Apsley House (the Duke of Wellington's), waiting for passengers for the East End. A thick fog hung over London, and a storm seemed to be coming on. The night was dark and gloomy. By the light of a neighboring lamp, I perceived a lady in an omnibus, who was not only unattended, but there was no other person in the carriage.

Her face, on which the lamp shone brightly, was as pale as marble; but her features were very beautiful. She was dressed as superbly as though she had just come from a ball at Almack's. There was a look of deep distress on her countenance; such a look as we never forget after it is once seen. The large blue vein on her forehead swelled out as if ready to burst. We rode on for a mile through the streets, now nearly deserted and silent, without speaking. In the presence of what appeared to me such great anguish, I could not think of words I dared to utter. In the light which shone in from the lamps as we passed along, her face wore an ashy paleness; and on that face there was an expression of such utter loneliness and desertion, of such evident sinking from rank and prostration of earthly hopes, that I needed but one glance to convince me, that she had fallen from the gay and heartless circle of fashion.

I ventured to ask if I could render her any service in a ride, at that late hour. She replied, "Oh! sir, whoever you are, for God's sake don't speak to me; I only want to die; you can't help me now."

As she uttered these words, she burst into tears. We rode on in silence, broken at intervals by her sobs and sighs. We passed through Temple Bar and reached St. Paul's, where I was to get out. But I was determined to go as far as the omnibus went, if necessary, to know whether my fellow-passenger was a maniac, or what. When we came to the Bank, the coachman stopped and inquired where we would get out. Again I asked if I could render her any assistance. "Yes, sir, you can, if you have any pity. Let me get out anywhere. I care not where I go if I can only find some place to lay my head."

I assisted her in getting out of the omnibus. She fell as she stepped down, and I caught her with one arm and her—*child* with the other. This new-born infant was wrapped in a Cashmere shawl—its only swaddling-clothes. The mother asked me to lead her to a place where she could sit down—the omnibus drove on, and not a human being was in sight. Near by was a flight of stone steps, upon which she was scarcely seated, when she fainted away.

XIX.

NO lamp was near us; it was past one o'clock; the rain had begun to fall heavily upon the pavements, and, save the feeble cry of the infant in my arms, and the distant rumbling of the omnibus, no sound was to be heard. I shouted for a policeman, knowing that one must not be far off, and down the street I heard his answer, followed by the heavy quick fall of his feet.

I inquired for a boarding-house. He said we must pass down two or three streets towards the Thames, to find one, and he would assist us.

"I will carry the lady," said he, "if you will spread this India-rubber cape (a garment which all policeman wear when it rains) over the child, and take care of it."

I spoke to the mother, whom I had raised from the step when she fainted, and had supported till now; and, as she partly recovered, the first words she spoke were, "Oh! where is my child—my child? Oh! God of heaven, has he stolen my child?"

I told her the child was safe in my arms, and protected from the rain. "Oh! then give him to me." She seized the babe, and, pressing it close to her heart, asked us to leave her. I said, "We will take you to a house where you will be comfortable."

"God bless you," she answered, "if you will."

She consented to let me take the child, and we hurried on through the storm, to a place of shelter. We were met by several policemen, each of whom stopped us, until he received the countersign from the one with us. At last we reached the house, and, after ringing the bell several times, the door was opened by a servant. We made known our business, and were admitted to the hall. The lady of the house was called, and engaged to furnish accommodations for the young mother. She took the child from my hands, and I paid her charges for a week, and turned to leave the house with the watchman.

The mother called me back from the door and said, "I can only thank you, sir. God bless you—God *will* bless you for this."

We left the house. As we entered the street the rain was falling heavily, and violent gusts of wind dashed by, with that dismal moaning sound, which is never so mournful, even in the wild woods, as in the dark solitudes of a large city late at night. But still, this was less dreary than the scene we had just left; and a load fell from my heart when I once more felt the night tempest sweeping by.

XX.

"POLICEMAN, whom do you think this lady can be?" "Why, sir," said he, "there is no knowing, of course, certainly; but I doubt not she has moved in fashionable life. Did you see how she was dressed? and how she spoke? Why, you can tell a lady from the West End only by hearing her speak once. You say she got in at Hyde Park corner. Why, I suppose she has been ruined by some heartless fellow, in Regent's Street. There are thousands of girls that are; and then they come to the East End, and starve to death, or die of neglect and privation. From one extreme to the other; this is the way with the London world. For my part, I am satisfied with the lot of a policeman."

I inquired if she could not be helped by one of the Charities. "Well, sir," said he, "we can do our best; but the Charities are all crowded. I have made three unsuccessful applications for persons in distress within the last two days. But, if you will write something about this, and let me take your letter, the chance will be fair."

I engaged to address a letter the next morning to the "City of London Lying-in Hospital, City Road, or any other London Charity." The policeman promised to call for the letter at nine o'clock. [By means of these exertions, this unfortunate mother received assistance; but her child died the night she came from the West End.]

I laid myself down on my pillow that night, worn out with fatigue. But too many confused images of the gay halls of Lord ——; of the revelry and splendor of the West End; and of the extreme suffering and wretchedness of that ruined female in the dark and dismal streets of London, crowded upon my fancy, to let me sleep.

In one night, I had seen the two extremes of a London life—opulence, gayety, fashion and song in the palace halls of an English nobleman; and the abject and hopeless misery of a broken hearted-female, who had fallen from such a circle, to fill a grave, dug by strangers in the Potters' Field.

Such is London—the West End, and Spitalfields—a nobleman and a beggar—revelry, mirth, beauty and fashion—a maniac victim of seduction, with her dying child.

BOOK V.

THE ESTABLISHED CHURCH.

Don't talk to me of its (the Established Church in Ireland) being a Church! It is a wholesale robbery.—*Burke.*

Let the English Church take warning. In these Democratic days *we want institutions for the poor.* . . . It is because we have in our towns no Church, no religious ministers, and no effective religious ministrations for the masses of the poor, that they are still in so wretched a condition.—*Kay's Social Condition and Education of the English People.*

Give us more bread and fewer Priests.—*Chartist mob at Norwich.*

The sums yearly raised by Dissenters for benevolent objects, reflect a lustre upon England brighter than all the glory of her arms.—Author of "*Natural History of Enthusiasm.*"

We certainly subscribe to the doctrine, that the church is the true and only fortress of Conservative principles.—*London Times, July* 31, 1841.

We cannot bring ourselves to suppose, that Sir Robert Peel has the slightest intention of sacrificing the rights of the farmer, to a thing so trivial and so temporary, too, as the popularity of the streets.—*Britannia, Feb.* 5, 1847.

But the principle is beyond all controversy—that on the safety of the *Church* of England, depends the safety of the *State* of England.—*Dr. Croly's Historical Sketches.*

THE ESTABLISHED CHURCH.

I.

CHURCH OF ENGLAND.—It consists of the reigning Monarch as the head—ninety-six archbishops and bishops, about thirteen thousand inferior clergy.*

* The following official list is taken from the Royal Almanac, of 1865 :

ENGLISH BISHOPS.		IRISH BISHOPS.	
NAMES.	Archbishops of	NAMES.	Archbishops of
C. T. Longley, D.D., *Primate of all England* £15,000	Canterbury.	Marcus Gervais Beresford, D.D., D.C.L.	Armagh, Clogher.
W. Thomson, D.D., *Primate of England* £10,000	York.	R. C. Trench, D.D.............	Dublin, Kildare.
	Bishops of		Bishops of
Arch. C. Tait, D.C.L...£10,000	London.	Joseph Henderson Singer, D. D.	Meath.
Chas. Baring, D.D.....£8,000	Durham.	William Higgin, D.D...........	Derry and Raphoe.
Chas. Rich. Sumner, D.D......	Winchester.		
Hen. Philpotts, D.D...........	Exeter.		Tuam, Kill- ala, and Achonry.
Con. Thirlwall, D.D....£4,500	St. David's.	Lord Plunket, D.D...........	
Thos. V. Short, D.D....£4,200	St. Asaph.		
A. T. Gilbert, D.D. ...£4,200	Chichester.		Ossory, Ferns, and Leighlin.
John Lonsdale, D.D.....£4,500	Lichfield.	James Thos. O'Brien, D.D.....	
Sam. Wilberforce, D.D..£5,000	Oxford.		
Lord Auckland, D.D...£5,000	F'th & Wells.		Cashel, Em- ly, Waterf'd & Lismore.
Jas. Prince Lee, D.D....£4,200	Manchester.	Robt. Daly, D.D.............	
R. D. Hampden, D.D....£4,200	Hereford.		
John Graham, D.D......£4,500	Chester.		Down, Con- nor and Dromore.
A. Olivant, D.D........£4,200	Llandaff.	Robt. Bent Knox, D.D........	
John Jackson, D.D...........	Lincoln.		
W. K. Hamilton, D.D...£5,000	Salisbury.		Limerick, Ardfert, & Aghadoe.
Robt. Bickersteth, D.D.£4,500	Ripon.	Henry Griffin, D.D.	
Hon. J. T. Pelham, D.D.£4,500	Norwich.		
Jas. C. Campbell, D.D.......	Bangor.		Killaloe, Kilfenora, Clonfert, and Kilm'c- duagh.
J. C. Wigram, D.D......£5,000	Rochester.	William Fitzgerald, D.D.......	
Hon. S. Waldegrave, D. D. £4,500	Carlisle.		
Hon. Philpott, D.D £5,000	Worcester.		Cork, Cloyne, and Ross.
C. J. Ellicott, D.D. £5,000	Gloucester and Bristol.	John Gregg, D.D...........	
E. H. Browne, D.D. ...£5,500	Ely.		Kilmore, El- phin, and Ardagh.
Francis Jeune, D.C.L..£4,500 (not a peer.)	Peterbor'gh.	Hamilton Verschoyle, D.D.....	
Hon. H. Powys, D.D...£2,000 (not a peer)	Sodor and Man.		

It is the established religion of the empire. It is maintained at an annual expense fully equal to the cost of carrying on the Government of the United States, previous to 1861. It furnishes " the means of grace," probably, to *one-tenth* of the population of the Home Empire. It is, therefore, the chosen religion of a small fraction of the English, Scotch, Welsh and Irish people. Most of its revenue is forced from British subjects by due process of laws, enacted for that purpose. Such is the Established Church.

II.

REVENUES.—It is impossible to arrive at any exact estimate of the revenues of the Church. They consist chiefly in the following items :

SCOTCH BISHOPS.

BISHOPS.	Sees.
C. H. Terrot, D.D.	*Edinburgh.*
T. B. Morrell, D.D.	*Coadjutor.*
A. P. Forbes, D.C.L.	*Brechin.*
A. Ewing, D.C.L., D.D.	*Argyll and the Isles.*
R. Eden, D.D.	*Primus. Moray and Ross.*
C. Wordsworth, D.C.L.	*St. Andrews*
Thos. G. Suther, D.C.L.	*Aberdeen*
Wm. Scott Wilson, D.D.	*Glasgow and Galloway.*

COLONIAL BISHOPS.

NAMES.		Bishops of
Augustus Short, D.D.	1847	*Ad'l'de,S.Au*
W. W. Jackson, D.D.	1860	*Antigua.*
Thomas Parry, D.D.	1842	*Barbadoes.*
John Harding, D.D.	1851	*Bombay.*
E. W. Tufnell, D.D.	1859	*Brisbane.*
G. E. L. Cotton, D.D.	1858	*Calcutta.*
Rob. Gray, D.D.	1847	*Cape Town.*
H. J. C. Harper, D.D.	1856	*Ch'st Ch. N. Z.*
P. C. Claughton, D.D.	1859	*Colombo.*
Geo. Hills, D.D.	1859	*Columbia.*
John Medley, D.D.	1845	*Fredericton.*
W. J. Trower, D.D.	1863	*Gibraltar.*
M. Thomas, D.D.	1863	*Goulburn.*
H. Cotterill, D.C.L.	1856	*Grah'ms T'n*
W. P. Austin, D.D.	1842	*Guina.*
Benj. Cronyn, D.D.	1857	*Huron, C. W.*
A. G. Spencer, D.D.	1839	*Jamaica.*
Samuel Gobat, D.D.	1846	*Jerusalem.*

NAMES.		Bishops of
Reg. Courtenay, D.D.	1856	*Kingston.*
F. T. Macdougall, D.C.L.	1855	*Labuan.*
Fred. Gell, D.D.	1861	*Madras.*
V. W. Ryan, D.D.	1854	*Mauritius.*
Charles Perry, D.D.	1847	*Melbourne.*
F. Fulford, D.D.	1850	*Montreal.*
A. R. P. Venables. D.D.	1863	*Nassau, B'a*
J. W. Colenso, D.D.	1853	*Natal.*
		Nelson, N. Z.
Wm. Tyrrell, D.D.	1847	*N'le, N. S. W.*
Edw. Field, D.D.	1844	*Newf'd land*
G. A. Selwyn, D.D.	1841	*N. Zealand.*
S. S. Crowther, D.D.	1864	*Niger Ter'y.*
Hibbert Binney, D.D.	1851	*Nov. Scotia.*
J. T. Lewis, D.D.	1862	*Ont'o. C. W'*
M. B. Hale, D.D.	1857	*Perth, W. A.*
		Rupert's L'd
J. W. Williams, D.D.	1863	*Quebec.*
E. H. Beckles, D.D.	1860	*Sierre Le'ne.*
T. E. Welby, D.D.	1862	*St. Helena.*
F. Barker, D.D.	1854	*Sydney.*
C. H. Bromby, D.D.	1864	*Tasmania.*
J. Strachan, D.D., LL.D.	1839	*Toronto.*
George Smith, D.D.	1849	*Victoria.*
W. Williams, D.C.L.	1859	*Waiapu.*
C. J. Abraham, D.D.	1858	*Well'n, N. Z.*
W. G. Tozer, D.D.	1863	*C. Africa.*
T. N. Staley, D.D.	1861	*Honolulu.*
J. C. Patterson, D.D.	1861	*Melane-i.t.*
Edw. Twells, D.D.	1863	*Orange Riv.*

English Bishops,		28
Irish do		12
Scotch do		8
Colonial do		44
Missionary,		4
Total		96

Church Tithes,

Income of Bishoprics,

Estates of the Deans and Chapters,

Glebes and Parsonage Houses,

Perpetual Curacies

Benefices not parochial,

Fees for burials, marriages, christenings, etc.

Oblations, offerings and compositions for the four great festivals,

College and school foundations,

Lectureships in towns and populous places,

Chaplainships and offices in public institutions,

New churches and chapels.

Rev. Dr. Heman Humphrey, whom all will acknowledge to have been as incapable of any design to mislead, as he was unlikely to be misled himself, tells us in his "Foreign Tour," that the incomes of the Archbishops of Canterbury and York were, thirty years since, over $250,000, and that he was assured by a gentleman in Durham, in whom he placed the utmost confidence, that the entire revenues of that rich Diocese might be fairly estimated at half a million of dollars.

The hamlet of Nottingham, in Kent, is liable to pay annually the sum of £8 13*s.* 4*d.* to the Dean and Chapter of Rochester. The clergy had granted to a Mr. Clayton, an attorney, the power to levy this sum on the hamlet, in consideration of £250 paid to them once in seven years, making Mr. Clayton's annual payment about £44 7*s.* 6*d.* Mr. Clayton, for the annual sum of £100, had granted to a Mr. Morris, a farmer in the vicinity of Nottingham, the power to levy tithes on the hamlet, which has been to the extent of ten shillings an acre, making his income on the six hundred acres in the limits of the hamlet £300 per annum.

When this gross abuse was fully understood by the people of the hamlet, a law-suit was instituted to rid themselves of the burden; but although in the entire hamlet there was no church or chapel of ease, or school, or church-service connected with the Establishment, yet the Court decided against the people!

In the report of the King's Commission the church revenue from this hamlet was put down at £8 13*s.* 6*d.*, while the people of the hamlet paid £400 every year. This is a single case, but it illustrates as clearly as a much greater number which might be adduced from the *ex-parte* and deceptive character of that report and all others from the same source.*

Mr. Colton's estimate of the Church revenue, thirty years since, exceeded $40,000,000.

A respectable-authority in England a few years ago, exhibited a table of facts showing that the administration of the Church of England to its hearers, costs as much as the administration of all other forms of Christianity in all parts of the civilized world, to over two hundred millions of Christians.

Again, I ask the question, who need be told that this prodigious amount is paid by the people and not by the aristocracy?

---

* Not long after the passage of the Reform Bill, an investigation into the condition and revenue of the Church was so loudly demanded by the people, that a commission on church revenues was appointed by the king to inquire into the matter, and present their report. The king being the head of the church was the last person in the kingdom who should have had anything to do in the appointment of this commission; this was proved by the result—for there was not a man on that commission who was not deeply interested in concealing from the people the real amount of church revenue. Their report was subjected to the severest scrutiny, and all parties were satisfied that they kept back everything they were not compelled to disclose. And yet this report, dated June 16, 1835, stated that the permanent gross annual revenue of the Church on the average of the three years ending 1831, was £3,750,000, or $18,187,500.

But this estimate, as the report acknowledges, did not embrace the vast sums derived from glebes, fines paid on the renewal of leases of bishops' and other lands, church rates, Easter offerings, fees on marriages, births and burials, and grants of Parliament for Church extension, which must have vastly swelled the aggregate. No certain knowledge of the amount of Church revenues can be derived from a report thus made out; not because the King's commission did not tell the truth, but because they only told a *part* of it. "This Report is incomplete," say the commissioners, "in that it does not embrace all the items which would be considered in a complete table of the revenue." So it appears; for instance: the entire annual revenue of all the arch-episcopal and episcopal sees of England and Wales, according to the Report, is less than $900,000, while the London *Times*, which is usually not far from the truth in such matters, said in 1835, that the annual income of the Bishop of London was $100,000, *independent of fines imposed for the renewal of leases*, "which occasionally happened to amount to a hundred thousand pounds at a single windfall," as it is called, and that "the income of the Bishop of London *will soon be sixty thousand pounds, or three hundred thousand dollars per annum.*

The poor man who raises ten bushels of wheat, must give one of them, or its equivalent, towards the revenue of a proud priest he never sets eyes on. A tenth of the gross income of the people goes into the pockets of the clergy.

Captain Ross, a Tory, in Parliament said, to the evident uneasiness of his friends, that one-fifth of the rent of the country went to the clergy. For it must be remembered that the tithe is a tenth of the gross income without any allowance for the expense of cultivation. If the poor man has any thing left, after being thus fleeced by his shepherd, and a child dies, he must pay the curate a burial fee, and last of all a fee for the privilege of erecting a tomb-stone over the ashes of his dead.

While his earnings are thus taken from him, how does the prelate expend his income? In building palaces, and rivaling the luxury and magnificence of princes. This is the *extortion* of the clergy.

III.

ARISTOCRACY is its twin sister. The Bishops are ex-officio members of the House of Lords, bear titles, use worldly civil power, and mingle actively in the affairs of the state, as peers of the realm—"It is no uncommon spectacle," says an English writer, " to see the Lord Bishops hurrying down to the House of Lords on what is called 'a field day,' to vote down the liberties of the people." As aristocrats of the land, they are every day becoming more and more opulent, while distress is overwhelming all the lower, and many of the middle classes. One and all, they were firm advocates of the Corn Laws, which were urging the people into famine and revolution. They are allied in their interests to the land owners, whose wealth increased just in proportion as bread was taxed into starvation prices. They resisted all propositions to make the necessaries of life cheap, for the splendor of their equipages— the magnificence of their dwellings and pleasure-grounds depended upon keeping bread at a high price—for a tenth of the produce of the soil coming into their pockets, it matters very much that wheat shall be made to sell for 80s. a quarter, and not 40s.—for the difference in price will double their income. Thus it becomes the interest of *thirteen thousand clergymen* to bring all their influence to support the aristocracy of the Empire—and we find the whole weight of the Established Church thrown into the scale of oppressive legislation. How wide asunder from the benevolence of the Gospel, is the organization of a church whose interests are so violently at war with the good of the people! We confess that in searching for anything apostolic in the practice of the Established Church, we meet with poor success. Thus to sustain its princely dignity, and continue its extortion in the midst of general distress, it must resort to oppression.

IV.

OPPRESSION.—The whole system of tithes and Church rates is one of oppression. The *London Times* of July 25th, 1831, said : " If venality be imputed to any class of Englishmen, look not to the columns of a newspaper for your proofs, look to the Red Book, to the Reports of Parliament, to the list of pensions and sinecures, to colonial functionaries, to mercenary lords, to pamphleteering, jobbing, mitre-hunting dignitaries of the Church, to the innumerable tribe of vermin bred within the folds of that poisonous mantle which has wrapped for ages and gradually numbed the Herculean power of England." Two years after, the same paper said : " The Church of Ireland is finally one which has for centuries, in any measure of severity, of exaction, of oppression, signalized itself by more than concurrence with the tyrannical spirit of the civil government. It is felt at once to be a weight upon the country, and a degradation."

The Church arrogates to herself the control of the Universities, where a son of a Dissenter is forbidden to enter ; because he cannot subscribe to the Thirty-nine Articles, he must be shut

out of the highways of learning. The Church takes the property and the education of the land under her own control.
Not satisfied with this, she claims the receptacles of the dead.
A Dissenting minister is forbidden to perform the funeral rites
over his own dead in the consecrated burying ground. The
child that has been baptized, educated, brought to the truth by
a Dissenting minister, grown up under his care, been consoled
by him in sickness, and cheered by him in the last fearful hour,
must die with the certainty that he will be interred by a
stranger, if he wishes to sleep in the old burying-ground where
his fathers rest; or (if no Dissenting burial place is near), be
buried on the world's wide common by his own minister. If
his friends will consent to have the hours of his bereavement
embittered by the presence of one who insulted and wronged
their dead while living, and treats them in their distress with
scorn, then, indeed, they can bury their loved and lost one in
the old churchyard. But if, as it often happens, the clergyman
of the parish is a fox-hunting, wine-drinking, godless man, and
the Dissenter, under the keen sense of oppression and insult,
under the deeper consciousness of the man's unworthiness and
heartlessness, refuses to have him minister at the burial of his
child, if he would have him rest with the ashes of his ancestors
—" with pious sacrilege," a grave he must *steal*. And if the
minister who has prayed with him—bound up his broken heart,
and spoken the words of truth and earnestness to him, perform
the service over the stolen burial, he is compelled to do it
standing without the paling of the churchyard, while the suffering friends listen from within. And this is the charity of
the Church of Christ—these the shepherds of the flock, whose
office it is, like their Great Master, " not to break the already
bruised reed !" This is Christianity ! The wild Indian of the
wood has more humanity ; the savage of the desert shows
more sympathy for bereaved men. *They* will not invade the
dead ; even the jackals wait till the living have retired to
their dwellings ; but not so with this Church of Christ—it casts
out the dead before they are interred, in the very face of the

living, if they have not subscribed to the Thirty-nine Articles.

v.

DISSENTERS are obliged to sustain their own churches and clergy, and pay just as much to the Established Church as its own members. Hence, to obey both his conscience and the government, the Dissenter must first pay a tenth of his entire income to the establishment, besides being called on frequently for Church rates, which are taxes ostensibly levied for keeping churches in repair and erecting new ones, to the extent of several millions per annum ; and finally, he must erect his own chapel and support his own minister. It is no small compliment to the Dissenters to say, that in addition to all these expenses, they raise more to support missionaries abroad, and benevolent enterprises at home, than the churchmen of England. The author of the *Natural History of Enthusiasm,* passes upon them the following just tribute of admiration : " The sums yearly raised by Dissenters for benevolent objects, reflect a lustre upon England brighter than all the glory of her arms !"*

---

* I might here record many instances of generosity among Dissenters, illustrating this remark ; I will allude to only one. I was told by two highly respectable maiden ladies, in Liverpool, that the various sums they were required to pay annually to the Church and State, amounted to $123 ; no inconsiderable part of this sum going into the pockets of the clergymen of the church, from whose ministrations they received not the least advantage, since they attended a Unitarian chapel. To me this seemed the more oppressive, for every shilling they were thus taxed for the Church, left them one shilling less to pay to their own minister, who devoted himself with great fidelity to his congregation. These ladies had long maintained themselves by keeping one of the most genteel boarding-houses in the upper part of the town ; and although their means could not be supposed to be so ample as to admit of any large offerings to the cause of benevolence, yet I had occasion to know, that the poor who came every day to their door, were not frowned empty away ; and that they contributed generously to the support of their own minister. All this was done with a Christian spirit, inspiring two sisters, who stand alone in the world, to deny themselves, that they may know the luxury of doing good to others. I was sitting with

It often happens that Dissenters refuse to pay the taxes levied on them to support the Church, since they regard it as helping to uphold a worldly and corrupt institution. They then suffer distraint on property. Anything on which the officer can lay his hands, be. it the last means of subsistence, the last comfort procured for a sick family, is taken. The distress thus caused is often very great, and such scenes are witnessed every day.

June, 1841, a man of the name of John Cockin suffered distraint on his property for refusing to pay 1s. 10d. for Easter offerings, in addition to his tithes. He declared that this was a tax never imposed on him before, and he would not pay it. The warrant for attaching his goods, process and all, swelled the amount to 11s. 10d., which the magistrates took *in dried bacon.* This was done by the agent of the Vicar of Almondbury, Rev. Lewis Jones.

The claims of the Church are never outlawed, although not enforced for years before. Unless they can be shown to have been abolished before the year 1180, they can be enforced with the certainty of being collected. Thus any titheable property, that has been suffered to go exempt for a long period, can be subjected to the tax when the clergyman pleases. These clergymen cannot even pay for the washing of their own surplices—the poor Dissenting minister, himself, is equally subjected to all these taxes with his own people.*

them one morning, as a friend entered to solicit charity for a family in distress ; what they had was freely given. After the person was gone, they spoke of the trials to their feelings they often experienced, of not being able to select for themselves the objects of their benevolence, rather than have those objects dictated by ecclesiastical law.

* Colton tells a story of a rector, who one morning made, what he professed to be, a *friendly* call upon a Dissenting clergyman who happened to reside in his own parish. The Dissenter was pleased to receive the call, since he hoped from the bland address of the rector, that he designed to open friendly intercourse with him, which had never before been extended, although he had lived for years in his immediate neighborhood. The Dissenter showed him his grounds, and took great pleasure in displaying his little premises and giving

VI.

OCTOBER 1, 1841 : "The Norwich Society for the Propaga-
tion of the Gospel in Foreign Parts," Lord Wodehouse in
the chair, was broken up by a Chartist mob. As one of the
clergy stepped forth to appease the tumult, he was hailed with
the shout, "*we want more bread and fewer priests.*"

In that shout was manifested the prevailing spirit of the mass
of the English nation, towards an institution which, for ages,
has over-shadowed the people with its magnificence and oppression. Everywhere in Christendom, the people are beginning to discover that they have long been robbed of the choicest
gifts of heaven. That not only have they been made uncom-
plainingly to surrender the fruits of the earth to the tyrannical
grasp of power, but that Christianity itself, the kindest and
best provision heaven has ever made for the souls of men, has
been turned into an instrument for his more complete degradation. The *poor* of England hate the *Church of England.* Its
magnificent churches and cathedrals are left vacant, and while the

him a history of his improvements. "There is about half an acre as you see,"
said the Dissenting minister ; "half of it is ornamented, where I take pleasure
with my thirteen children, and the other half furnishes vegetables to feed them.
You would hardly believe it, but this little patch, under the culture of my own
hands, goes a great way towards supplying the table of my numerous family."
"Indeed, sir. And how many years has it been so productive ?" "Some half
a dozen or more." The vicar confessed himself greatly pleased, and having
ascertained all he came there to know, withdrew, wishing his Dissenting brother
a "good morning."

Now for the result ! Immediately after, the rector's steward sent to the Dissenter's study a bill for tithes on the little garden of £6, or nearly $30 per
year, for six years previous, and the same for the then current year, amounting
in all to $200. The rector was a single man, and had a large salary. The
Dissenting clergyman had a family of thirteen children, and a small congregation, who could afford him with the greatest economy but a slender support.
But the tyranny of the English Church is such, there was no relief for the outraged man. To pay this large bill, swept away every comfort he had gathered
around him, and reduced his cheerful family to want and sorrow. And yet
this is " Apostolical !"

jewelled priests minister at the altars, humble dissenting chapels are crowded. In the time of our Saviour the rich were the enemies of the Church—the poor *now ;* the titled and the luxurious are its advocates and supporters, and the lower classes its antagonists.

It may be well to inquire into the cause of this growing hatred of the poor towards the Established Church ; why it is that "more than one-half of the whole number of those who profess serious religion" (Dr. John Pye Smith) prefer to withdraw from the establishment, and worship within humble chapels, while they not only bear the burden of maintaining their own services, but are just as heavily taxed to support the Church of England as her own members. Why it is, that dissenters are continually and more rapidly increasing in power, wealth and influence ; why it is, then, when the bishop dashes by with his gorgeous equipage, the starving wretch, as he shakes the dust of the chariot from his tattered garments, murmurs to himself, "this splendor costs the sweat and toil and famine of me and my brethren." "Why is all this?" "There is a reason for it somewhere." Christ came to the poor. The neglected multitude, the starving widow, the abandoned leper, were his associates. The haughty priests shook their mitred heads at him, and called him a *friend of publicans and sinners.* The elevation of the mass was the grand design of the Saviour and his religion—he came to heal the broken-hearted—to preach deliverance to the captive. Ancient philosophers and heathen priests had passed unheeded by the lowly dwellings of the poor and forsaken, but the Son of God proclaimed himself the restorer, the comforter, the brother of all earth's neglected children. Feeling that their deliverer had at last come, they crowded around him, caught hold of his garments, pressed upon him in his retirement, and wept at his feet, as the Gospel with its new and abundant consolations was spoken in their ears.

All this is felt by the despised and depressed classes, and if they have read their Bible. or heard its truth preached, how can they help contrasting "The MAN of sorrows," "The FRIEND of the poor," as he wandered in poverty through the valleys of Canaan, seeking out the dwellings of the suffering, satisfied with the shelter that covered them from the storm, if he could pour light and consolation into their souls—with the proud prelate, who rolls up in his stately coach to the House of Lords to vote against reform, or to the doors of the massive cathedral, where, once a year, he tells the few noble hearers gathered there from the fox-chase, that the Dissenters are very great sinners—that the Corn Laws are a great blessing to the country, particularly to the poor; and that he (the speaker) can trace back the office of bishop in one unbroken chain to the chair of St. Peter. It would be strange if the poor should not institute the comparison—it would be still stranger if they should see much resemblance between the carpenter's son with his twelve fishermen, and the Primate of all England with his princely bishops.*

---

* To the *poor* of England, as the depressed and neglected multitude, the Established Church does *not* preach the Gospel. Within its pale little provision is made for them. They feel this, and they feel it deeply. So apparent is all this to casual observers, that foreigners often speak of the absence of the poor from the churches. In M. Leon Faucher's *Etudes sur l'Angleterre*, the author, a late minister of State in France, says: "Place yourself on Sunday, in the midst of Bridgate Street in Leeds, of Mosely Street in Manchester, of Lord Street, or Dale Street, in Liverpool; what are the families whom you see, walking to the churches silently and gravely? It is not possible to deceive oneself; *they belong almost exclusively to the middle classes.* The operatives remain on their doorsteps, where they collect in groups, until the services in the churches being concluded, the taverns will open. Religion is presented to them with so sombre an aspect and with such hard features—she affects so well not to appeal either to the senses, or to the imagination, or to the heart—that it ought not to be a matter of surprise if she remain the patrimony and the privilege of the rich."

Mr. Kay, in speaking of the neglect of the religious education of the poor, says: "We want a class of clergy who could enter *daily* into the lowest haunts without disgust, and with whom the poor could converse *daily* without shyness or fear, and to whom they might relate their troubles without difficulty, and with a certainty of being understood and of meeting with sympathy.

"The greatest part of the poor of our towns are now never visited by a religious minister, or are visited so seldom, that the minister always enters as a

VII.

CHRISTIANITY is the purest democracy on earth. Man as a living soul, and not as a noble or a king, receives its attention. It seeks the greatest happiness of the greatest num-

stranger. Even when the poor man is visited by a clergyman, it is by a man of so strangely different a rank of life, that the poor man knows his clergyman cannot comprehend his peculiar wants or difficulties. The clergyman is, therefore, received with shyness, and with the constraint which the visit of a great and wealthy man always inspires in the house of a poor and humble one. As the operatives in Lancashire are in the habit of saying, "there is no Church in England for the poor; there is only a Church for the rich."

"How seldom, too, in the course of a year, are the poor of the cellars, garrets, or lodging-houses of the towns, visited by any religious minister! How often are these poor creatures never visited at all! And yet, how else is religion to be spread among the masses of our town poor? Sermons will not do it. Constant personal intercourse between the ministers of the Church and the poor can alone succeed in effecting this result. That intercourse under the existing state of things is often quite impossible. The number of clergy is too small. The social rank of the clergy is too much removed above that of the poor. Another class of clergy is required. Most of the town churches, too, are virtually closed to the poor. Go into the churches and see how little room is reserved for the poor. It is as if the churches were built exclusively for the rich; and as if the English Church thought it was of much less importance, that the poor should enjoy the consolations of religious worship, than that the rich should do so. In the Roman churches, there are no closed pews and reserved places. In their churches all men are treated as equals in the sight of their God. In the Roman churches, the poor are welcomed with an eagerness, which seems to say—the church was meant especially for such as you; and in the Roman Church, many of the priests are chosen from the body of the poor, in order that the ministers of religious consolation may be able the better to understand the religious wants of their poor brethren.*

"Let the English Church take warning. In these democratic days we want

* In illustration of this, I quote from the *Roman Catholic Directory* for 1865, to show how rapidly the Catholic Church is gaining in Great Britain.

"The issue of the *Roman Catholic Directory* for 1865, under the authority of the late Cardinal Wiseman, gives a concise view of the progress of the Church of Rome in England and Scotland during the past year, and especially its progress in London. The ecclesiastical staff immediately under Cardinal Wiseman, numbers no fewer than one thousand, three hundred and thirty eight priests (including seventeen bishops) for England, and one hundred and eighty-three priests for Scotland, (including four bishops) making a total for Great Britain of one thousand, five hundred and twenty-one priests. There is thus an increase during the year of no fewer than seventy-one priests in England, and five in Scotland—in all, seventy-six. In Eng-

ber. In its light the peasant and the monarch stand on the
same level. Now the simple reason why the lower classes hate
the Church of England is, that it reverses the entire spirit of
Christianity. It opposes the progress of the democratic principle, in which they and the world are so deeply interested. It
is the most oppressive aristocracy in England. Its exclusiveness and pomp equal that of the nobility ; while the tithes and
taxes it wrings from the poor man, who is struggling to live,
render it more obnoxious than the hereditary Aristocracy itself.
Wherever new churches rise, new burdens are created for the
people around them. And the clergyman who issues his war-
rants on Saturday, to force the collection of his tithes, is not
very likely to win the poor man's heart to love of that Saviour
who came to preach the Gospel to the poor, without money and
without price.*

institutions for the poor ; and especially do we want religious institutions for
the poor ; and it is partly because we have in our towns no Church, no religious
ministers, and no effective religious ministration for the masses of the poor, that
they are still in so wretched a condition."

* In Ireland this oppression is not borne with so much moderation. England
has been obliged to keep a standing army there to execute her injustice. Lord
John Russell declared, that without this army not a penny would be collected
from a single Catholic in Ireland for the support of the Church.

The Irish blood is often too hot to submit tamely to these violations of home
and property : this enormous tax to support what they most bitterly hate. Who

land, there are nine hundred and forty-one churches and stations; in Scotland, one hundred
and ninety-one, making in all, one thousand, one hundred and thirty-two. Thus, there is an
increase of thirty-four churches in England, during the year. There are also fifty-eight monasteries in England. There are none avowedly as yet in Scotland. There is an increase during
the year, of two of these institutions. There are one hundred and eighty-seven nunneries in
England, and fourteen in Scotland : in all, two hundred and one, showing an increase during the
year, of five in England, and of one in Scotland. There are ten colleges in England and two
in Scotland, which is the same number as last year. Cardinal Wiseman, in order to illustrate
to his audience at Mechlin, the progress of his operations in London, showed the number of
churches, nunneries, monasteries, hospitals and orphanages, for 1829, 1851 and 1863, and, bringing down these figures, so far as we can with certainty, to the present date, we see the more
readily, the steady and rapid progress which the Church of Rome is making, especially in the
metropolis of the kingdom :—

Years.	Churches.	Nunneries.	Monasteries.
1829	29	1	0
1851	46	9	2
1865	117	31	15

I wage no war against Episcopacy, nor against the religious doctrines of the Church of England. Nor do I apply any of

that ever read it, has forgotten the slaughter of Rathcormac? Having procured a military force from the government, Archdeacon Ryder headed the troops himself, and led them down to the cottage of widow Ryan, to force the collection of £5 tithes, which she had not paid because she could not. It was regarded by the populace as a barbarous cruelty upon a poor widow, and they pressed him to desist. "He gave orders first to draw swords, next to load, and at last to fire. He was obeyed. Nine persons were killed, and as many wounded."

There were 2,900 Catholics in the parish, and only twenty-nine Protestants, and half of these were members of the Archdeacon's family. The tithes of the parish were between $7,000 and $8,000 a year. The "Minister of the Cross" shot down more persons than his whole congregation amounted to, exclusive of his own family! The heart-sickening details of the widow searching among the dead bodies for her son, her finding him with his mouth open and his eyes set in the fixedness of death, the closing of his eyes, and the arranging of the body in the decency of death, amid the blood where he lay, are all too terrible to be minutely described! Another widow had two sons killed in this ecclesiastical slaughter. "When their lifeless, but still bleeding bodies were brought into her house, she threw herself on them, and exclaimed, in Irish, 'They are not dead, for they are giving their blood.'" And when the terrible truth forced itself on her that her noble boys were no more, she went mad!

This bloody massacre was to get £5 worth of corn, due to the Archdeacon for tithes. Stanzas have been composed to commemorate the bloody scene, which shall yet be sung at the funeral of the Church Establishment in Ireland. The last verse runs thus—

> "The widow knelt, and she muttered low,
> ' On the men of Rathcormac, wo! wo! wo!'
> The curse of the widow who shall bear:
> God of the childless, hear her prayer!"

He will hear it, or the Bible is a fable, and Heaven a lie. The song will be incorporated in the barbaric literature of the lower classes of Ireland. The fearful tragedy shall be handed down from generation to generation, making each Irishman a sworn Hannibal to the English Church until it is overthrown. It shall yet ring in their wild battle cry as they pour on their foes. That murder scene shall be emblazoned on their banner, and nerve many a heart to deeds of wilder strength, long after the descendants of him who committed it shall have crumbled to dust. Cowered by the tremendous physical force that continually frowns on them, they remain silent. Yet each of these deeds of oppression and murder is treasured up in their hearts, handed down from father to son, and waits the day of vengeance! Whether Ireland shall ever be free and independent or not, we cannot tell, but that she will have a bloody reckoning with England, unless her oppressive hand is removed, we cannot doubt.

my remarks on the Church of England to the Episcopal Church of this country. That Church I honor.* But the unholy alli-

* Among the rare instances in which American citizens in foreign countries have disgracefully turned their backs on the spirit and principles of their Institution, was a distinguished American Bishop of the Episcopal Church. At a sumptuous banquet of Prelates of the Church of England, the following toast was proposed in honor of the guest—the American Bishop:

"The Right Reverend Dr. ——, Bishop of —— ——, and the Church in America," with " three times three."

In a speech replying to this toast, the Bishop says: "The Church in America stands unsupported, unconnected with the State. I need not draw any comparison. I hold it to be your great privilege that your Church and State are connected, and inseparably connected, as I believe and hope, in God's name, for ever." (Cheers.)

How the Bishop could thus coolly record his own shame, his falsehood to his country, and his puerile servility to the prelates who flattered him, is to me quite astonishing. I make no comments on this strange paragraph. I only say to those of my countrymen who regard a union of Church and State as one of the greatest calamities that could befal us, *Keep your eye on such men !*

Yet all this, anti-republican as it is, we could have passed without notice, and only pitied the bigotry and servility displayed in it. But there is one thing not to be pardoned, and which will awaken the indignation of every man who has a drop of the blood of the Puritans running in his veins. In a speech made by the Bishop in St. Mary's Hall, Coventry, is found the following remarkable passage, which I have taken the liberty to underscore:

"I have lived in a land peopled by those who emigrated from this country. It is the *fashion* to call *some* of them the Pilgrim Fathers—men who *fancied themselves somehow straightened* in the enjoyment of religious liberty—who, in the claim of greater freedom in God's worship and service, set out for distant shores, and planted themselves in a region now called New England: I enter not into the inquiry as to the *character of these men, the justice of their complaints,* or the *motives* for their proceedings—*I will accord to them all that charity can ask.* They went from here, as they thought, and truly believed, the true followers of the Gospel of Jesus Christ; preaching, *as they thought,* the very principles of the Reformation—but without a Church—without a Liturgy,—*with no transmitted authority from God to administer in holy things.*"

The result of this sacrilegious invasion of the prerogatives of the Church, he makes to be the prevalence of "Unitarianism, Atheism, and Pantheism, in New England."

Now, I venture to say, that no native-born American, for the last seventy years, has dared to utter so contemptible a *sneer* at the Pilgrim Fathers; and yet he is "willing to accord them all that charity can ask." And what "charity," Sir Bishop, do the Pilgrim Fathers ask of *you?* Charity ! No other Ameri-

ance of the Church with the State—the corruptions and oppressions that have grown out of that union, and, above all, the

can has been found so false to his country, and those who left him the rich heritage he enjoys, as not to render them a proud and cheerful *reverence.* Charity
from a Bishop of the Church of England to the Pilgrim Fathers!

You say it is the *fashion* to call *some* of them *Pilgrim Fathers,* intimating,
in no obscure language, that it is the *soubriquet* of the ignorant and the superstitious. You add, " Men who *fancied* themselves somehow straightened in the
enjoyment of their religious liberty." A *fancy* indeed, that cost them dear.
The war-whoop of the Indian—the roar of the wintry storm—a desolate unpeo-
pled continent, methinks were a sad relief from *fancied* wrongs.

Poor, credulous, superstitious men, to leave the bosom of the mother church,
whose *slightest* fault was that she was a *dry nurse!* You "will enter into no
inquiry as to the *character* of these men." Indeed! You will in charity for-
bear—with that species of insinuation which is the worst calumny's best weapon
—lest painful truths should be divulged! Meek minister of Christ, how much
you can overlook even when you cannot forgive! But seriously, Sir Bishop,
do you venture at this day to wag your mitred head at the "Mayflower," as she
struggles along the middle Atlantic, surrounded by all the terrors of the midnight storm? Can it be that insulting fling was meant for that frail, yet God-
protected vessel, as she rocks in Massachusetts Bay—her icy deck crowded with
men kneeling in solemn covenant with God, who, alas! had given them "no authority to minister in holy things." Poor deluded men! under *"fancied"*
wrongs they had fled to our inhospitable wilderness, and having "no authority
to minister in holy things" they must live without Christianity. No cathedrals
—no rich livings—no widow's tithes—no poor man's church rates—no fines on
the renewal of leases—no fox-hunting clergy—no starved curates—and above
all, no Bishops deriving their authority from St. Peter through *all* the Popes—
none of these things to constitute them a Church of the living God!

You have the honor, sir, of being the first one who has sneered at the Pilgrim
Fathers, while enjoying the priceless privileges of moral and political liberty
won by their blood. Far from my humble pen the presumption of undertaking
to defend these noble men! There are their graves, but the dead are not in
them—they live in the hearts of their countrymen. Around them cluster the
noblest associations of freedom. The civil and religious liberty they left us we
hold and will hold forever, though there are found men in our midst so false to
their birth, so servile to foreign despotism, as to talk depreciatingly of them, and
fulsomely, in a company of English hierarchs, about the glorious privilege of a
union of Church and State!

False-hearted American!—unworthy priest! Leave, then, a country which
reveres the Pilgrims, and abhors an " Established Religion" you esteem " so
great a privilege," and go back to the government you so congenially revere—
the institutions you so affectionately eulogize, and spend your sympathizing

Church as an enemy of the interests of the working classes ; as an adversary of the spirit of liberty in England, will have my uncompromising opposition.

There are many reasons why the Establishment is odious to the British people—many reasons why the poor hate, and will continue to hate it—many reasons why it should go down. It is one of the last strongholds of Feudalism ; and whatever may be the fate of the Government, the Establishment must be swept away, just as the Corn Laws were, and for the very same reason. It is a strong bulwark I know ; it has gathered round it the patronage, the wealth, and the power of ages ; and it will struggle hard before it gives over the conflict. But it is now drawn into the field, and there is no retreat from the final battle ; neither is the issue doubtful. For a spirit has been awakened in our times among the masses, which has always in past times been confined to a few—a spirit which will not brook the despotism that has hitherto controlled the world—a spirit that clamors for change, because change is necessary to the advancement of the race ; a spirit which has given birth to the grand improvements which have marked the progress of modern civilization, and which is determined to blot out every vestige of that vast prison-house, in which humanity has slumbered in darkness and chains for thousands of years.

prayers for a Tory ministry which you boast your Church brought into power, for they will in return plunder the poor of the realm, and tax the starvation of dying thousands and tens of thousands, to fill the insatiate pockets of the order, of which nature so admirably fitted you to be a member and an ornament !

I have thus spoken of the Bishop's remarks, to show the spirit of aristocratic hatred to free institutions that pervades the Established Church. If these be its exhibitions in an American, nurtured and bred in the principles of liberty, overcoming even the love of his native land, what ought we to expect from those who are instructed in the principles of aristocracy, strengthened by love of country ? Just what has been described in the body of this work—oppression of the poor—contempt of their rights—worldliness and irre'igion. In England we fear them not. In this country, as that Bishop will find, a mitred head can poorly sustain the withering scorn the sons of the Pilgrims will pour on their heads, for such base betrayal of them in the land of their oppressors.

VIII.

REASONS are plain why I say that the crisis of the Established Church is at hand. *First.* The well-known and acknowledged fact, that it is a system of corruption, aristocracy and oppression. Of *corruption*, in that the hierarchy riot on the millions wrung from the laborer, and the ecclesiastical emoluments, being in the patronage of political men, are very often bestowed upon persons destitute either of piety or morality. Of *aristocracy*, in that the bishops are, *ex-officio*, members of the House of Lords, peers of the realm, and, of consequence, identified with them in all their interests, feudal tastes and overbearing pride ; and of *oppression*, in that they receive immense revenues from the people, and roll in wealth, while the flock to which they are overseers, pine in want and poverty. *Second.* That all this is for the first time being understood in its true character by the middle and lower classes of England.

A lie may long survive if it is believed to be a truth ; but a *known lie* must be overthrown. The Church of England, then, as it stands connected with the civil government, constituting part of the oppressive system that bears so heavily on the multitude, and with whose fate seems interwoven the *fate* of the government, claims our particular attention. For the person who wishes to understand the workings of the social system in England, and ascertain, with what accuracy he can, the probable issue of the crisis England is approaching, must not overlook in his estimate an institution of such enormous power—one so intimately allied with the civil and social structure of the nation—as the Established Church.*

---

* The assertions I have made above in regard to the Church, would be evident enough from her constitution and practice. It started in sin. Henry VIII. was its founder ; and if "a corrupt tree cannot bring forth good fruit," we should not expect anything but evil from such a stock. The history of the rupture between England and Rome, *misnamed the Reformation,* is a curious affair ; and into it we shall not go very minutely. It is perfectly understood

IX.

PERHAPS the chief merits of this question will be found fairly illustrated, in the following extracts from *My Private English Diary*, containing an account of an interview with John Thorogood, who had been "made an example of," to vindicate the right of the Church of England to force British subjects to pay their money to support a religious establishment which they condemn and abhor :

CHELMSFORD, *July*, 1840.

Yesterday I came to this place, which is thirty miles northeast of London, chiefly to see John Thorogood, who is a victim of the tyranny of the Established Church. I have spent several hours with him in the Chelmsford Jail; and I have seen no man for a long time for whom I feel more sympathy and admiration. I found my way to the jail, and asked permission to see Mr. Thorogood. The keeper reluctantly turned the key and unbarred the door.

by all parties, that this rupture was merely the effect of an amorous passion on the part of the English monarch. In other countries the Reformation originated with the people; but Henry, under scruples of conscience (says Rotteck, the keen-sighted German historian), wished to separate from his wife, Catharine of Arragon, the widow of his brother Arthur, who was growing old, in order to marry the beautiful Anne Boleyn, whose favor he was unable to obtain at a lower price. The Pope, chiefly from love to Charles V., opposed the divorce, which Henry then caused to be pronounced by his pliant clergy. This step was followed by the Papal excommunication, and a complete rupture with Rome. Such was the origin of the Church of England; and as if it were not incongruous enough to have a church start from such a source, in the first grand article it constituted the *king its head*. A Henry VIII., a Charles II., a George IV., the representative of Christ on earth ! The greatest *murderer* that ever escaped from the gallows; the most corrupt *libertine* that ever filled the royal palace with courtezans; the most profligate and heartless man of his time, the representative of the immaculate Son of God ! Nominating all the bishops, possessing thousands of livings, and convoking and dismissing synods at his royal pleasure ! From such bold encroachments in the outset on the simplicity and purity of the Apostolic Church, we should expect to find a secular, selfish establishment, acting not for the poor but the rich; not for the elevation of man, but his more complete subjugation. Commencing in pride and lust, it would necessarily live by extortion, and end in oppression. The extortion of the Church is seen in its enormous REVENUE.

"Yes, sir," said he, "you must come in, I suppose, but I wish the authorities would take this Thorogood away; for once in a few minutes, day after day, and month in and month out, some one comes to the door, 'Can I see John Thorogood, sir?' 'Can I see Mr. Thorogood, sir?' 'I have come to see this famous Thorogood;' and I have got sick of his very name. Why, if you were to stay here one week, you would think there was nobody in all England worth seeing but John. But I don't complain of him or his wife—*that's* all well enough; still I don't want to be bothered with John any longer."

The jailer led me to Mr. Thorogood's apartment, and I introduced myself. He seemed to be about thirty-five or forty years old, with a stout and well-made person. His countenance wears a kind but resolute expression, and his forehead denotes a considerable degree of intellect. He is a mechanic, and has always moved in the common walks of society; but he is a man of extraordinary intelligence and great firmness of character. I told him that I had come to Chelmsford to see him; that I considered him a persecuted man, and wished to know something of his history.

"Yes, sir," said he, "I *am* a persecuted man, and I thank you for coming to see me. I am an obscure and unworthy individual, but the Providence of God has placed me in circumstances very trying, and I have endeavored to act like a freeman in Christ. I said I was glad to see you, and I am; and I thank you for the sympathy you manifest in my behalf: not because I begin to grow irresolute and faint-hearted; for I should be just as firm, I think, if I stood alone; but then, you know, it does one good to see the face of a friend, and take hold of his hand, when one is in trouble or persecution for conscience' sake.'

"How long have you been confined here, sir?"

"Eighteen months, sir; and all for what some consider a very small matter. They say, John Thorogood had rather lie in jail eighteen months than pay five and sixpence Church rate. Just as though I cared anything for that five and sixpence. Why, I will give any of those gentlemen half a sovereign or more at any time for a good cause; but I am not in Chelmsford Jail for five and sixpence at all. I am here because I will not surrender my liberty of conscience. That is the highest and most inviolable of all human rights. I can bear oppression until you invade the sacred ground of native moral rights; and then I cannot, and will not, give way to the wicked claims of despotic civil rulers.

"But I will tell you something about the history of this matter, and then you can judge for yourself. I am, as you well know, a dissenter. For many years I felt it my duty to oppose the Established Church. I wept over its corruptions, its abuses of power and truth, its tyrannical oppressions of the consciences of good men ; and still I paid my Church rates, although I received no advantages whatever from the institution I supported. I regarded this payment of Church rates rather as a civil duty.

"But after suffering a good many trials of feeling, at last I became satisfied it was wrong for me in any way to give my countenance to the Establishment, and I refused to pay five and sixpence Church rate. I was summoned before the Ecclesiastical Court to be tried, and, of course, condemned by my enemies ; for in England, when the Church prosecutes a suit at law, you must know that they are both judge and jury. I thought and prayed over the matter, and concluded it was best for me to pay no attention to it.

"The result of it all was, that for contempt of Court, as it was called, I was thrown into this jail, the 16th of January, 1839, where I have remained ever since, and where I will remain till I die, rather than surrender the principle for which I am contending. That principle is no less than that for which Protestant reformers in all ages have contended ; the very principle for which England broke away from her allegiance to Rome ; for which Huss and Jerome, and ten thousand others, went to the stake ; the same principle for which John Bunyan lay twelve years in Bedford Jail ; the greatest, the dearest principle for which man ever contended—the high and sacred right of conscience.

"I cannot believe that I owe religious allegiance to any man : God is my only master. No man, or body of men, have a right to place any restrictions upon my religious liberty. The free exercise of conscience in matters of religion is a right which man can neither give nor take away. Religion is sacred to conscience ; conscience is sacred to God, and all human interference is sacrilege. Religion is seated in the will ; it is essentially voluntary ; exaction either of profession or payment is destructive of it. To establish religion by law, is first to corrupt and then to destroy it. The Established Church is one of the greatest structures of wrong the world ever witnessed. Why, who does not see this ? it is as plain to me as a self-evident truth.

X.

" THE other day Sir Robert Inglis, the zealous advocate of the High Church party in Parliament, came to pay me a visit ; and I asked him a few questions which perhaps he did not expect, for he was not exactly prepared for them. I said to Sir Robert : 'Is it not a wrong to refuse Dissenters interment in the national burial-grounds, except their friends are willing to have the deceased Dissenter give the lie in his death to all he had said and done while living, which he would do if he consented to be buried with the forms of the Church ? Is it not wrong to exclude him from the national schools and universities, except he conform to the Church ? Is it not wrong to compel the Dissenter to contribute to support a Church which he conscientiously disapproves ? Is it not an act of oppression, the greater because it comes from the stronger and wealthier party, and because, too, he has to support his own Church ?

"'And is not his Church as dear to him; are not his Church privileges, his liberty of conscience, the religious rites and worship of his own Zion, the affection and comfort of his pastor, and wife, and children, all as dear to the Dissenter's heart as to the churchman are his ? Do you not, sir, commit great wrong when you take from me those rights and privileges which you prize so dearly ? If the golden rule is to be our standard of action, you cannot outrage it more palpably, than by throwing me into jail because I will not quietly give away my highest rights as a man and a Christian.

"'Do I not suffer the greatest wrong, when any party seeks to prescribe to me in religion, either what I shall believe or how I shall express my faith ? Has not compulsory payment produced nearly all the evils which the best friends of the Establishment acknowledge and lament ? Has it not placed its ministry beyond the wholesome influence of the people ? Has it not dishonored religion by making the Church the creature of the State ? Has it not attracted the worldly, and the indolent, and the inefficient, to the Church as its ministers ? Who does not know that the Prayer-book contains little besides the Mass-book translated into English ? That the Pope offered to confirm it, if the Church of England would join that of Rome ? That Episcopal clergymen of great reputation have declared such a union of the two Churches practicable ? That the efficiency of Episcopal ordination is derived entirely through the Popish prelates ? That at the accession of Elizabeth, 9,011 Catholic priests, out of 9,400, joined the Church of England ? and who supposes that they gave up their Papacy by doing it ? The Papists and Protestants worshipped together in the English Church until they were prevented by the Pope; and at the Reformation, Parliament transferred the entire powers exercised by the Pope in this country to Henry VIII. and his royal successors.'

"I spoke to Sir Robert about a good many other things. I thought I would tell him something that he would not be very apt to forget; and I expressed myself with great freedom. There was a trap laid in London, by the High Church party the other day, and Sir Robert was sent down here, to spring it. My friends there had said, I was not comfortable here; and the Tories wished to get a confession from me, that I was. I had received intimation that I might expect certain persons down here, about the time of Sir Robert's visit, and I was on my guard when he came.

"He asked me, if I was not comfortable here. Said he, 'Mr. Thorogood, you seem to be surrounded by a good many conveniences and comforts.' 'No, sir,' I answered, 'I am not comfortable, and never can be, so long as my liberty is taken away. You degrade a man; you trample on a man's highest rights, and then ask him, if he is not comfortable.'"

XI.

"WELL, Mr. Thorogood, how long do you expect to remain here?" I inquired.

"That, sir, is a question I cannot answer. My friends in Parliament are constantly bringing the matter before the House; they are laboring manfully and zealously in my cause, and keep me advised of all their proceedings. I receive scores of papers and pamphlets on the subject. They will do all they can; but I do not expect relief for a good while. For if the Church party should give up, and consent to my liberation, they would abandon the whole question: they would never be able to heal the wound such a decision would inflict upon the Establishment.

"They are right in saying, 'The question is not whether we shall let an honest and worthy man go out of his prison and enjoy his freedom;' for they all would be glad, undoubtedly, to see me liberated; but the question is, 'Shall we surrender the rights of the Church? Shall we concede the great question of Church-rates tithes, and government patronage? If we let this man go, we must give up the Church; and the consequence of it would be, a dissolution of the union of Church and State.'

"It has always happened, I believe, that every great question which has ever yet been disposed of, has been settled in this way. Nothing has pained me so much as to see how insensible the great mass of the Dissenters are, to the infinite importance of this question. Why, sir, multitudes of them have come to me, and besought me to give it up; they said, 'Why, John, you are only *one* man!' So was Luther only *one* man; and suppose *he* had given up.

"Look back on the history of the world, and you will find that *one man* has worked a revolution. One man is enough to start a reform; but he must have help to carry it on. Oh! brethren, I say to them, if you would all come along with me; if the millions of English Dissenters would take the same stand that I have, what a spectacle would be presented! Why, we would gain our cause at once. To assert our rights would be, to secure them; it would be a pretty sight, surely, to see half the people of England in jail! Oh! would to God the faint-hearted and policy-bewitched Dissenters would go along with me. I want to see no violence; none is needed. We could dissolve the Unholy Alliance of the cross and the throne, as peaceably as we effected the revolution of 1688.

"It is a mystery which I cannot unravel, why the Dissenters submit to these abuses. They will get up great meetings; they will make enthusiastic speeches; they will write flaming pieces about the corruptions of the Church; they will clamor violently about *rights of conscience*, and yet not a soul of them has the courage to take the stand that poor, ignorant John Thorogood, the shoemaker, has. But they will have to do it before they ever get their liberty."

While he was speaking, his wife came into the room. "Here, Mary," said he, "I want to introduce you to Mr. ——. He lives in the United States, that blessed land, where there is no Established Church, no Church-rates or tithes, except what a man is willing to tax himself."

She is a very neat, pretty woman, and worthy to be the wife of John Thorogood. I asked her if she was not almost discouraged and disheartened.

"Oh! no, sir; far from it," she answered. "I was at first of a mind that my husband should pay the five and sixpence, and not go to jail; and it came very hard not to have him at home with us, nights; and I thought I could not bear up under it. But he talked to me a good deal; and we prayed about it; and at last, I could agree with him; and I feel now, that I would rather see John Thorogood die, than to give up his religion. He don't need any cheering up; his courage is as strong as it can well be. But if he ever gets down-hearted, I can raise his spirits for him. No, sir, he shan't give it up now. It's cost too much already, to have nothing come of it. I can come and stay with him from morning until nine o'clock in the evening; and the children can come too. We have a good many kind attentions from friends and strangers, and we are working for *liberty of conscience for all England*. No, sir, we can't give up."

XII.

IT was a sublime spectacle, to see two humble, simple-hearted Christians taking such a lofty stand: a spectacle which may challenge the admiration of the world. If I were an Englishman, I think I should be more proud of that sight, than of the glorious structure which they call St. Paul's Cathedral.

John Thorogood has all the elements of a reformer. If his learning and rank corresponded with his resolution, he would work such a revolution in England, as it is to be feared will be effected now only by violence. But, so long as idolatry of rank prevails so exclusively among all classes, it is out of the question; "It would be in bad taste" to let a man who has moved in John Thorogood's humble sphere, lead on a great reform. I must confess that I have seen no spectacle on this side of the water, which has so excited my surprise and indignation, as this. Let the world, who have so long dreaded the power of the English government, and admired its philanthropy in breaking the chains of negro slavery, and its zeal in sending missionaries to barbarous climes to tell the glory of the Saviour's love, contemplate the British lion with his paws upon John Thorogood, in Chelmsford Jail.

XIII.

BUT daylight is beginning to break over the gray battlements of this Feudal castle. The tramp of the gathering host comes on the listening ear of prayer and hope ; and soon —yea, those now living shall see it—the gloomy turrets of the Prison House of God's Poor shall reel to the shock of the Reformers, and the worn and weary prisoners shall come forth to bathe in the sparkling ocean of divine light and love, which is yet to roll round all the world.

What a vision of beauty and splendor will dear Old England then unfold to the gaze of nations—when " her officers shall be peace, and her exactors righteousness"—when her redeemed millions "shall call her walls Salvation, and her gates Praise !"

BOOK VI.

THE THRONE AND THE ARISTOCRACY

IN CONFLICT

WITH THE DEMOCRATIC SPIRIT.

CHRISTEN the babe, Archbishop proud,
  Strange servant of the lowly Christ,
Thousands are to *your* purse allowed—
  For *Him* the smallest loaf sufficed.
Though holy water's scanty now,
  My lord, you may dismiss your fears;
Take, to baptise the infant's brow,
  A starving people's bitter tears!
    Starvation Anthem for the Royal Christening.

In 1835, when Sir Thomas Potter represented to the Duke of Wellington the great distress of the manufacturing districts, and said, that if some remedy was not applied an outbreak would take place, the Duke replied, "*I have the means of putting that down.*"

Well may'st thou *stand*, when nations wheel
  Their cannon towards thy throne!
But when thy starving millions feel
  A foe in *thee* alone,
Nor throne, nor lords, nor martial power,
Can stand the onset of that hour.

Who can tell what dangers, and what calamities may lie hid within what remains of the present century! Who can tell how intense may be the distress, how fierce the animosities, or how unscrupulous the factions that may be let loose upon us.—*Edinb. Review.*

THE THRONE AND THE ARISTOCRACY.

I.

THE Throne is the fountain of all Rank and Power in the Empire. Whatever honor or emolument a subject may be clothed with, in the Church or the State, flows from the Supreme Head. Such is the theory of the British government, and such it has been since the Battle of Hastings, 1066, when William the Conqueror established the Norman Line on the Throne of England, and from whom Victoria (the fifth English Queen in her own right) traces her blood.*

---

* SOVEREIGNS OF ENGLAND SUBSEQUENT TO THE NORMAN CONQUEST.

Sovereigns.	Commencement of Reign.	Years of Reign.	To whom Espoused.	Where Buried,
NORMAN LINE.				
William I.........	1066	21	Matilda of Flanders...........	Caen, Normandy.
William II........	1087	13	.. ..	Winchester.
Henry I..........	1100	35	Matilda of Scotland..........	Reading.
Stephen..........	1135	20	Matilda of Boulogne..........	Feversham.
THE SAXON LINE RESTORED.				
Henry II..........	1154	35	Eleanor of Guienne...........	Fontevrault.
Richard I.........	1189	10	Berengeria of Navarre........	Fontevrault.
John	1199	17	Earl Montague's daughter..... / Avisa of Gloucester........... / Isabella of Angoulême........	Worcester.
Henry III........	1216	56	Eleanor of Provence..........	Westminster.
Edward I..........	1272	35	Eleanor of Castille............ / Mary of France...............	Westminster.
Edward II........	1307	19	Isabella of France............	Gloucester.
Edward III	1327	50	Philippa of Hainault..........	Westminster.
Richard II	1377	22	Anne of Luxembourg.......... / Isabella of France.............	Westminster.
THE LINE OF LANCASTER.				
Henry IV.........	1399	14	Mary Bohun.................. / Joanna of Navarre...........	Canterbury.
Henry V.	1413	9	Catharine of France..........	Westminster.
Henry VI.........	1422	39	Margaret of Anjou	Windsor.
THE LINE OF YORK.				
Edward IV........	1461	22	Elizabeth Woodville..........	Windsor.
Edward V.........	1483	..	.. ..	Unknown.
Richard III.......	1483	2	Ann Nevill...................	Leicester.

(241)

II.

NO queen was ever born to so magnificent an empire ; few have been more prosperous in their reigns, happier in their families, or more respected and beloved by their subjects. Once only has the shadow of death fallen on the brilliant family whose record is summed up thus :

THE QUEEN (Alexandrina) VICTORIA, Queen of the United Kingdom of Great Britain and Ireland, only daughter of his late Royal Highness Edward, Duke of Kent, born May 24, 1819, succeeded to the throne on the decease of her uncle, King William IV., June 20, 1837. Proclaimed, June 21. Crowned Sovereign, at Westminster, June 28, 1838. Married, Feb. 10, 1840, at the Chapel Royal, St. James', to her cousin, Field-Marshal, His Royal Highness Francis Albert Augustus Charles Emanuel, Duke of Saxe, Prince of Saxe Cobourg and Gotha (b. Aug. 26, 1819, d. Dec. 14, 1861), K. T., G. C. B., &c. *Issue*—I. VICTORIA ADELAIDE MARY LOUISA, Princess Royal, b. Nov. 21, 1840, m. Jan. 25, 1858, Frederick William, Crown Prince of Prussia, K. G. *Issue*—1. Frederick William Victor Albert, b. Jan. 27, 1859. 2. Victoria Elizabeth Augusta Charlotte, b. July 24, 1860. 3. Albert Wilhelm Heinrich, b. Aug. 14, 1862. 4. A Prince, b. Sept. 15, 1864. II. ALBERT EDWARD, Prince of Wales, b. Nov. 9, 1841, m. March 10, 1863, Princess Alexandra Caroline Maria Charlotte Louisa Julia, of Denmark, b. Dec. 1, 1844. *Issue*—1. Albert Victor Christian Edward, b. Jan. 8. 1864. III. ALICE MAUD MARY, b. April 25, 1843, m. July 1, 1862,

THE FAMILIES UNITED.

Sovereigns.	Commencement of Reign.	Years of Reign.	To whom Espoused.	Where Buried.
Henry VII	1485		Elizabeth of York............	Westminster.
Henry VIII......	1509	24 37	Catharine of Aragon.......... Anne Boleyn................. Jane Seymour................ Anne of Cleves............... Catharine Howard........... Catharine Parr..........	Windsor.
Edward VI........	1547	6	.. ..	Westminster.
Mary I............	1553	5	Philip, King of Spain.........	Westminster.
Elizabeth	1558	45	.. ..	Westminster.

THE UNION OF THE ENGLISH AND SCOTCH CROWNS.

Sovereigns.	Commencement of Reign.	Years of Reign.	To whom Espoused.	Where Buried.
James I...........	1603	22	Anne of Denmark............	Westminster.
Charles I.........	1625	24	Henrietta of France	Windsor.
Charles II.........	1661	24	Catharine of Portugal.........	Westminster.
James II....	1685	4	Anne Hyde.................. Mary of Modena.............	Paris.
William III....... } Mary II............ }	1689	18	Mary, daughter of James II...	Westminster.

THE UNION OF THE TWO KINGDOMS.

Sovereigns.	Commencement of Reign.	Years of Reign.	To whom Espoused.	Where Buried.
Anne	1702	12	George of Denmark..........	Westminster.
George I...........	1714	13	Sophia of Zell...............	Hanover.
George II.........	1727	33	Wilhelmina of Anspach.......	Westminster.
George III........	1760	60	Charlotte of Meklenbg. Strelitz	Windsor.
George IV.... ...	1820	10	Charlotte of Brunswick	Windsor.
William IV........	1830	7	Adelaide of Saxe Meiningen...	Windsor.
Victoria	1837	..	Albert of Saxe Coburg........	

His Royal Highness Prince Frederic William Louis of Hesse. *Issue*—1. Victoria Alberta Elizabeth Matilda Mary, *b.* April 5, 1863. IV. ALFRED ERNEST ALBERT, *b.* Aug. 6, 1844. V. HELENA AUGUSTA VICTORIA, *b.* May 25, 1846. VI. LOUISA CAROLINA ALBERTA, *b.* March 18, 1848. VII. ARTHUR PATRICK WILLIAM ALBERT, *b.* May 1, 1850. VIII. LEOPOLD GEORGE DUNCAN ALBERT, *b.* April 7, 1853. IX. BEATRICE MARY VICTORIA FEODORE, *b.* April 14, 1857.

III.

ARISTOCRACY AND ENGLAND :* they are synonymous terms, and they will remain so until the whole fabric of Feudalism is overthrown in the British Empire.

The House of Lords consists of 425 peers and 28 bishops. There are 14 peeresses in their own right, of whom 1 is a duchess, 3 countesses, and 10 baronesses. There are 22 Scotch peers, and 88 Irish peers, who are neither peers of Parliament, nor representative peers.

The House of Commons consists of 656 members—England having 498 : Scotland, 53 ; and Ireland, 105.

The Navy has 327 admirals, 782 captains, and 1,350 commanders.

The Army has 5 field-marshals, 71 generals, 139 lieutenant-generals, 361 major-generals, 900 colonels, 900 lieutenant-colonels, and 1,100 majors.

The Cabinet Ministers, the Judiciary, the Diplomatic Corps,

---

* *Debrett's Peerage* for 1865 shows that there are 24 dukes, 34 marquises, 197 earls, 57 viscounts, and 215 barons of the United Kingdom, 117 of whom are baronets, 430 have been married, the remaining 97 still being in a state of single blessedness; 80 have obtained academical honors at Oxford, whilst 50 have been receivers of the same from the sister university ; only 9 peers are in holy orders, 2 of whom are bishops (Bath and Wells, and Tuam, Killala and Achonry): 743 of the younger sons of peers have obtained honors of various distinctions, have had or still hold government appointments, or, like 974 of the daughters of peers, are married. There are only 14 peeresses in their own right. Last year there died 4 dukes (Athol, Newcastle, and the second and third Dukes of Cleveland), 1 marquis (Bristol), 8 earls (Aberdeen, Gosford, Poulett, Morley, Cadogan, Stair, Carlisle and Clare, this last title becoming extinct), 1 viscount (Sidmouth), 4 barons (Ashburton, Manners, Rodney and Somerville), 1 lord bishop (Ely), and one peeress in her own right (Ruthven).

the Chief Officers of India and all the Colonies—in a word, the enormous list of offices of emolument and honor throughout the British Empire are held or conferred by THE ARISTOCRACY. For this privileged class the Government exists, and for them *alone*. It is an Aristocracy pure and simple—not a Democratic element enters into it. It is the richest, the most powerful, the most splendid aristocratic organization of which we have any knowledge in human history. Nor is it possible to conceive a condition of society, or a series of events, that can ever produce its equal or its like on the face of the earth !

IV.

WHAT is this British Aristocracy made up of—princes and princesses of royal blood, dukes and duchesses, marquises and marchionesses, earls and countesses, viscounts and viscountesses, barons and baronesses, bishops, admirals, generals, ambassadors, lord-lieutenants, judges, governors, and members of Parliament ?

The answer is short. *They are the people that own and rule the Empire.* Nobody else has much to do with it. The fee-simple of most of the land is in the Nobility.

The family estates of many an aristocratic house cover immense regions, exceeding in extent ordinary German principalities, and yielding revenues far greater. The annual income of the Marquis of Westminster, who owns all that part of London in the vicinity of Euston and Berkeley Squares, is $5,000,000, and that of the Duke of Buccleugh, is half that amount ; that of the Duke of Roxborough, is $2,000,000. The Duke of Sutherland owns half of Scotland ; but his revenues are somewhat less than any of the above, since the greater portion of his lands are irreclaimably barren. Some idea may be formed of the resources of the Duke of Buckingham, whose estates and effects were sold at Richmond, from the fact that his liabilities were not less than £1,500,000.

Although the lords receive directly no compensation for

their services as the hereditary legislators of the realm, yet the immense patronage derived from their position is ten times more than equivalent. Through their influence they procure for themselves pensions of profitable places in the civil and military departments of the government, obtain commissions and preferments for their sons and nephews in the army and Church, and secure high and lucrative posts at Court for their wives and daughters. Out of the whole number of British peers, there are not fifty who do not themselves hold, or have not immediate relatives holding, valuable public offices. The Duke of Beaufort has a brother and an eldest son in the House of Commons, a son in the Life-Guards, nine brothers and cousins in the army, and three in the Church, and is patron of twenty-nine Church livings. The Duke of Bedford has two brothers in the House of Commons, a cousin who is Accountant-General of the Court of Chancery, eight brothers and nephews in the army and navy, and one brother in the Church, and is patron of twenty-seven Church livings. These two cases are proper samples of the character and extent of aristocratic patronage. It is true that military commissions are objects of sale in England, but yet it requires great personal influence to obtain them ; and the official staff of the army is recruited mainly from the sons, nephews, and cousins of peers, deprived by the laws of entail and primogeniture of their fair share in the family estates. The extent to which nepotism and personal favoritism in the distribution of public offices have been carried in America, has justly excited great complaint. But these things, as known among us, are mere child's play compared with what is practised in England. There they ramify through every sphere of the public service, civil, military and ecclesiastical ; and, what is worse, they are chiefly used to bolster up the family interests of a class whose wealth and other advantages, if rightly improved, would, without the aid of government, put within their reach every honorable station in professional or in public life.

The government of Great Britain is called a limited monarchy, but if it received its denomination from the predominant element in its administration, it would more truly be termed a limited oligarchy.   Practically, the Aristocracy is always more or less in submission to popular sentiment, but potentially they have the direction of public affairs in their own hands.   The majority of the Cabinet almost always consists of the peers of the realm.   Of the present Cabinet, with Lord John Russell at its head, one-half belong to the House of Lords, and every individual of the other half is connected either by birth or marriage with the peerage.   A majority of the seats of the Lower House, are, or at least may be, filled by the nominees of the Nobility.   The colonial governors, and the ambassadors at important foreign Courts, are almost universally selected from the ranks of the Aristocracy.

v.

THE peerage of England as a body, though there are many miserable and most disgraceful exceptions, are now of high personal character.   Even most of those who have no lofty guiding principle, have a quick sense of honor, and a scorn of base actions.   As a class, they are not corrupted by vice, nor are they enervated by that effeminacy which has sapped the strength of favored classes in so many other lands.   They are both intellectually and physically robust, and they share abundantly in all those qualities which are comprised in the expressive word *manliness.*   Most of them have undergone long discipline in the Senate or at the bar, or on the camp-ground, or the quarter-deck, and have thereby acquired the stamina of character which qualifies men for high posts and arduous duties, and which not " all the blood of all the Howards " would be able of itself to give.   No class of men in England have better developed physical organizations, while the beauty of English women of rank is incomparable.

The British nobleman has much of that chivalrous spirit which long descent through honored generations naturally inspires, with little of that over-bearing pride which springs from a contempt of inferiors. Arrogance and hauteur, a vain love of ostentation, and other like traits, are seldom among his characteristics ; on the contrary, his intercourse with the world is usually distinguished by courtesy, urbanity, generous confidence, and graceful simplicity. His ordinary personal appearance exhibits no mark of affectation. The relations that exist between the English Nobility and their tenants, are often of a friendly and pleasant nature, totally differing in character from the same relations in Ireland. The British proprietor generally feels a personal interest in his tenant; an interest founded in the fact that the ancestors of both have lived and died on the same hereditary domains. And this interest is not confined to the landlord personally ; it is not at all unusual to see his wife and daughters visiting the dwellings of his tenant, to mingle in his family joys and sorrows. Not a few noblemen build, at their own expense, schools and churches on their estates, and manifest some solicitude for the well-being of those subject to their influence. But they are perfectly innocent of any idea of raising the subjects of their benevolence beyond the doom of hard work and absolute dependence.

VI.

SUCH, however, is but the sunny side. Let us probe deeper, and come to the real essence and spirit of what British Aristocracy consists—what are their true feelings—what their determination. They are not ignorant of the burdens and distresses of the people, nor of their feelings and determination under their wrongs. They are aware of the rapid advances reform has already made, and the increased confidence of those who urge it. The encroachments on their ancient prerogatives and power are felt. The still more radical changes proposed, do not elude their scrutiny. Quiet and dignified as they may appear, they feel under their feet the mighty undulations of the mass on which they have so long trod. The ominous sounds arising from starving millions—the clear, practical language of men who have just learned both their rights and their strength, are not unheard by them; the perils with which they are be-girt, thickening every year, are not unwatched. They are also conscious that taxation, the cause of this discontent and suffer-ing, must be increased to meet the exigencies of the times, or their revenue decreased. Placed in this dilemma, beset by the dangers that are augmenting every hour, it is not to be sup-posed they are without feeling or purpose. Inaction is not to be entertained a moment. But the thought of surrendering their power, is repelled as equally unwise and unworthy. Too much pride, and too much interest, are involved in the surren-der. A reform thorough enough to allay the discontent of the people, and relieve their distresses, would deprive the nobility of their emoluments and influence, and tend to reduce them to the rank of citizens.*

The same spirit governs the Church, with her immense rev-enues. A certain Lord Bishop not long ago said, in Parlia-ment, " Reduce the revenues of the Church, and no man of rank will enter it." Self-interest holds the whole Aristocracy and Hierarchy together—a bond of union minor differences will never sunder. But united though they be by interest, and held together by love of rank and influence, yet different portions of them have very different anticipations, in view of the terrific and increasing struggle to cleave down the tree of hereditary despotism. One part, destitute of intellect and virtue, look back on the long unbroken family line, of which they form a

---

* When Lord Stanley, though willing enough to support reform in the corpo-rations, opposed all reform in the Church, one remarked: "It is very natural; for he would have to give up livings, worth £22,000, or more than $100,000, a year. The Duke of Rutland, in eighteen weeks, had drank in his house 200 dozen of wine, 70 hogsheads of ale—burned 2,330 wax lights—630 gallons sperm oil. In that time, there had dined at his grace's table 2,000 persons, 2,421 more in the Steward's room, 11,312, in the servants' hall, etc. The income of some of the richest noblemen in England is over $5,000 a day. Such estates will not be given up without a struggle.

part—its wealth and power—and fancy there can never be a change. Unable to appreciate the spirit of the age in which they live, thoroughly imbued with the spirit of feudalism, they look with ineffable disdain on the demands of the people. In the British realm it has ever been the duty of the people to submit to their aristocracy, and leave the laws and government to their jurisdiction. The power belonged to them, and the people had nothing to do but to obey, and receive what was given as the gracious benefaction of those who had an exclusive title to all the emoluments of the kingdom. It has been so for centuries ; and, arrogant and senseless, they vainly dream it can be so still. They forget that a change in the spirit and wants of the age demands, and will have, a change in its institutions. Magnified to themselves, and blinded by the glare of their own titles, they do not measure the full force that is bearing down on them. Wrapped up in the mantle of feudalism, they sit proudly within the crumbling structure, hoary with age, and gaze on the pictures, and heraldry and symbols, around them, till the past seems revived; and the wild uproar of the starving populace without is changed into the acclamations of humble and obedient serfs.

This class believe all reforms quite unnecessary. Why should they not cling to that which gives them rank and wealth? What has succeeded in the past, will do for the present. They verily believe the same relation that formerly existed between the lord and his serf to be the right one, and may still be preserved.

VII.

THIS stupidity seems impossible, amid the turbulent elements that are so rapidly assuming shape around them. But, it may be remembered, a title does not prevent a man from being a fool : nay, if he was half a one before, it immediately supplies the deficiency. The less wisdom he possesses, the more inflated he becomes with his rank, and the more profound his

wonder at the audacity of the starving wretches, presuming to
clamor for bread.   Among such men, notwithstanding his military genius and success, we should have placed the Duke of
Wellington ; unless we chose to explain his conduct, as some
others did, and regard him as returning to second childhood, his powers reduced and weakened by age.   On no other
ground can we account for the false and stupid statement, that
although he " deeply lamented the distress that prevailed in
some parts of the country, *there was no distress arising from the
want of food.*"   The noble Duke would probably not believe
there was a scarcity of food, till, like La Fayette, he was leading the National Guards against an army of women, besieging
the court and the palace, with that most terrific of all popular
cries, " *bread, bread.*"   On no ground but *half* idiocy could be
justified the declaration, " that the reduction of taxes had
been carried as far as it could be, and that of all the constitu-
tions ever devised by man, that of England, with the unreformed
Parliament, was the most perfect ;" or the still stranger language and cruelty to the Paisley operatives, who sent a depu-
tation to him, begging him to hear their complaints, and relieve
their sufferings, when he told them, he was not desirous of
hearing any such account, and that he was not one of her majesty's political advisers.   And yet, in anticipation of the approaching winter, he did advise her to prorogue Parliament.
This noble Duke refused to grant even his hearing to the petition of famishing men ; or reply to it in any other form, than by
telling them, he was not desirous of listening to the tale of
their woes !   He refused to extend even private charity, to
10,000 men, women and children, who were then living on a
penny-a-head per day—and yet the noble duke received annually
from his countrymen a stupendous income.   Such are still
the views and feelings of many of the nobility of England—
foolish, heartless and cruel as they are !   Such men, if left to
themselves, will never come to their senses till their castles are
on fire over their heads, and an infuriated and avenging populace is treading down their rich heritage in blood !   Such men

hold the offices in the royal gift, have a seat in the House of
Lords, and a vote on all measures of relief for the country.

VIII.

BUT there is another portion of the higher classes of England who possess clear heads and far reaching penetration. They see the unalterable tendency of things, and the
perils around them. These men, when in power, are the throne
and the government. The Queen is a mere wax figure in their
hands, the motions of which are governed by the wires they
hold. Men more entitled to rank for intellect, never existed.
Accomplished, learned and dignified, they reflect honor upon
the throne. They have carried England through storms that
made her reel, and lifted her out of abysses from which other
empires never emerged. It is true, love of rank, wealth and
power, holds them in subjection, but does not render them ignorant of the position they occupy. They are conscious of the
futility of resisting openly the encroachments of the spirit of
the age. They also see the danger to the present system of
government, in yielding to it. They know that any reforms
that would reach the people, to benefit them permanently
would in the end overset the entire aristocracy and hierarchy
of the realm. Many of the nobility are liberal and benevolent,
and would alleviate the distresses of the people by lightening
their burdens. They would consent to smaller incomes to remedy this horrible state of things—but they would give the people *bread,* and not *power.* Thus some of them voted against the
Corn-Laws, and commercial restrictions, while at the same time
they oppose granting the lower classes political privileges. Of
this number was Macaulay, who could once make Parliament
tremble at his eloquence, as he pleaded for the Reform Bill.

But their number is small. Most feel, that something even of
political power must be surrendered to still the increasing
clamors of the people, but how much, or rather how little, is the
question. What they give, they know they can never retake.

The little the people get, they will hold. Thus, to yield anything is to take a step towards that result which, of all things, they would escape, if yet anyhow possible.

But independent of the interests involved in this contest, they have no confidence in the sagacity or integrity of the people to select their own rulers, and devise plans for their own relief. They most sincerely despise any such pretensions on their part. This feeling of contempt belongs to the whole class. It is a necessary part of such distinctions in rank, for all the wisdom, learning and accomplishments of the nation, they believe to exist within their magic circle. This contempt of "the lower classes" is the most dangerous feature in the aristocracy of England. Sooner or later it will be visited upon them in returned contempt. The benevolence—the real kindness of a large portion—their abstract love of liberty, and their political penetration, would lead them to a more liberal course in the present crisis of affairs, were it not for this contempt for the *vox populi*. It makes them underrate the power of the poor millions, and hence feel less alarm than they ought. The following paragraph, published anonymously in England, is doubtless a correct exhibition of the feelings and policy of the Government.

" In the first place, that as no state of society is essentially and permanently durable, it is the wisdom of legislators to be aware of this tendency to alteration, and not too long to resist such remedies as the altered state of the country may demand.

" In the second place, that in all such changes, however, care should be taken to apply them only to undeniable and pressing exigencies—to avoid the use of all terms fitted to suggest or to foster the hope of universal alterations—and always to be aware that change is essentially of a restless and extravagant character, and constitutes one of the great dangers against which, in its extreme tendencies, the wisdom of legislation has been authorized to guard.

" And, in the last place, that as this desire for universal change is a morbid and delusive state of the public mind—

and has an essential tendency to defeat all the purposes at which it professes to aim—and in reality to render impossible any good and substantial improvement whatever, it ought to be treated as a malady of a peculiarly dangerous and insidious nature, and repressed by all the means which legislative wisdom can devise as best suited to the case. At the same time, as, from its nature, it is not a malady which can be met in most cases by violent remedies, it is best assailed by preventive measures, and among these, perhaps the chief is, the avoidance, on all occasions, of any such terms or notions as may beget the idea that all things are in a state to require alteration, and which, consequently, seem to consecrate the very work of destruction, by the fallacious and ambiguous terms that veil its malignancy."

IX.

THE practical maxims of the British government, however modified and explained, are all embodied in this short paragraph. Hence it is evident they never intend to grant the just demands of the people. Afraid to oppose them openly, they endeavor to accomplish their object by trickery and deception. They know that violent measures will excite violent measures in return. They also know that to yield to any one demand is to grant that reform is necessary; that this will awaken greater expectations and enlist stronger opposition. Their political skill and self-control prompt them to a middle course—to appear to grant while they really withhold; or if compelled to surrender, to do it with the plainest intimation that this is all that can, with any reason, in safety be permitted.

The English government must hold together *as it is*, or meet an entire overthrow. Lord Eldon was a consistent politician when he resisted *every* change, because he was aware all the English institutions hung together; that restrictions on trade could not be removed without giving commerce a prospect of ascendancy over the landed interests; and the landed interests could not be weakened without taking from the Church and Aristocracy their support.

This was true, but he looked on only one side of the question—what they were *losing*, and not on the fiercer opposition they were arousing by resisting reform—an opposition that might eventually scorn petitions and haughtily give commands. He looked on what was *assailed*, and not on *who* and *what* were assailing.

As an illustration of this contempt on the part of the nobility for the lower classes, exhibiting itself at every turn, and thus defeating their own plans by revealing the spirit that actuates them, notice the following extract from *Blackwood's Magazine*, which spoke the sentiments of the Tory party in eulogizing Metternich, the prince of aristocrats :

"The secret of his success as a minister seems to have consisted in being faithful to that conservatism which never failed any man who had the good sense to adopt, and the firmness to maintain it. *The march of mind, rights of the rabble, and the statesmanship of the streets, has been treated by Metternich at all times with due contempt.* He has not suffered popular clamor to extort a single concession, nor popular conspiracy to dictate to public council. If he had been minister of France ten years ago, he would have sent her rabble patriots to the dungeon, and saved the Bourbon throne. If he had been minister of England as many years since, he would have crushed the Whigs, silenced the roarers for reform, and by calling on the property of the country to protect itself, and the good sense of the nation to control the absurdity of the populace, he would have rescued us from ten wretched years of party strife and national humiliation ; from unequaled avarice of pelf ; from statesmanship which had no other object than office ; power exercised only for party ; economy which has added 7,000,000 to our public incumbrances ; *and reforms which menace us with a Republic.* He would be to our age, what Pitt was to that of our fathers."

X.

HERE is the true spirit of Toryism, exhibiting the hatred of popular rights which ministers veil under a treacherous smile. We might speak of the *expediency* of Metternich's policy even in Austria *in the long run*, for Metternich's policy cost Austria her magnificent empire in Italy after he was dead. *One* generation does not always settle the results of a bad principle. Truth can often afford to wait the adjustment of her claims, for " The eternal years of God are her's."

We might also speak of the difference between the middle and the lower classes of the two nations. But we are tempted to make a short quotation from the *father* of this Mr. Pitt, whom *Blackwood* places beside Metternich, who " *would have silenced the roarers for reform*," and treated the rights of the rabble with due contempt. In his speech on " Conciliation with America," the Earl of Chatham thus swoops on the Tory ministry who would preserve the Metternich policy of laughing down the popular cry of " No Representation, No Taxation." " Yet when I consider the whole case as it lies before me, I am not much astonished, I am not much surprised that men who hate *liberty* should detest *those who prize it:* or that those who want virtue themselves, should endeavor to persecute those who possess it. Were I disposed to carry this theme to the extent that truth would fully bear me out, I could demonstrate that the whole of your political conduct has been one continued series of weakness, temerity, despotism, ignorance, futility, negligence, blundering, and the most notorious servility, incapacity and corruption. On reconsideration, I must allow you one merit—a strict attention to your own interests, in which view, you are sound statesmen and able politicians. You well know that if the present measure (reconciliation with America) should prevail, that you must inevitably lose your places. I doubt much whether you will be able to keep them on any terms. Such, then, being your precarious situation, who can wonder that you should put a negative on any measure that must annihilate your power, deprive you of your emoluments, and at once reduce you to a state of insignificance, for which God and nature designed you."

XI.

NEVER was this language more applicable to the Tories than now. Well may they sneer at *the rights of the rabble*, and strive to *silence the roarers for reform*, when, if the Reformers prevail, *they* will be deprived of their emoluments, and a large, useless and indolent class be " reduced to the state of insignificance for which God and nature designed them."

Notwithstanding the universal distress everywhere unsettling society, and the no faint intimations of a fiercer storm discernible on every side, notwithstanding the sagacity and apparent concessions of Sir Robert Peel, we see the determination still is to resist the just demands of the people. Said the *Britannia* in reply to some alarm expressed by a Tory paper, that in consenting to any modification whatever in the Corn Laws, the Premier was giving up the interests of the Aristocracy : " We cannot bring ourselves to believe that Sir Robert Peel *ever* will give up a single iota of Conservative principle, although he may *accommodate agitators with some slight changes in the present tariff*. No ! Sir Robert knows his *own interests too well*." Yes, this is the policy. However Tories may tremble at the present posture of the government, nothing in the aspect of affairs seems so dreadful as an entire change in the system by which their rank, and wealth, and power, alone can be maintained. But this change they know *must* be the result if they yield to the spirit of reform, for the more it gets the more it asks, until the last abuse is rooted out. The past shows this to be their fixed purpose ; for *not a single reform has been granted willingly;* it has been wrested from them with the most painful difficulty, by the moral power of the people. The Catholic Emancipation Bill, which simply asked that a man's religious belief should not disfranchise him, was stormed all the way through Parliament. The unjust opposition to it arose, not so much from dislike to grant the Catholics of Ireland the rights of citizens, as from the fear of encouraging the spirit of Reform. The same fear fought the Reform Bill through both houses : nor would it ever have passed, even after being so mutilated and deformed that it was a promise without a fulfilment, *had not still greater fear seized the noble lords*. They found that a resolve, firm as their own, and backed by still greater and more desperate power, had been made that the Bill *should* pass.

The Tories would not have been so greatly opposed to some little alterations, provided the suggestion had come from themselves ; but if they began to yield to the people's demands, when and where should they stop ? The spirit which is abroad in the land, is an active and fearless spirit. This they know, and are also aware that the whole system by which their emoluments and power are secured, is one of corruption and oppression. They know too well the rottenness of the entire structure they have built for themselves, to expose it to the angry eye of an oppressed people. Therefore, however they may appear to concede and smile in great good will, behind it all is the fixed unalterable purpose to bury themselves in the ruins of their corrupt system, rather than surrender the rank and emoluments it confers.*

---

* In *My English Note Book,* for 1842, I find the following on the political character, position and policy of Sir Robert Peel and his party—

Toryism is now dominant in the British Empire. Sir Robert Peel is Premier of England. He furnishes another illustration of the feelings and designs of the more intelligent portion of the Aristocracy. Gifted with no ordinary sagacity, he finds himself encompassed with no ordinary difficulties. He does not expect, we imagine, to remove them, only to afford present relief. Holding not his rank by succession, but taken from the mass of English citizens, he understands somewhat the spirit and tendency of the age. Not like the thousand and one titled fools who verily believe the feudal age can be restored, and the people whipped back to their kennels, and the spirit of reform and democracy extinguished by force and formulas, he knows it is onward, with a power that nothing can stay. He sees too, that the financial condition of the country requires new taxes, and the removal of restrictions on corn. He knows that manufactures and com

XII.

SUCH were the views I expressed in the beginning of Sir Robert Peel. How far I forecast the inevitable result of affairs at the time, and how accurately I estimated the exigencies of his position, subsequent events determined. History, when truthfully written, is the safest of all tests to apply to human opinion. It was clear to my mind, in 1840, that Sir Robert Peel would be glad to take the reins of government, to extricate England from the embarrassments into which she was being hurled, by the imbecility and the reactionary policy of Melbourne; and one of the most singular phenomenon,

merce are declining, and that free trade alone can revive them. He knows that the intelligent part of the nation are in favor of radical alterations in the Tariff. He is also aware of the inequality and injustice of the present system of representation. Neither has he forgotten the history of the Reform Bill, and the danger of res'sting the popular will, beyond a certain point. He is conscious that Ireland cannot be governed by a Tory ministry, acting on Tory principles, and he does not attempt it. So far is plain—why not then do what a just policy demands? *He fears his party*, composed of high Tories, hierarchy, and the great landed interests. To remove commercial restrictions with a liberal hand, would give commerce an ascendancy over the latter. This would reduce the revenues of the landocracy, and through them the income of the Church. His party are jealous of these interests.

On the other hand, are an awakened and indignant people, declaring in no baby tones that it is better 30,000 land owners should be deprived of a few luxuries, than that twenty millions should lack the necessaries of life—should grow desperate with want, and send the torch of revolution through the land, or lie quietly down to be devoured by famine. He understands the import of this *people's language.* He knows that this at least is one of those cases in which words are indeed things. Thus he stands between two hostile parties, each menacing him with vengeance if he betrays their interests. He is truly to be pitied. No man in the empire possesses his powers—but they are not equal to the task before him. An impossibility he cannot accomplish. Yet he attempts it when he would silence the clamors of the people, and, at the same time, secure to the Aristocracy their privileges and power.

In this dilemma, knowing he cannot still the storm, and lay the tempest that is bursting over the land, by words, he declares a reduction in the Tariff necessary, and urges with all the power he can master his income tax through Parli-

even in English politics, exists in the fact that, while Sir
Robert Peel, and every other enlightened statesman in England, felt the necessity of adopting a more liberal and enlarged
policy in the administration at home, and in her relations
abroad, he was compelled, in order to get into power, to advocate doctrines far less liberal than he afterwards was forced to
carry out, when he became the pilot of the ship.

He defeated Melbourne in a fair battle, by bringing the question of Free Trade and Protection side by side in the struggle ;
and he, all the while, the advocate of the aristocratic side.
The cause of his victory was not because England wanted
more class legislation, or was in favor of conservative or Tory
principles ; for he was no sooner in office than he began a sys-

ament—boldly declaring that his party must accept his scheme *entire*, or find
another prime minister to do better for them if he can. But his Tariff Bill
will afford only partial relief, and the Income Tax will, *in the end*, come out of the
people. The land owner will pay it, and then reimburse himself, by increased
rent and reduced wages of his tenantry. Besides, it is designed only to meet
the *increased expenditure* of the government—*not to reduce the taxation* which
already crushes the people. It is as a substitute for *more* taxation, not to *lessen*
that which exists. His whole scheme is a *sedative* not a *cure*, and he knows it.
But he must do what he can. The increased expenditure must be met—the
slaughtered regiments in Affghanistan must be replaced. But the necessaries of
life have been taxed, he candidly says, all they can bear. The only resort, therefore, is to introduce an extraordinary *transient* remedy for a *permanent* and *a
growing* evil : and this is the end, even of Sir Robert Peel's statesmanship. This
trifling he must practice, or increase at once the burdens of the people ; or strike
at the entire system of oppression, and thus be hurled from the helm of government down to the ranks of the Chartists. To save himself and his party, and
in the meantime prevent insurrection and civil war, he endeavors to put off
the evils he cannot cure, and hopes that future remedies may be found for
future exigencies. *He* can take heed only for present—the future must take
care of itself.

Whatever convulsions are threatened in the future, the Aristocracy are determined to hold fast to their emoluments and power. The strongest of all motives,
personal fear, has failed to alter their determination. Yet they are troubled,
and dare not look the future in the face—hoping for some change—some relief
not now discernible ; they evade as long as possible the final struggle to which
the people are urging them. They forget that when a *forced* crisis comes it
always involves the destruction of those who neglected to provide for it.

tem of reform so gigantic, that even the Whigs themselves raised the cry of alarm, that the old landmarks were in danger of being swept away by this new freshet. He was the first statesman England has had since the time of Cromwell, who dared to follow out his honest convictions ; namely, that the labor of the country could endure no more taxation, and that the property of the nation, which had been so long protected into over-grown wealth, must begin to contribute a larger share towards the expenses of the administration.

With a stern courage he laid his Income Tax upon the rich with one hand, while with the other he relieved the poor of one of their enormous and insupportable burdens. It was with him, at all events, whatever were his motives, an earnest conviction that England had long enough tested the doctrine of protection, and that, bound under it, she had, by a long course of class legislation, legislated the few into princely wealth, and the many into abject wretchedness. England was starving, and the poor had been made, by centuries of oppression, so poor, that nothing more could be filched or sponged out of their emptiness. He was forced by famine, against which rounded periods and elegant appeals could furnish no remedy, to make a bold movement ; and, like a good hunter on the full run, leap the ditch. He astonished the Whig party and shocked his own, by coming out all at once with the proclamation of a principle, which none but Reformers like Cobden had dared to propose. He had been the pet and the hope of the landed aristocracy for years. At last he checkmated his antagonists, and satisfied the nation for awhile, by proclaiming the absolute necessity of removing all tax whatever from bread by unrestricted free trade in corn.

His opponents listened to the announcement with astonishment, and the Tories were petrified ; but, as a statesman, he stood at that time in a position which reminds one of Napoleon, on some of his early battle-fields, when the only means of safety were those counseled by desperation.

XIII.

SIR ROBERT PEEL knew what England must come to, and he dragged her to her destiny. It was a signal for the most malignant assaults from the high Tory party. His motives were assailed in all quarters. Even the Whigs, who had, in some of their more fanciful moments, dreamed of some such political millennium, traduced him for giving realization to their dreams ; and the *London Herald*, which took up the cause of a desperate Nobility, lashed the adventurous states-man furiously through a hundred malignant columns. But it was a brave act for all that ; and wherever he showed himself to the famishing multitude of England, his name called forth a shout which the people never send up to any but their bene-factors. All over the Continent this great man gave a new impulse to the cause of enlightened legislation, which it were vain to have hoped for from any other source. Before twelve months had elapsed, nineteen European States, and among them even the despotism of Austria, Russia, Sardinia, Naples and Rome had removed most, and in nearly every instance, all restrictions upon the free importation of bread. There was not a Cabinet in Europe whose policy was not affected by the action of the British Parliament ; and there was scarcely a hillside, even in far-off Italy, where the press had never yet swung its gigantic arms with freedom, that the peasant did not send up a shout of gratitude and honor to the great Eng-lish statesman, who had taken the foremost rank among the politicians of Europe, in the pathway of reform. Hencefor-ward humanity, or to use a less hackneyed phrase, *men* had begun to be regarded as items of more importance in the coun-cils of cabinets. Their hunger and their thirst began to occupy some space in the calculations of statesmen. The veriest slave journal of Austria began to discourse learnedly, of this new theory of freedom of intercourse between nation and nation, and between man and man. In a word, the whole Continent

felt the electric shock of that movement, and the abolition of
the Corn Laws was a greater triumph to the cause of freedom
in Europe, than has ever been achieved by any of the sanguinary battles that have drenched the bosom of the Old World
with human gore. Not long after this great reform in British
legislation, the Anti-Corn Law League, which had been struggling heroically for fifteen years or more, through gloom and
opposition, held their last great festival and sold off their
property at auction, because the business of the association
had ceased. The great object it had proposed to itself from
the time of its foundation had been victoriously achieved ;
there was nothing more to be done, and the instruments with
which the power had been wielded, that had produced the
effect, were put up under the hammer. Soon after this, Richard Cobden, the chief of this reform, and upon whom posterity
will gather the honors of its achievement, received the great
testimonial of the great British nation ; and he went upon the
Continent to recruit the vigor of fifteen years of exhausting
labors in the cause of the people. His journey through the
kingdoms was a complete triumph. Wherever he went he was
greeted by an ovation. Gifted, like most public men in Europe,
with that priceless grace—a knowledge of continental lan-
guages, he responded at all the dinners and festivals that were
given to him, from Paris to Naples, in the tongue of the
people among whom he sojourned ; and if my readers had
listened to him, as I had the fortune to do, when the ministers
of the King of Sardinia, the bankers and great merchants, the
Reformers and literary men of Genoa, accorded to him that
public honor, they would have felt how much nobler to send
before one's self the fame of having deserved well in the cause
of the multitude, than to appear all-glittering in the gems, and
stars, and crosses of honor, which have been made the symbols
of the highest honors, which even despotism itself could invoke.
I was particularly touched on several occasions like these, in
hearing Mr. Cobden speak so magnanimously of the efforts of
Sir Robert Peel. He accorded to him more honors in the cause

of reform than justice would have exacted, for all Europe knew that to Richard Cobden, and not to Sir Robert Peel, the chief honor belonged. But he, like other great men, felt what little men never can feel, that posterity is sure to do them justice, and that no anxiety or thirsting for premature or undeserved popularity can ever give them lasting fame.

XIV.

LOOKING, then, at the conflict going on in British Society between the Aristocracy and the People, the thoughtful man will say : All this must end in something. It is not to vanish in smoke. A crisis of some sort England is fast approaching. Local outbreaks and sudden discontents from some unpopular measure may be quelled. But the movements in England now are of a different character. It is not the surface that is ruffled, but the profoundest depths of the nation's soul are stirred. Beginning with reluctance, and advancing by slow degrees, every measure of resistance in the power of government, except extreme physical force, has been employed to quell them. This last she dare not now use. It is too late, if it ever would have done. To employ it now would turn England into one great slaughter-house. All the power vested in a proud aristocracy and prouder throne has been expended, while the spirit of discontent has steadily increased. Every year presents sadder sights. Every Parliament struggles in deeper water. Every petition takes a louder and a firmer tone. *Reform or revolution—thorough reform or thorough revolution—England must have.*

She may choose between the two. I know there are many things favorable to the stability of the English throne—that England contains many elements of strength, which in certain stages of her history would have to be taken into the calculation, in order to draw right conclusions of her fate. But all these may be cast out when we find a counter power at work, which reduces them to nothing in its mightier, its resistless progress.

In the commencement, these great forces, which rest in the hands of every government, furnish grounds for conjecture concerning the issue. Before the antagonist powers have tested their respective strength, all reasoning concerning the result must be wholly problematical. But when the test has been fairly applied, and physical strength is found to be utterly powerless in the struggle, then it requires no prophet's ken to read the result. He that can weave the simplest web of thought can come to right conclusions. This test has been applied to England. Her great resources have been called into the field. Their action is seen in the attempts to bribe the leaders and divide the forces arming against her. It is seen in the effort to draw off the suffering part of her population by extensive emigration ; and more than all, in the partial reforms she from time to time grants to prevent an explosion. All these things combined have had their effect. In ordinary circumstances their success would have been complete. They have delayed the concentration of the forces gathering for the onset. They have drawn off hundreds of thousands to hush their murmurs in foreign lands. They have distracted the counsel of the leaders—deceived the most wary—bribed or intimidated those esteemed the most incorruptible and firm, and baffled for awhile the hopes of the ~ood. But all these combined, are found too feeble to arrest the force levelled against them. Through, and over all obstacles the movement gathers strength and momentum every hour. Hence these resources of the government are to be thrown out of future calculations. Found too weak in the outset, they are to be disregarded now.

xv.

REFORM or revolution England must have. Which of the two, and how soon either will occur, is the only question? This is plain, and to feel its force we have only to consider the

cause of the present suffering and discontent, and the extent
and progress of the movement they have occasioned. If the
cause continues and increases, the distress and agitation will
also continue and increase, till the time will come when redress
must be granted.

Oppressive taxation alone supports an idle and profligate
oligarchy. To remove this is to grant the reform the people
demand. Not to do it, is to retain all the elements of ruin that
now threaten, and will soon rock the kingdom like an earthquake. England cannot stand still.

In the first place, the increase, till recently, of the national
debt, with the excess of expenditure over the revenue, exhibits
this downward tendency of things. Says a Tory writer in
Blackwood: " Every country in Europe is accumulating debt—
every one is anticipating its means, and the results must be
convulsions, sooner or later, but inevitable."

Again he says : " The national debt is the cause of the general discontent, and worse than slavish suffering of the peasantry of the land ; the fount of those unquenchable fires which
burst up in chartism, socialism, and a hundred other wild and
ominous threateners of general evil." This debt is now nearly
£4,000,000,000, and nearly $150,000,000 are required to pay
the annual interest.

It has been settled that no sinking fund can be applied to
liquidate this debt but a surplus revenue. Says M'Culloch,
" An excess of revenue above the expenditure, is the only sinking fund by which any part of the national debt can be dis-
charged." But, for many years, the expenditure has generally
exceeded the revenue, so that an increased tax is necessary to
meet this increased expenditure, without paying one farthing
of the public debt.

But from what source is to come the money to meet this increased expenditure, to say nothing of the national debt?
From taxation ? But if the people are now taxed all they will
bear, and the expenditures of peace must be met by the extraordinary measures resorted to only in the extreme exigencies

of war, whence is to come the money for those great emergencies into which, sooner or later, England must be plunged? From loans? The people will be taxed to pay the loans. From new commercial restrictions? They were working ruin to the nation, and some of them had to be removed. From direct taxation? The people declare they will not submit to what is now laid upon them, and it requires no uncommon sagacity to see that it needs but little more to precipitate them in angry masses on the government.

To liquidate this debt by repudiating it would plunge the nation at once into bankruptcy. Every system of Insurance, Exchange and Banking in the realm would be ruined. This mighty robbery might relieve the sufferings of one portion, but it would add to those of another. Besides, if it struck only the higher classes, they, holding the government, would repair their losses from the pockets of the people. So long as a government is oppressive in its action, take what course it will, it reaches the pockets of the people at last.

XVI.

LET distress increase as it has done, and must do, with the increase of population, the unsteadiness of manufactures, and high price of bread, and in a few years not all the physical force in the world can control the people. This distress must have an end. Yet the laws which support the privileged classes of England created it all.

If the Church will give up its immense revenues, and relieve the people from tithes and church rates; if the nobility will surrender the privileges which secure their incomes at the expense of the poor, England can be saved from revolution. But this extensive reform would send her far towards a republic. It would be the death blow to the Aristocracy of England, if not to royalty itself. To refuse this reform, is to increase the discontent and suffering already existing. But this distress, on which is based one of our arguments that reform or revolution is the fate of England, must have an end. It had an end in France, and in the language of *Blackwood's Magazine:* "One of the lessons to be palpably derived from the catastrophe of the French war, is, that *where substantial grievances exist in any nation, they will be enabled, sooner or later, to make their own remedy!*" This truth is working its fulfillment in England. Discontent is not only spreading broader and deeper every year, but it is acquiring the boldness of famine, and the energy of despair. It will precipitate a crisis—a crisis formed to annihilate the difference in the balance of the two interests of the higher and lower classes.

The millions will no longer famish. Starvation will find some means of relief, although great changes be the result. Discontent will break out into Socialism, Chartism—anything that promises food. We shall in the next two Books have to speak of children given up to toil like brutes for bread—of crimes perpetrated to escape famine—of virtue sacrificed for the same price—of starving laborers, of wretchedness, want and despair in every part of the land. We shall have to speak of convulsions that threaten to rend England asunder—her mills silent and deserted—her foundries empty—her torch and dagger meetings, crowded with desperate men : her shores dark with men, women and children fleeing from the horrid fate of dying by famine, and we again say, all this must have an end.

XVII.

WITHHOLD reform a little longer, and the scenes of Paris will be renewed. Says Carlyle, "When the thoughts of a people, in the great mass of it, have grown mad, the combined issue of that people's workings will be madness—an incoherency and ruin." Again, in speaking of the discontent among the lower classes of England. "To us individually, this matter appears, and has for many years appeared to be the most ominous of all practical matters whatsoever—a matter in regard to which, if something be not done, something will do itself one day, and in a fashion that will please nobody." It was the lack of bread that upset the Bourbon throne. Louis XV. foresaw the storm that was darkening the firmament of France. Riding one day through the forests of Senart, he saw a coffin borne on the shoulder of a squalid and half starved peasant. He stopped and asked for whom it was? He was told "for a wretch like myself." Again he asked of what he died, and as the short but fearful reply was returned, "of hunger," Louis put spurs to his horse and disappeared. Think you not, as he dashed through the forest, that the phantom of a falling empire passed before his vision! The political parties in Paris might easily have been dispersed had not the common people lacked bread.

Nothing passes power into the hands of the lower classes sooner than hunger. The leaders of the Parisian mobs understood this, and one wrote epigrammatically—"*Tout va bien ici: le pain manque*," all goes well here—there is a lack of bread. The first attack of the populace was on one who said, "A man could live on seven sous a day;" and yet 10,000 in Paisley alone have lived on one penny a day. Two millions in Ireland are now living on less. The first insurrection in Paris was quelled only when 400 corpses were strewn over the streets. Then came attacks upon tax-gatherers, and those who were suspected of preventing the free introduction of grain. The bakers were next slain, for supposed deception in weights. The first man hung at the lamp post was Foulon—hung for the crime of saying, when told of the people's distress, "Let them eat grass!" Yet this was not more insulting than the reply of the Duke of Wellington to the hungry thousands of Paisley. One speech, that "there was no need of reform," drove the common people to the verge of civil war. "*Rien*," says Madame de Stael, "*ne dispose le peuple au mécontentment comme les craintes sur les subsistances.*" Nothing spreads discontent faster than the fear of famine; and nothing, we might add, imparts such desperate courage and force.

An army of women swarming around Versailles by night, crying, " Bread ! Bread !" could not be resisted. Their cry in the National Assembly, whither they had forced themselves : "*Du pain, pas tant de longs discours !*" is the same the women of England are uttering in the ears of Parliament. " Give us bread, and not speeches !" was their cry, and they gave it. Grown desperate with want, they cooked even a horse that had been slain in the *mêlée*, and ate it. They were hungry enough to eat it without the cooking. The people of France demanded precisely what the people of England are now demanding— increase wages, or cheapen the necessaries of life. The refusal in the one case wrought madness and revolution, and it will in the other, unless relief comes soon. However different the characters of the two people may be, they are alike in this— they will never consent to starve to death so long as there is bread in the land. The extremity of suffering, after looking in vain to the proper source of relief, will *relieve itself*.

A few women, in a single night, changed the whole aspect of France—made certain the overthrow of a throne, and brought in a reign of blood that blanched the world. Hunger can do *anything*. It makes exigencies for which no skill can provide. The tread of the multitude impelled by this wildest of all im- pulses, sends terror to the firmest heart. There is an appeal in the cry for food that reaches the heart of every man. It is too sad and desolate to awaken anger. Besides, there is a justice in their claim that arms them with double strength.

XVIII.

DEBATE or sneer as noble lords will, England is now in this state. Every man that will stop long enough to listen, can hear the roar of the multitude that will *not* be quieted : while the laws that make them beggars, load the tables of their oppressors with luxuries. Good heavens ! is England infatuated that she will believe no crisis is near ? Give me the single truth that there is a God on high who beholds the actions of men, and I want no more to say in the face of the world than that England must repent or fall.

But while this cry is passing over the land, and these dangers are thickening every hour, where are these hierarchs and oligarchs from whom reform alone can come? " Collecting tithes and preserving game !" But other business is preparing for them. Some twenty full-grown millions of gaunt figures, with their haggard faces, have started up to ask, as in forest roarings, these washed upper classes, after long unretrieved centuries, virtually this question—"How have ye treated us? how have ye taught us, fed us and led us, while we toiled for you? The answer can be read in flames over the nightly summer sky. This is the feeding and leading we have had of you—emptiness of pocket, of stomach, of head and of heart. Behold there is nothing in us—nothing but what nature gives her wild children of the forest—ferocity and appetite— strength grounded on hunger. Did ye mark among your rights of man, that man was not made to die of starvation, while there was bread reaped by him? It is among the RIGHTS of man." This question is virtually put by the people of England at the present day. What else meant the 10,000 assembled in one meeting in Manchester, solemnly pledging themselves to pay no more taxes? What else meant these 26,000 on the hills of Acerington, declaring themselves ready for anything that would bring relief; and the riots in Cork, Ennis and Tipperary, where the only attacks, as in Paris, were on the receptacles of grain? What else meant the petition of three millions and a half suffering men and women, carried in solemn procession to the House of Parliament? This *is virtually* putting the question, and England *must* answer it. What! is she rocked in such profound slumber that the howl of famishing millions cannot arouse her? Will the simple declaration in the forests of Senart, that a man died of hunger, send a king of France trembling through its shades ; and yet English statesmen look calmly on while thousands are starving around them?

We might speak here of the burning, over twenty years ago, of the Parliament House, representing the oppressive government ; the Royal Exchange, representing the wealth of the few ; the firing of York Cathedral, representing the oppressive and harlot Church ; and last of all, the conflagration of the Armoury of the Tower, representing the military and feudal power of the Aristocracy ; all binding the people in fetters of iron. All these are no faint omens where the coming storm shall strike. I know it is called accidental ; but chance makes no such combined selections. Neither is plunder sought where no treasures are garnered. The incendiary's torch is significant when it selects such objects for its destruction. It points clearly and distinctly to the *sources of evil.* The truth is, all these declare, in no ambiguous language, that the patience of the people is well nigh exhausted, and a tremendous collision near, unless government legislate, or rather *unlegislate,* fast. Said Raumer, twenty-seven years ago, in speaking of the tendency of things in England : " Without helm or master the ship is lost. With bad pilotage she may, indeed, be run on the French rocks ; but to avoid this danger by doing nothing, is a very ostrich-like means of security."

XIX.

POPULAR tumults, it is true, in England have not shaken the government as they did that of France. And why ? When the first outbreak in Paris revealed the fires that had long been smouldering out of sight, the preventive means of the government had all been exhausted. Deferring the crisis by every measure in their power, when it came they had nothing left with which to appease the populace but physical force. In that day of darkness and vassalage, the common people writhed under oppression till an arbitrary government could inflict no more—till even the bayonet and the scaffold could be contemplated with more calmness than their actual calamities, and then they rose in the might and madness of despair.

England, on the contrary, had not exhausted her preventive means when open discontent first showed itself. Hence, she has been enabled to delay the crisis she cannot escape, by dealing these out, one by one, sparingly as she could; but they are well nigh exhausted. On her own showing, the necessaries of life will bear no more taxation. The income tax does not pretend to relieve the present distress. Nothing will do it but an entire change in the principles and policy of the government. When she has no more preventive measures with which to deceive and soothe the people, England will rush to revolution as fast and as fiercely as France.

To some this may seem only the language of an excited imagination; but I am of that number who believe that such suffering as now makes England stagger round her throne cannot long be harmless. The simplest logic in the world will prove it. The causes that originated this distress will continue and increase it. Until these are removed, discontent will continue and increase with the increase of population, till it can be borne no longer. But their removal would be the reform the people are contending for, and when granted, it would sink the oligarchy of England forever. She may choose, we repeat, between the two.

XX.

THE whole structure of the Aristocracy is based on pride, sensuality, indolence and injustice. The deeper such a foundation sinks, the higher the suffering it creates will rise above it. Physical force, which England has seemed to rely on when all other means failed, is useless here. It is too late to begin to shoot down starving rebels, and place the realm under military law. It may seem to do in Ireland just now, under the terror of Fenianism; but authority, the strong arm of physical power, can no longer allay discontent. Applied, it will be "a mere taste of the whip to rearing coursers which makes them rear worse. When a team of twenty-five millions begin rearing, what is Dominie's whip!" Neither whip nor reign will govern them. Bounding madly on, they will strew throne and government in their path.

This is not all prophecy or wild conjecture. It is a faithful description. This state of things has actually begun, and needs but to go on as it has commenced, and more and worse than we have hinted at will have come. The ground-swell of discontent that betokens a fiercer movement at hand, has surged up to the very throne, and its retiring murmur, as it goes to gather its might for a darker flow, all may hear that will.

This argument, drawn from the universal and rapidly increasing distress of the people, to prove that the government must reform or be revolutionized, is a fair and valid one. If the past can be relied on in judging of the future, I have predicted nothing aside from reason. Local outbreaks and partial distress may have been quelled, but when the spirit of reform has penetrated the entire realm, till there is the simultaneous and steady action of millions on a single point, governments have always been compelled to retreat or fall.

XXI.

BUT we have a still stronger argument to prove my first statement, that England must thoroughly reform or revolutionize—an argument those will appreciate who have watched the spirit and tendency of the age. This tending is to equality among all classes ; that is, equality in civil and religious rights. Physical want becomes dangerous only when it reaches a certain extremity. But slavery is always dangerous ; especially when men have learned their rights and are resolved on regaining them. The right to *live* on the bread they reap, all men understand. But this a man may know, and still be a slave ; but when in the pride and majesty of a man he steps on the same level with his oppressors, and, firm in the consciousness of right, says—I stand here or die—there is aroused in him a spirit that neither bribes nor threats can subdue. This is the attitude the lower classes of Europe are assuming, and those of England have already taken.

The struggle for principle is a longer, stronger and steadier one than the struggle for bread. It is true that famine often teaches men their rights; it makes them keen-sighted and think fast. As the starving man beholds the lazy lord roll by in his chariot, he very naturally asks himself the question, " Why is it that I must starve, to enable that man, with no more bones and muscles than myself, to riot in abundance ?" He is not long in coming to the conclusion—there *is* none.

Famine, together with the progress of civilization, has opened the eyes of Englishmen to their true position. They begin to see what fools they have allowed a few indolent spendthrifts to make of them, what oppressions they have tamely borne, under what disabilities they have labored, and what robberies they have silently submitted to ; and seeing it, they are resolved to have a change. They ask now, not only for bread, but their rights as men. The system that supports the oligarchy of England, is not more a system of starvation than of slavery. While with one hand it takes bread from the mouths of the poor, and clothes from their backs, with the other it seizes their civil and religious rights. Tyrants know that men cannot be coolly plundered till they become slaves. Englishmen can no longer so easily be made slaves ; hence the plundering of them is getting to be dangerous.

Yet the final result is not inferred from the simple fact that the people of England have learned their rights, and demanded them, although we apprehend the argument in this case would be a sound one ; but from the fact, that having been refused their rights, a fair trial of their strength has been made with the few and found to be on the side of the many. In my statements on the progress of democracy, I think it is fairly proved that the march of the people is onward with a strength that clears all obstacles ; that the principles of liberty are spreading on every side, and fixing themselves deeper and firmer in the human soul. Said Raumer : " The power of the nobility *has* declined, and is declining. The result of the long struggle between the patricians and plebeians of Rome was their perfect equality, and incontestably this is the tendency of modern Europe."

XXII.

INDEED, Great Britain, in many respects, resembles the Roman Empire—as much as the different periods of their existence will allow a resemblance. The social organization of Rome was based on absolute domestic slavery. That of England on the same slavery—different only in degree. The internal government of the former was simply a war between the patricians and plebeians when external war did not absorb their mutual hatred. Whatever the plebeians won by threats from the patricians, the patricians repealed on the first safe opportunity. The poor were continually crying for " panem et circenses," bread and entertainments. Nine-tenths of the property belonged to the other fraction, composing the privileged class. Their external policy was also similar. Conquest and spoliation were the history of both—oppression and slaughter the result. By tyranny and utter disregard of human life the power of both maintained. Becoming distracted at home, Rome could no longer protect her provinces abroad. England will soon be in the same dilemma. The struggle between the higher and lower classes was often interrupted, but never abandoned, until they both stood on the same level. The same struggle is witnessed in England, and the result will be the same, although the difference in civilization and religion will bring, we trust, in the latter case, a more favorable issue to the plebeians.

That this struggle is now shaking England, no one will doubt, whatever he may think of the issue. As Carlyle says : " What are rights and what are the mights of the discontented working classes in England, is the question at this epoch. For we may say beforehand, this struggle dividing the upper and lower societies in Europe, and more particularly and notably in England than elsewhere—this too, is a struggle that will end and adjust itself as others do, and have done, by making the right clear and the might clear." But we may now say " the right and the might" are both made clear. All, but tyrants, agree where the *right* is. Nature, with her ten thousand tongues, utters it, while the history of the past few years tells where the *might* is. At the outset, this last was a question to be settled. Truth is not always immediately the strongest : but the progress of reform in the last few years has settled it—*the right and the might are both with all the people of Europe.*

XXIII.

ALTHOUGH unnoticed, the right in England has for centuries been slowly acquiring the might. Not the people, but their representatives were the first who dared whisper of popular rights, and in the question of monopolies, when Elizabeth yielded, obtained their first triumph. Charles I. dared to hurl Hampden and Elliot from their parliamentary seats into prison for saying less than every Chartist and Liberal in England says with impunity. In that struggle between freedom and despotism, the King and Throne both fell, and with them the House of Peers. Although there was a reaction, then was fought the great battle of the world—the battle between tyranny and liberty—reason and prejudice.

America was its fruit, as also the revolutions that soon after passed over Europe. I might show, step by step, how freedom has made progress among the subjects of Great Britain. Resisted at every step, it has never yielded a single inch. The Catholic Emancipation Bill, though fought by the aristocracy, from first to last, with a desperation deserving a better cause, did pass. The Reform Bill was cast indignantly from the House of Lords, and tossed in scorn to the people, but the people sent it back with a shout that rocked the nation, and it passed.

The Duke of Wellington was compelled to eat his own words, and the King to swallow in silence his indignation. The people again triumphed. Nor is this all : the people ask still more. Then they demanded the correction of flagrant abuses ; now they claim general suffrage. A petition of 3,500,000 was carried to Parliament. Like all that preceded it, which asked for reform, it was scornfully rejected, and thrown back to the people. Like all others, it will come back with a shout and a threat that will suddenly change the opinions of noble lords and country gentlemen, or provoke a collision that will be felt the world over, and be remembered while governments shall stand.

XXIV.

HOW would Elizabeth have regarded a Chartist meeting? How would Charles I. have treated a petition for Universal Suffrage, and a reform in every department of government? How would George III., or even King William, have regarded this last petition? Yet they seem as natural and reasonable as the first faint prayer for redress. Astonishment or opposition makes no alterations. Rejected, they return, backed by stronger power, and fortified with firmer resolution. And, if like causes produce like effects—if the law of progress holds good, a great Reform Bill will pass in England as certainly as the sun will rise over her hills—smoothly or roughly, as the case may be. If the oligarchy, finding that all is going at this rate, shall abide the collision, then revolution must follow. If this be not plain, we know not what is. It requires no political skill to read one of these two results.

If the past can be relied on, this mighty spirit of progress must have way—peacefully or stormfully, it is on, right on, with the strength of awakened millions. Shattering that it *may* reach, and shattering *what* it reaches, it passes to the throne and seat of oppression. It is invulnerable. We see no power to arrest it, which has not already been employed. Everything has been tried—persuasion, threats, bribery, deceit, promises, all : and yet its triumphant march is onward still. I stand not alone in this opinion. Says Lord Brougham : " Where no safety-valve is provided for popular discontent, to prevent an explosion that shall shiver the machine to pieces ; where the people—the wealth and glory of the British nation—where this most important order of the community are without a regular communication with the legislature—where they feel the load of such grievances, and feel too the power they possess, moral and intellectual, and let me add, without the imputation of a threat, physical ; then, and only then, are their combinations formidable ; when they are armed by their wrongs far more formidable than any physical force ; then, and only then, they become invulnerable." In another place he says, " the support of the people must be sought if government would endure." I know these words were uttered long ago, before the Reform Bill was passed. But they are as true to-day as then—truer.

The riots and tumults in England and Ireland are natural and reasonable. The people are not to blame for them, but the government for resisting their just claims. The English government is teaching her subjects the most dangerous of all lessons—that she is their enemy—that she is not their protector but their spoiler ; cares not for their happiness, but cares only for their money and their toil. Nor are we alone in saying that to the government which seizes with unrighteous hand the inalienable, eternal rights of the people, is to be charged the guilt of these fierce outbreaks and fiercer threats. The trampled worm will writhe, the hunted deer turn at bay : and shall the smitten soul of man never rise on its smiter ?

" Who, indeed, can tell what dangers and what calamities may lie hid within what remains of the present century ! Who can tell how intense may be the distress, how fierce the animosities, or how scrupulous the factions that may be let loose upon us !"—*Edinb. Rev.*

XXV.

SAID Lord Brougham : " Those portentous appearances—the growth of later times—those figures that stalk abroad, of unknown stature and strange form, union of leagues, and mustering of men in myriads, and conspiracies against exchequers, whence do they spring ; and how come they to haunt our shores ? What power engendered those uncouth shapes ; what multiplied the monstrous births till they people the land? Trust me, the same power which called into frightful existence, and carried with resistless force the Irish volunteers of 1782 ; the same power which rent in twain your empire, and raised up thirteen republics ; the same power which created the Catholic Association, and gave it Ireland for a portion. What power is that ? Justice denied, rights withheld, wrongs perpetrated, the force which common injuries lend to millions, the wickedness of using the sacred trust of government as a means of indulging private caprice, the idiotcy of treating Englishmen like the children of the South Sea islands, the frenzy of believing, or making believe, that the adults of the Nineteenth Century can be led like children or driven like barbarians. This it is that has conjured up the strange sights, at which we now stand aghast. And shall we persist in the fatal error of controlling the giant progeny, instead of extirpating the execrable parent ? Good God ! will men never learn wisdom even from their own experience ? Will they never believe till it be too late, that the surest way to prevent immoderate desires being formed, aye, and unjust demands being enforced, is to grant, in due season, the moderate demands of justice ?"

But even Lord Brougham would probably now wish to define his own language, " *moderate* demands of justice," and would unhesitatingly decide that what the People demand is the " *immoderate* desires.*" But shall the miserable reform which does scarcely more than acknowledge the robbery without abandoning it, the scanty pittance doled out grudgingly to the starving millions be called granting " the moderate demands of justice ?" But the language of Brougham is as applicable now as ever. And if to refuse to accede to just demands, will, in the end, cause unjust ones to be enforced, what shall be the final success of those just demands ?

It is too late to talk of quieting the people by what noble lords would call " moderate concessions." The prophecy of Brougham has come to pass—the " *immoderate* desires," as he would term them, will be " enforced." Once I thought imme- diate relief in the earlier stages of public discontent would have quieted the people. But I am convinced it was a false view. Nothing short of a great and radical Reform Bill will satisfy the British people in this year M.DCCC.LXVI. Lord John Russell cannot cheat the three kingdoms this time with accus- tomed impunity. The tendency of England and the tendency of all Europe, as De Tocqueville says, is towards the equaliza- tion of the higher and lower classes.

XXVI.

EVERY nation is, sooner or later, to reach the crisis where the reins of government are to be thrown into the hands of the people, and the latter to rule for themselves. Whether it result in anarchy or order, is not the question. Tyrants and people are yet to stand and stare each other in the face, and the long bloody arrears be settled up. The fierceness of the conflict, and the ruin of the victory, are to be in pro- portion to the oppression that preceded them, and the reluct- ance with which it was abandoned. As Macaulay has said : " the greatness of the outrage attendant on a revolution, only shows the greater necessity of a revolution." The only hope for England is to attempt to guide, not resist, this awakened energy. It is a fearful thing to trample on the human mind. There is no danger like that of endeavoring to scourge the newly emancipated spirit back to its prison and its chains. It is the frenzy of madness for a government, with the wrong all on its own side, to attempt with words and formulas, or even physical force, to arrest the avalanche rush of millions towards their rights.

The memory of injuries treasured up through long centuries of oppression, the pangs of present suffering, the rage under insult and falsehood, the scorn of betrayers, the consciousness of right, the energy of despair, and the strength of God, are all on their side.

The movements, hitherto often lawless and distracted, are now combined and regular, and directed by a single feeling on a common wrong. And what is opposed to all this? An imbecile and rotten government—drunken with pride and black-spotted with crime—conscious of wrong, and backed only by a few cannon they dare not use, and laws they cannot enforce, and upheld only by the base motives, love of power and love of money.

XXVII.

OVER such frail barriers the tread of the multitude will be like the march of the storm. The throne and crown-mitres, heraldry and titles, they will fling about them like withered leaves, those playthings of the tempest. When the last hope of relief is abandoned, and respect for the laws, and reverence for ancient customs, and fear of death, are all broken over, and maddened men have got the first taste of blood and power, you can chain the lightnings of heaven, or the in-rolling tide of the sea, as easily as them.

Such fears, I know, are called idle, by those who talk dignifiedly of law and order. The apparent repose and firmness of the surface cheat the wisest politicians into the dream of security, till they feel the ground actually heaving beneath them. They forget the clap is never heard till the bolt has struck. It is this blindness which has strewn the earth with the fragments of ancient monarchies. Kings and rulers can be stupid sometimes, for the owl and the bittern sing of it in the mouldering desolate palaces of fallen empires.

Having shown, as I think I have in this book conclusively, both from her financial prospects and the extremity of suffering which must increase under the present policy of government, and more than all, from the steady resistless progress of democracy in England, that she must reform or be revolutionized, I will add only one other argument. It is drawn from the government of God. There is a throne above that looks down on thrones below. And if it be true, that God keeps a record of the doings of rulers on earth, and the judgment day to nations is in this world, England has indeed reason to be afraid.

Obeying no law but her own imperious will, she has conquered without justice, and slaughtered without mercy. Her throne, based on the necks of the people, has grown hoary with oppression. No enlightened nation has ever in time of peace inflicted such suffering upon its subjects. The records of no nation present so dark, so bloody a picture as that of England's jurisdiction over Ireland. Her very Church has robbed the poor, and imprisoned the widow and him that had no helper, under the blasphemous pretence that she was doing God's service.

And if it be true that God visits the iniquities of rulers on their own heads, and the cry of the poor reaches his ear, and he does break the arm of the oppressor, then the doom of Babylon is written on the walls of her greatness unless she repent.

XXVIII.

BESIDES, the government of England is based on a lie—a great lie—that the many ought to suffer for the happiness and luxury of the few. The Creator cares for his truth. It may be buried so deep by the strong hand of oppression, that it may seem lost forever; but there is a day appointed for its resurrection. Surely, though it may be slowly, it works its way back to light and power. Centuries may roll by, and the few who have buried the truth may rejoice in security, for its grave is grown over, but it will yet arise and stare its murder-

ers in the face. " All men are born free ; and equally entitled
to life, liberty and the pursuit of happiness"—is the great truth
which despots have tried to prove a lie, but which is to be the
rallying cry of an enslaved world.

It is not always to be that nine-tenths of mankind are to die
from starvation, in order that the remaining fraction may be
able to die of surfeit. Equality among all classes is the goal
towards which the world is straining, and it will reach it.
What tumults and chaos and blood lie between them and it no
man can tell. But if needs be through these it must be reached
—through them it will pass—and armed with the Almighty's
decree, press enslaved mankind to freedom. How fast, or how
slow is to be its march, none but the God of nations can tell.
We only hear the mighty tread of the advancing multitude.
We only know that it is a part of the Almighty's plan to bring
the world back to competence and happiness, and England
must wheel into the movement that shall accomplish it. Vainer
than a dream is the expectation of arresting this onward movement of the race. The world (to repeat from my own Introduction) shall not be dragged back to its former darkness and
slavery. The power to do it has passed forever from the hands
of despots. War, anarchy and madness may drench the earth in
blood ; but civilized man is no longer to sit tamely down under
oppression. Its silent, deadly tooth is no longer to sink unre-
sisted into his bruised and bleeding flesh. The world has
heard the shout of freedom and is straining on its fetters. It is
saying to its oppressors, the cup of trembling you have so long
pressed to our lips we will drain no more forever. *We are
men!*

To this crisis every careful observer acknowledges the world
to be tending. Of all the monarchies of Europe, England is
nearest this crisis. There the struggle has already commenced.
The great battle-field of human rights is spread out, and the
governments of the Old World are anxiously awaiting the issue.
If the feudal principle fall there, it must fall everywhere.

XXIX.

IN lifting the veil from English society to reveal the terrible shapes that lay beneath it; in going over the painful details of oppression and suffering inflicted by a heartless few to increase their pleasures and their pride; especially in speaking of the fearful, but inevitable crisis to which all things are steadily tending, I may seem to some readers to have been betrayed into an asperity of language that would seem inconsistent with the feelings such disasters should awaken. But while I would not avert the crisis which shall relieve the people from an oppressive government and heartless church, whatever be the means by which it must be reached, I pity the stupidity and selfishness that will probably make it so terrible.

Freedom is dearer than life: it is a part of our nature, and burns on forever a sacred flame. " I have lived," says Emerson, " to hear that blessed name taken in vain, used in caricature, uttered with a sneer. It will not be so always. Prophets proclaimed it, noble men died for it, and felt the price cheap. None counted how much gold could be coined out of fetters. Dimly seen, imperfectly understood, its dimmest shapes, its shadowy visions even rising amidst bloody clouds, have been heralds of joy. Not brighter and more glad to the forlorn and weary traveler the first rays which look out through the golden dawn, than to commonwealths and men the day-break of liberty. I may regret, to be sure, that a dagger should ever have been hidden in a myrtle bough; I may mourn that in the name of liberty the least wrong should ever have been done; would that the blessed form needed never but voice soft as the gentlest evening wind. More deeply should I mourn, my tears more hopeless, if I saw her assailed, nor hand nor voice lifted in her defence. Nay, as in the worst superstitions I welcome the divine idea of religion, as through dreams and filthy tales of mythology I see and bless the living God, nor ever feel more sure that God is, that truth is, and that man is made for God and truth ; so in and through frantic excesses of an incomplete and infantile freedom, I see, I feel, that freedom is, and is sacred, and that it is everything to the soul of man. Carry me to Paris in the frenzy of its first revolution ; carry me to St. Domingo in the storm of its insurrection ; carry me to Bunker's Hill and its carnage ; carry me to Thermopylæ while its three hundred wait the sure death ; set me beside those whose names may scarce be uttered without contempt and hate—a Wat Tyler ; set me where and with whom you will, be it but man struggling to be free, to be himself, I recognize a divine presence, and wish not to withhold my homage. Pardon me, but in the slavish quietude of the ages, I see nothing but despondency. Freedom, be it wild as it may, quickens my hope. The wildness is an accident which will pass soon ; that slavish quietude is death. There is a grandeur in the earthquake or volcano ; in the dark, dank, offensive vault —something else."

XXX.

A FEW years ago, in addressing the following Memorial to the Queen, an English operative expressed the feelings of his whole class :

" It is not unknown to you, Madam, that among large bodies of my fellow-subjects, there prevails an ill-defined, but strong opinion, that Whigs and Tories are alike their natural enemies ; that, in fact, all the middle and upper classes are in one grand conspiracy to trample on and oppress them. Let an attempt be made to pass through the fearful approaching winter without some grand legislative effort made to relieve the industry of the country, and the spirit of Chartism—aye ! and something worse will once more raise its head, and neither churches nor yeomanry, neither bayonets nor sabres, will put it down. We have had Jack Cades and Wat Tylers in England, and these have been put down ; we have had great gatherings in Birmingham, riots in Bristol, Ludism, Radicalism, and physical force Chartism—and all these have been appeased and subdued. But we have yet to see another spectacle, which comes as surely as the sun rises to-morrow, should the Corn Laws be maintained. In the midst of a 'run of gold,' and the fear of a national bankruptcy, thousands upon thousands of starving men, rising up like grim and appalling shadows ; men hunger-worn with savage hatred in their hearts, demanding not bread alone, but their rights, and trampling alike upon public credit, national honor and general safety. Oh, let not good easy souls persuade you that in England such a thing is impossible ! It is perfectly possible. The materials for such a frightful catastrophe are ready ; the train is laid, and wants but the lightning's flash to set it on fire. England is strong in the natural spirit which regards order as heaven's first law ; but when hunger and hatred are combined, and these concentrated in masses, the public opinion which respects the laws falls powerless before them." Are these, we ask, vain forebodings ?*

* The following noble Lyric was written for this work.

SONG OF THE ENGLISH CHARTIST.

[Affectionately inscribed to the Author of " The Glory and Shame of England."]

THE lord sits high in his old stone tower,
    And the blood-red wine is there :
The lord hath smiled at his ancient power,
    And he lists to an ancient air.
Its stern wild music swelled of old,
O'er the marble arch and the roof of gold,
From the harp of a gray-haired minstrel rolled,—
    And around the festal board,
Like a cheerful flash of morning light
    The blood-red wine is poured.
Ha ! the Chieftain starts from his velvet throne
With a flush of rage and a stifled groan :
The ancient air in its silver fall,
And golden rise, which filled the hall,
    Hath sunk unto a breath :
For a wilder, deeper, grander tone
Comes leaping upward—fearful—lone—
    And terrible as Death.

XXXI.

SOME new Duke of Wellington, or some other noble lord may declare there is no distress in the land for want of food, and no need of reform; yet no one who has looked on England with open eyes will believe him. Discontent, deep and bitter, must follow such a state of things as I describe in this work. Men's hearts are not made of steel, that no amount of suffering can move them. All men are not martyrs in resignation; and hence, so long as England carries on her extensive scheme of oppression, there must be the reaction of discontented, indignant men. There must be *feelings* when the iron enters the soul, which will result, sooner or later, in determinations and actions.

Crushed between the Church and State, the working classes are reduced to want, the small farmers are slowly consuming

> A mighty Song
> Of woe and wrong—
> It rushes abroad like the roaring of fire—
> And a bleeding, quivering heart the lyre
> Of that fierce Song.
>
> " Revel on! revel on! we have waited long,
> And writhed like a worm under feudal wrong:
> We have fed your veins with the strength of ours,
> We have built with our groans your iron towers:
> But a stern, deep voice comes rushing down
> Like the voice of God with a ' Wo to the Crown:'
> We have heard the mighty music roll
> Like a surging sea through the Vassal's soul;
> And an answer sweeps through the troubled night,
> With a shout for the voice and a shout for the Right.
> Revel on! revel on! while yet you may!
> Glitter on! glitter on! in your bright array!
> Hear ye not? hear ye not, through your marble arch,
> The iron tramp of the Million's march?
> See ye not that the flame of our vengeance plays
> In your hall like a Vulcan's lurid blaze—
> When the earthquake wakes in a giant-start,
> And breaks the chain which has bound its heart?
> Revel on! revel on! in your olden power,
> As we bide with a smile the coming hour!"

away, and general distress is spreading through the entire population, so that, however ministers may strive to urge on the government, a deep and powerful feeling, like the undertow of a wave, continually drags it back to the bosom of agitation. Yet from the mere narrative of the *condition* of men, we can but poorly estimate the suffering it creates. It is a principle everywhere true, that we can never appreciate the distress of others till it becomes our own. Could we look with the eye of God into the hearts as well as hovels of the destitute poor—hear, as he does, the secret language and desolate prayer *they* utter in the solitude of reflection—know all the agony the spirit embraces in its moments of despair, and behold all the sad sights the future presents to the parent, as the gaunt form of famine stands on the threshold of his house, withering up the very hearts of the inmates, we could better describe the feelings of English subjects under their mighty wrongs. The same injustice and suffering produce different feelings in different classes.

It depends very much on a man's education and natural spirit, whether he rises on his oppressor and strikes in self-defence, or retreats sadly away to some place of peace. Some, with the first lash of the tyrant, bound madly on his bosom, and conquer or die. Others if they *can*, flee the scourge and the conflict. Others wait, and bear, and, guided by principle rather than passion, calmly ask for justice, believing in the omnipotence of truth. Others still will lie down in despair, and abandon themselves to brutish habits, neither asking nor expecting a change. All these varieties are found in England. The first are those who, having little hope of success if they should attempt to resist oppression, and preferring the tranquillity of other lands to the agitation of their own, take up their household goods and depart. But they who leave are not all of those embraced in this class; for multitudes, impelled by the same feeling, would gladly forsake their homes if poverty did not prevent them. Seeing this discontent and fearing its effects, England, some years ago, offered a premium for emigration. Not only did she employ agents to persuade, by false representations, her subjects out of her dominions, but she directly appropriated funds for this purpose. Money was scarce enough, the Premier knew, but he would gladly incur a deeper debt for his country, if by it he could sweep away the agitated millions around him. But the cruelest of all her acts to drive off her subjects, is the compulsion of her infirm and helpless paupers into wretched exile. In one year, between June of 1835 and July of 1836, the Poor Law Commissioners of England reported that 7,075 *paupers* were expatriated at the cost of £39,340, or about $196,000. A more brutal deed was never justified by a civilized nation. Whenever a good opportunity offered itself, these paupers, old and infirm, were shipped off like cattle, in vessels hired to convey them to other countries, where their miserable food and miserable burial would not be charged to the government. Is not this more inhuman than shipping off slaves to New Orleans or the Georgia plantations. Our own coasts have never rung with wilder farewells than have gone up from the shores of England's despairing emigrants. Multitudes have thus been banished for the flagrant crime of being poor, when their poverty was brought on them by the robbery of those very persons, who thus wrenched them, like neglected branches, from the parent tree.*

* I am here half tempted to give what lays at my hand, the Statistics of *Pauper Exportation* to the United States by the British government. Of her exportation of criminals, secretly and clandestinely, to our shores, I need hardly speak. Ever since our Government was founded this has been British policy. In multitudes of cases condemned men, indicted persons, or people who had become obnoxious or dangerous, whom the Colonial authorities would not receive, have been shipped to this country—supplying us with murderers, burglars, forgers and thieves ; while of the pauper class the number has amounted to *tens of thousands.* We all know that this mean, unfriendly and contemptible conduct of the British government went so far, that our General and State Governments had to resort to laws of self-protection, when the most earnest and repeated protests and expostulations had failed. The records of our criminal courts in every State of the Union, show the enormous excess of imported over native pauperism and crime. It is also well known from authentic sources, that by far the larger share of imported paupers and criminals was of the class sent away by the authority or money of the government, or both.

England lets them toil as long as that toil wrings from the ground or manufactory the luxuries she enjoys, and then, when old and infirm, she ships them to strange lands to find for themselves graves. The Southern planter fed and clothed his decrepid, aged slaves. The humane man refuses to knock in the head the horse that has carried him for years, because he can do no more work. But England, more cruel to her subjects than the master to his slave or the man to his beast, not only plunders their pockets, but wrings their hearts with anguish; and when her merciless extortion can force out no more, she casts forth the exhausted and helpless wretch into the wilderness to die.

XXXII.

SIR ROBERT PEEL did not propose any plan of emigration, for by looking over the statistics he discovered that voluntary emigration was increasing fast enough, without the aid of compulsion. The artisans and manufacturers, whom English injustice has driven to our shores, have helped to enrich us, and added to that prosperity which enables us to offer a still wider asylum to their brethren. If to enrich her nobles England will send away her industrious subjects, we will gladly receive them.

But our charge against England is, that much of this is not voluntary emigration. The oppression and distress that force them abroad, is as much the act of government as the special acts of confiscation and banishment. The result is the same, both to the government and the sufferers—the means only are different by which it is reached. We have no objection to voluntary emigration; but let the emigrant's choice be between freedom and equal rights at home, and the promise of a better fortune abroad. Let him go borne up by hope and the spirit of adventure, and not crowded out by dire necessity from the home of his fathers.

The pains and regrets they suffer in their departure are not regarded by those who despise their low estate. Yet the heart of the poor emigrant clings with as much affection to the land of his nativity, as the heart of a peer. Nay, more so. His associations—his friends—his knowledge, are all confined to the town in which he lived ; and that is his home, his *old country home.* We know not the anxieties—the resolutions made and abandoned—the fear to cast all that he loves on the uncertainty of the future—that fill the heart of the emigrant. Perhaps it is a poor family that is leaving, and the circumstance of their departure is accompanied by no outward display. A little cart, on which is piled a few humble utensils, is the only vehicle that leaves the quiet cottage. Behind it are the coarse-clad children, looking eagerly into their mother's face to learn what all this means. To her, that little green spot never looked so green before. The sunlight never fell on that humble roof so lovingly before. The silent trees and the little garden grow dearer every moment, till she at length sobs out her farewell and turns to depart. The father stalks on with a moody brow, not venturing to turn back for a last look. To his home he might bid adieu, but between him and it are the beings he loves more than his life. The ties that bind the humble laborer to his home are not easily sundered ; the associations of childhood and riper years are not all broken up without pain. It is a strong necessity that does it.

XXXIII.

EVERYBODY remembers how pale England turned a few years ago, at the sight of the Chartist Petition. Who were those 3,500,000 signers of the People's Charter? Not the wealthy, nor the great, nor the indifferent man of leisure, who forgot the next moment that they had given their names ; but the working people of England—the mass of British industry, starving in one of the most productive portions of the earth— men who meant something by their act. Hence, its fate is not uncared for, but watched as men watch the issue of a battle on which their fortunes are staked. From every hovel in the kingdom is a father looking out with listening attitude, to catch the answer a haughty government shall return to his prayer. Hopes are bound up in that Charter, dear as life and freedom.

Loaded with 3,500,000 British names it is drawn towards London. It has reached the city, and before Lincoln's Inn the procession is forming to carry it to St. Stephen's. Borne on the shoulders of sixteen strong working-men, followed by four thousand more, it moves through the busiest thoroughfares of the city, and rolls on towards the House of Parliament. Crowds gather on the corners of every street to gaze on the unwonted spectacle. Banners float in the breeze, and the heavy tread of the working-men of England is borne ominously to the ears of the assembled Commons. They too start, and from the windows gaze on the approaching pageant. More fearful than the army of women that roared around Versailles, demanding bread, until the king shook in his palace, they come steadily on to ask for BREAD AND THE RIGHTS OF MAN. It is the PEOPLE shouting in the ears of their own Commons, and uttering truths that shall yet make the world change masters. Too bulky to find entrance even through the ample doors of the House, it is divided up and carried in fragments into the lobby. Pyramid like, that parchment is piled upon the floor. In their eagerness these men have overstepped the bounds prescribed to them, and are actually on the floor of the House—a startling omen we think of the way, and the only way they will ever find entrance there—in their own persons, and in the tumult of those excitements which do not stand upon trifles or formality.

What now, ye Commons of the people! In that Charter are bound up the hearts of 3,500,000 souls. Trample on it, and you trample on 3,500,000 bleeding hearts. Scorn it, and you scorn so many determined men. Smile, and the insult may be paid in blood. We envy not the political sagacity or patriotism of the man who could sit unmoved in Parliament, while that scene was passing before him. Feargus O'Connor, who had suffered calumny and imprisonment, and toiled through the disastrous year to get that petition to Parliament, sat in the gallery watching its fate.

Parliament would do nothing, and now those sixteen bold men, on whose shoulders rested the hopes of the people, having finished their task, turn away ; and the four thousand who thundered behind them, having fulfilled their mission, also turn away ; and all over England, on wings of lightning is borne the tidings, "Refused to hear it." Beware, lest the bayonet be again whetted in Birmingham, and England have new illuminations of the people, fed by blazing dwellings. We wonder at and admire the spirit that can turn peaceably away after being treated with such contempt ; not back to their workshops and fields, but back to their starvation and despair.

XXXIV.

AND what is this petition that the Commons of Great Britain will not permit to be defended by its friends, but must hurry it away into silence and obscurity ? It first describes the abuse of the elective franchise. It declares that "when representation is denied, taxation should be resisted." It condemns bribery and threats at election. It complains of the oppressive taxation to support a debt incurred without the will of the people, and for the overthrow of liberty—and of the increase of that debt in time of peace. It complains of an extortionate Church, whose prodigality they are compelled to support. It speaks of the deplorable condition of those who signed the petition—the unparalleled suffering of the lower classes everywhere, while the upper classes spend profusely as ever. It declares these abuses and this destitution, calmly, plainly, truthfully ; and demands immediate reform—immediate relief. It demands also, vote by ballot—annual Parliaments—equal electoral districts—the repeal of the Union, and universal suffrage —and closes by boldly intimating the fearful effects that must ere long result, unless their petition is heard.

This is all. It contains not a complaint that is untrue—profers not a claim that is not right—and yet only forty-nine out of three hundred and thirty-six were found to vote even that the petitioners might be heard in their own defence. They asked simple justice, and were hurled back from the threshold of their own House, by those who styled themselves their representatives. The great bugbear in the petition was universal suffrage ; Whigs and Tories together shouted down the doctrine, declaring they would never entertain it. And what was the overwhelming argument, noble and wise legislators used against free suffrage? " The people were unfit to hold the power." Will the people believe they are not as fit to use it, as the selfish landlords who use it against the interests of the country? You cannot convince men that they do not know what they need as well as their oppressors. Strange that a free vote should not be as safe as a bought one, and yet we know that a large portion of the members obtain their seats by bribes.

Macaulay, once the champion of liberty—the defender of the Long Parliament—the eulogizer of Hampden and the Puritans—the condemner of Charles, whose head rolled on the scaffold for his tyranny—this man became a mouth-piece for Tories and Whigs against the people, declaring he never would vote to give free suffrage to them. Why not, Mr. Macaulay—do not you enjoy it ? Mr. Macaulay is learned in history, and always drawing instructive lessons from the past. But did he ever read of 3,500,000 people calmly, intelligently, uttering their grievances to their assembled rulers—boldly, yet respectfully presenting the charter of their rights, and appealing to the God of truth and the soul of man for their justice, and baffled at last? Has he studied the philosophy of history, and the spirit of the age so superficially as to believe such a charter, backed by so many millions of men, can be dissipated by a few passages of oratory, on the unfitness of the people to vote for their own rulers ? Is the French revolution entirely forgotten—the petition that 3,000,000 of people once before sent across the Atlantic, based on the same grand principle, that

taxation and representation should go together. Has he forgotten the noble band of Irish Volunteers, demanding and
getting their rights. Has he ever known such a tide rolled
back, and the united people hushed into trembling silence by a
speech.

XXXV.

THE sinking of the Bourbon throne and the French aristocracy in the bloody abyss of revolution ; the waving
of the star-spangled banner over thirteen free States, till the
shout of freedom swelled over the Alleghanies ; the independent
legislature of Ireland, extending its protection over the suffering people, are facts in history Mr. Macaulay would have
done well to recall before he thought, in this age of the world,
to send 3,500,000 people, chidden and abashed like whipped
school-boys, back to their homes.

But he said " there would be no security to property should
the petitioners' prayer be granted." Strange language this
for a wise man. And what security did he expect from
wronged and insulted men, denied justice as well as mercy ?
Did he forget the midnight sky made red by the burning of
" secure property," amid the terrors of Birmingham riots ?
Birmingham has been in a blaze ; fields have shone in the light
of their burning harvests ; Guildhall has felt the incendiary's
torch, and the Tower of London tumbled in one blazing ruin—
all of it this " secure property." " Government, too, would be
in danger," said Macaulay : how much more so by granting
the people justice, than by driving them to despair and madness by oppression and starvation ?

It was once thought Macaulay was unshackled from the
feudal and bigot spirit that blinds so many of the aristocracy,
who will believe, against the evidence of their senses, that the
people can be kept in awe by symbols and formulas. I remember once to have read a speech of his on the passage of the
Reform Bill, in which occurred this bold and startling para-

graph : " The arguments of these gentlemen, be they modified
how they may, out of all their variations, could be reduced to
this plain and simple dilemma : When the people are noisy it is
unsafe to grant reform ; when they are quiet it is unnecessary.
But the time has come when Reformers must legislate late because bigots would not legislate early ; when Reformers are
compelled to legislate in excitement, because bigots would not
do so in a more auspicious moment.   Bigots would not walk
with sufficient speed ; nay, they could not be prevailed upon to
move at all, and now Reformers must run for it.   By fair
means or foul, *through* Parliament, or *over* Parliament, the
question of reform must and will be carried."   This is truth—
every word truth, and worthy the utterance of a prophet of
freedom.   But why did not Mr. Macaulay use this language
afterwards on the presentation of the People's Charter.   Such
a declaration of principle England never heard before, appealing, as it did, to the consciences of men, the Word of God, and
the history of freedom for its truth.

In every particular where Macaulay showed an argument
for the passage of the Reform Bill, the Reformers showed the
same argument applicable to the People's Charter, and increased a hundred-fold.   By refusing to move then, he was
only making it certain that he and his successors " would have
to run for it ;" and in his own language, we yet say that
" *through* Parliament, or *over* Parliament," the people's Charter
must and will be carried.

XXXVI.

ONE glance back to 1832.   Earl Grey seeing that all was
lost if the Reform Bill was not carried, resigned.   This
only increased the danger of impending revolution.   King
William was troubled ; all England was troubled ; discontent
stalked through the realm.   Earl Grey was recalled, and
Parliament re-assembled.   New peers were about to be created,

to get a majority in the House of Lords. But reform or ruin was the only choice left them. It was too late to prate of the danger to old-established forms from the encroachment of the people. *It must come*, and the noble lords must vote for it. All the arguments they had used were valid as ever. The declaration that all was lost if they yielded to this invasion of their ancient prerogatives was true enough. Yet the bill *must* be passed. The mandate had gone forth from a power above the throne. The terrific murmur of the people, as they came thronging by thousands and tens of thousands to the doors of Parliament, stifled even the voice of covetousness ; paleness sat upon every countenance—the last speech was made. "Through Parliament or over Parliament it must be carried," had just died away on the ear, and "shall the question be put." The darkness of night was around the ancient pile wherein sat the rulers of the people. Underneath the open sky the dense expectant mass were swaying to and fro with ominous sounds. The tired artisan had forgot his rest, his rights were dearer than his sleep—the question *was* put—the bill passed. It was sent to the king, and willingly or unwillingly he must sign it. It became a law, and the shout of a victorious people shook the island.

This struggle and success was to England what the victory of Cromwell and the long Parliament was to the world. Step by step did the popular will gain ground till it controlled both the throne and Parliament. The timorous lords were right— this was only one of a succession of triumphs that awaited the cause of human freedom.

The bill, modified and emasculated it is true, passed, and England for a while breathed free again. But the code of human rights was fairly in the hands of the people, and they were reading it from one end of the land to the other.

Carlyle well says : "What are the rights and what are the mights of the discontented working-classes of England, is the question at this epoch. It is a struggle which will end in making the right clear and the might clear."

XXXVII.

FOURTEEN long years of suffering and starvation rolled
drearily away, and a final onset was to be made on the
Corn Laws by a starving people goaded to despair by outrage
and wrong. The same battle was to be fought between Aristocracy and Democracy ; and Democracy was to win. Another
and a greater statesman than even Earl Grey held the fortunes
of the British Empire in his hands.

It is painful to behold the dreadful writhings of feudalism in
the strong grasp of the awakened people. It reminds us of the
Russian mother who was followed at night by famished wolves.
Unable to save all, she first threw out her youngest child to
appease their hunger, and hurried on. The howl died away
for a moment as they scattered the limbs of the infant among
them. But with their hunger only half appeased, they again
bounded on the track. Another and still another child was
thrown to them, till the last was gone, and the mother, fleeing
over the trackless waste, alone escaped. So do the Aristocracy,
when pressed on by the famishing people, throw out one by one
their darling children to still the clamor that is thundering
behind them—but it is all partial relief. The starving people
are still pressing hard after, and will not be tranquil till all
is given up. The long steady course of the wolf, on the track
of his prey, is not so tireless as the pursuit of man after his
stolen rights.

Thus far we have shown that Democracy has advanced in
England—not only in its demands but its conquests. The past
is plain. Nothing has checked its progress. It is onward with
a strength that prostrates all opposition, and WHAT SHALL THE
END BE? The question is not destined to remain long without
an answer,

XXXVIII.

TWENTY more long years of suffering and sorrow have now
rolled drearily away since the overthrow of the Corn Laws,
and the masses of the British people have been steadily sinking

into deeper wretchedness and gloom. Sydney Smith, but a few years ago, said, " There is, no doubt, more misery and acute suffering among the mass of the people of England, than there is in any kingdom of the world. There are thousands house-less, breadless, friendless, without shelter, raiment or hope ; millions uneducated, only half fed, driven to crime and every species of vice which ignorance and destitution bring in their train, to an extent utterly unknown to the less enlightened, the less free, the less favored, and the less powerful kingdoms of Europe." What would that great and humane writer say now ?

The million I know have been crushed into helplessness ; but their cause has been taken up by a new and more formidable body of Reformers than England has ever before had to deal with. They are not to be trifled with. They have undertaken the emancipation of the oppressed. The barriers of power are melting to their touch. The ponderous gates of the prison-house of humanity will swing open at their approach. They will call forth and concentrate all the slumbering energies of the timid and the doubting. They constitute a force, around which swing all the discordant elements, and separate parties that have been working for the same thing in not the same way. Their words are charmed words, combining and har-monizing multitudes. Their action and their language authen-ticate their commission. The people feel it, and in them behold the pillar of fire that is guiding them to liberty.

XXXIX.

LIBERTY has seen its darkest day in England. The dying year closed over the ashes of Palmerston, the strongest foe of the people, and witnessed the accession of Russell, the feeblest friend of the Aristocracy. From his ministry nothing can be hoped by the privileged class in Church or State. Feudalism cannot lean on him. If he should put forth his last and strong-est effort in her cause, he would do her more harm than good.

She wants no nerveless advocate now. She is too decrepid to go alone—she is too timid to risk herself to do anything.

There has been a prolonged lull in the political world of England. No striking signs indicated an approaching storm. There was no desire for hastening the conflict. The Aristocracy was glad enough to have everything remain as it was ; no news was good news. Nothing was everything. Masterly inactivity had become feudal statesmanship.

The Reformers saw that their hour was coming. Events in other nations were helping them on. The toiling millions had given their cause over to the great Liberal leaders ; helpless in their destitution, hoping little, but praying all the time to the God of the poor.

But ominous sounds were heard from other nations. There came rolling up from the purple shores of the Mediterranean the shout of political redemption from twenty-five million Italians. The last Bourbon footfall had died away in the Halls of the Doges ; the shivered fragments of the Pontifical Sceptre lay scattered among the tombs of the Cæsars.

The wild shouts of twenty-five million freed serfs—exulting in their freedom, standing on their broken fetters—came rolling down from the ice-plains of Russia.

The wand of Liberty's Enchantress had been waved over our Western world, and the sword of the last rebel against the Great Republic lay broken among the broken chains of his slave. Two nations born in a day.

XL.

THESE were the world-reverberating sounds that broke upon the shores of Britain, and shook the foundations of her feudal castle.

Meanwhile the voice of Peel—the last great champion of Aristocracy—still lingered in the ears of its doomed worshipers ; while the clarion voice of Cobden—the prophet and high-priest of Democracy—had not yet died away in the desolate hovels of the countless multitude.

Aristocracy was without a leader. Neither they nor the Liberals would trust Derby or Gladstone—the only two men in all England, perhaps, who could still arrest the rush of feudalism to its wreck. A tacit but transient truce was proclaimed. Russell, whom nobody wanted, except as a *pis aller*, was called to the helm. The vessel was tranquilly floating, not a sail was unfurled ; any body on deck could stand at the wheel—one hand could play *dummy* as well as another. *The decks were not yet cleared for action.* But a new British Parliament is assembling, and not to try, but be tried by an indignant People.

Lord John Russell! a pilot for a calm—an aristocrat without the pride or chivalry of his class—an insipid eulogist of Popular Liberty, still clinging with feeble grasp to the skirts of his brave martyr-ancestor—a stone in the bed of the stream, not strong enough to resist the current, or weak enough to go with it—yet grown smooth by the polishing but harmless flow of the waters—stepping out of Sodom only to turn back to gaze on its doomed towers—a Premier untrusted at home and despised abroad. What can such a pilot do for the fair vessel slowly drifting into shoal water? Nothing for the Aristocracy, except to surrender their colors on the field—nothing for the Liberals, but to keep a stronger man out of the way—nothing for the wolf-million, but to reach forth his shrivelled hand to throw a bone, or worse, a tasteless sop to this Cerberus. If this be the game, something " live," with " warm blood," must go.

Oh! were I the holder of the broadest acres and the proudest coronet of England to-day, I would, in the presence of all this imbecility and all this danger, scream for Peel!

" Where, where was Roderick then ?"

XLI.

IN closing this Book, I cannot withhold the following tribute to two of the most illuminated Statesmen of our times.

I have gathered from authentic sources in England and America the following important facts, now for the first time communicated to the public, in regard to the almost simultaneous repeal of the British Corn Laws, and the enactment of our celebrated tariff of 1846, framed by Mr. Walker, then Secretary of the Treasury, on the request of Congress.

Mr. Walker had throughout his life advocated the policy of a tariff for revenue, and not for protection; but what policy he would recommend, as Secretary, was not known until he recommended the Revenue Tariff, designated *here* as the "Free Trade Policy."

During the year 1845, we had clear premonitions of the pending famine in Ireland. This great fact, perhaps, precipitated the Free Trade movement of Sir Robert Peel, then at the head of the British Cabinet. Meantime, an unofficial letter was addressed by Sir James Graham, special friend of Sir Robert, to Mr. Walker, suggesting the peculiar state of affairs in Ireland, the probable movement of Sir Robert for the repeal of the Corn Laws, indicating the great difficulty of the passage of that measure through Parliament, and stating that if Mr. Walker intended at any time to recommend the Free Trade Policy to Congress, it would greatly aid Sir Robert's movement, if the American Secretary would advocate a similar policy in his forthcoming Report.

As Mr. Walker had always advocated the Free Trade Policy, and issued Treasury circulars with similar views, he would have, doubtless, maintained these principles in his first Report. Perhaps, however, as no American Secretary of the Treasury had ever recommended the Free Trade Policy, it is quite possible that Mr. Walker's first Report might have been less bold and decisive had he not been aided by the fact, that such a Report would probably ensure the repeal of the British Corn Laws.

Mr. Walker's first Report, was made to Congress on the first Tuesday of December, 1845. Parliament did not meet till late in January, 1846, and on the 26th day of that month Sir Robert Peel, to the amazement of the Tories, but to the delight of the nation, made his great speech in favor of a repeal of the Corn Laws. In that speech he quoted extensively from Mr. Walker's Report, and based his movement, to a great extent, on it, as indicating the adoption of a reciprocal, liberal commercial policy by England and America; the former repealing the Corn Laws, and the latter reducing the Tariff; but as was shown by the sequel, trebling our imports, exports and revenue. Mr. Walker's Report was printed by the vote of both Houses of Parliament, it being the only Report of any Foreign Secretary that had ever thus been placed on the files of Parliament. It is quite clear from the sequel, that neither of these great measures could have been adopted without the support each received from the other.

Sir Robert Peel commenced political life as a Tory and Protectionist, then, and still, almost synonymous terms. He remained at the head of his old party until January, 1846, when with bold and manly eloquence he discarded at once the whole protective policy, and, renouncing all the favorite theories of his life, introduced his bill for the repeal of the Corn Laws. He was deserted by the great body of the Tories and Protectionists, and retired from the Cabinet. But he remained in Parliament, carrying with him a small body of the most enlightened of his former followers, included among whom was his special friend Sir James Graham, who was selected by him to correspond with Mr. Walker.

The death of Sir Robert Peel, in 1850, was a great calamity to America, to England, and the civilized world. At the period of his death, he stood at the head of European statesmen. His oratory was clear and argumentative, generally dealing in the logic of facts, but rising occasionally into impassioned eloquence. Such passages were rare and brief; but they showed that beneath the dry logic of statistics, there reposed deep feeling and sympathy with the masses of the people. He knew how greatly they had suffered from the exactions of the landed aristocracy, and the starvation prices of breadstuffs and provisions caused by the Corn Laws. It was a sliding scale of distress and misery, causing the death of thousands of the poorer classes, driving thousands more to the dark recesses of the poor-house, and inflicting unspeakable pain upon millions more who barely escaped starvation. During the last four years of his life, in various public speeches, Sir Robert Peel made touching allusions to these events, and rejoiced that, while many of the nobility and landed aristocracy had deserted him, the hard-hand of labor was strengthened in its toil, and that millions remembered him with gratitude. Indeed, during his latter years, he exhibited great sympathy with the working classes; principles clearly allied to true Democracy.

Connected with these sentiments were the kindest expressions of feeling toward America; and had he lived, it may be safely averred that our commerce would never have been pillaged by British Confederate cruisers; nor would the angry message of the late Lord Palmerston, our bitter enemy, have ever crossed the Atlantic in regard to the Trent. Let us hope that Mr. Gladstone, the present Lord-Chancellor of England, a pupil of Sir Robert Peel, and, perhaps, destined to be the Premier of the British Cabinet, will, as regards this country, soon follow in the footsteps of his illustrious master.